AFRICA IN THE MODERN WORLD

Edited by GWENDOLEN M. CARTER
Indiana University, Bloomington

Angola: Five Centuries of Conflict
by Lawrence W. Henderson

The Cameroon Federal Republic
by Victor T. Le Vine

Dahomey: Between Tradition and Modernity
by Dov Ronen

Ethiopia: The Modernization of Autocracy
by Robert L. Hess

Guinea: The Mobilization of a People
*by Claude Rivière; translated by
Virginia Thompson and Richard Adloff*

Liberia: The Evolution of Privilege
by J. Gus Liebenow

Malawi: The Politics of Despair
by T. David Williams

Rhodesia: Racial Conflict or Coexistence?
by Patrick O'Meara

West Africa's Council of the Entente
by Virginia Thompson

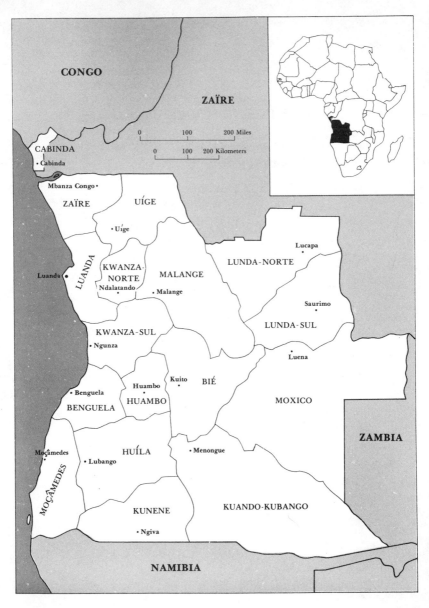

Angola (with postindependence administrative divisions and nomenclature).
Diário de Notícias, Lisbon, July 7, 1978, p. 5.

ANGOLA

Five Centuries of Conflict

LAWRENCE W. HENDERSON

Cornell University Press
ITHACA AND LONDON

International Standard Book Number 0-8014-1247-1
Library of Congress Catalog Card Number 79-5089
Printed in the United States of America
*Librarians: Library of Congress cataloging
information appears on the last page of the book.*

To Ki

Foreword

Angola occupies a strategic position in changing southern Africa; it is also a focal point of current West-East interactions. It shares borders with three countries of particular significance to the West: Namibia, long occupied by South Africa and facing an uncertain future; Zambia, bordering on battle-torn Zimbabwe Rhodesia; and Zaïre, whose central position and vast, largely uncoordinated territory make it a key area for the stability of much of the continent and yet a continually disturbing one. All three of these countries and Angola itself have rich mineral resources, exploited, insofar as they are, largely by Western entrepreneurs. Yet Angola has an avowedly Marxist-Leninist government that depends heavily on Soviet aid and Cuban troops and supplementary personnel.

When Angola and Mozambique—former Portuguese colonies in southeastern and southwestern Africa—became independent after Portugal's army coup in April 1974, the future of Rhodesia Zimbabwe[1] and even of South Africa became more uncertain. Some anxious critics see the two communist-supported countries as political pincers which may ultimately push Western economic interests out of this profitable area. Others view them as the most hopeful evidence that black nationalism can ultimately supplant white minority control with majority rule in southern Africa.

No other country in Africa has had so tumultuous a road to independence as Angola. In part this is because of deep ethnic-cultural cleavages between the Bakongo, Mbundu, and Ovimbundu, each primarily based in a broad geographical belt of the country—north, center, and south—and each dominant in a different nationalist movement—the National Front for the Libera-

1. The former name of Zimbabwe Rhodesia.

tion of Angola (FNLA), the Popular Movement for the Liberation of Angola (MPLA), and the National Union for the Total Independence of Angola (UNITA)—in the long and bitter struggle against the Portuguese. Also, the clash between the three nationalist movements has impinged on East-West rivalries. The ultimate victor in the race for recognition in 1975, the MPLA, with its strategic position in the capital, Luanda, had received support from the Soviet Union almost from its founding in 1956. The FNLA, allied closely to Mobutu's Zaïre, was favored by the West, and in particular by the United States. UNITA, based near South African–controlled Namibia, ultimately sought the support of that country when its hopes faded for a share in a coalition government. Nothing, it turned out, was so effective in securing diplomatic support for the MPLA from African states as the ill-conceived invasion of Angola by the troops of the feared and hated apartheid regime in support of MPLA's opponents. The United States repudiated South Africa's action and denied the latter's claim that it had encouraged the intervention.

Angola, ravaged by battle, still torn by ethnic divisions that give rise to continued conflict, and fearful of further South African attacks, clings to its Cuban reinforcements, which in turn stand in the way of American recognition of the MPLA government. Yet Gulf Oil continues to reap a rich harvest from offshore drilling in Cabinda, Angola's northern enclave beyond the Zaïre River, a harvest whose royalties to Angola's MPLA government are its economic mainstay, and the MPLA is eager to welcome more American investment in its exploitable resources.

While current attention naturally focuses on such issues, Angola's past history, its cultural patterns, and its distinctive characteristics are the bases of its long-term development and ultimate significance. With consummate skill and with understanding based on many years of personal experience of the country, Lawrence Henderson has provided the background without which this complex society cannot be understood or appreciated. It should be read by everyone concerned with the volatile situation in southern Africa.

GWENDOLEN M. CARTER

Bloomington, Indiana

Contents

Maps

Tables

Acknowledgments

I acknowledge that I cannot be coldly or academically objective about Angola. I learned to know and love Angola and its people by living in that former Portuguese colony with my family for twenty-two years. Our two sons are Angolan by birth and our two daughters also grew up there. Our colleagues and closest friends were Angolans of all races, creeds, regions, and social strata.

We always resided in central Angola along the Benguela Railway, but from 1960 to 1969 my professional responsibilities gave me an office in the capital, Luanda. During that period I represented the Protestant missions and churches of all Angola before the Portuguese government officials, and so was provided the opportunity to visit widely in that vast territory and to become acquainted with peoples of all regions.

It is impossible to acknowledge by name the hundreds of Angolans who have contributed to my information and understanding of that land; however, those who knew Jessé and Teresa Chipenda will not begrudge my singling them out for special recognition and gratitude. They transmitted to us their pride in traditional Angolan culture at the same time that they worked unstintingly to give to their children and to thousands of other Angolans the skills to live productively in the European culture. When the Rev. Jessé Chipenda died in the São Nicolau Prison Camp in 1969, we grieved, but were confident that his tremendous contribution to his country would someday bear fruit in an independent Angola. It is now clear that we were too optimistic about the time it would take to realize Pastor Jessé's dream of a free and peaceful Angola. Ten years after his death, Angola is still in conflict and the São Nicolau Camp where he died is crowded with another complement of Angolans.

I have dedicated this book to my wife, Ki, whose special gifts of friendship and hospitality made all Angolans feel welcome in our home. She reminded me frequently in the course of this project that I was writing about people and not just about political or military events.

Our daughter Kathleen M. Ashley has patiently read and criticized this manuscript step by step and forced me to reorganize and rewrite the more awkward and obscure passages. As a good teacher, she resisted the temptation to rewrite whole passages in her more fluent and graceful style. While acknowledging her indispensable assistance in giving a measure of coherence and clarity to the manuscript, I must acknowledge that the final draft is my own and therefore the inelegancies and obscurities are my responsibility.

In the academic community, I acknowledge especially the advice and encouragement of Gerald J. Bender, Joseph C. Miller, Douglas Wheeler, and John Marcum. Their research and writings as well as personal comments and suggestions have contributed to my understanding of Angola and inspired me to work harder to produce an accurate and balanced account of Angola in the modern world.

Of the many missionary colleagues, Protestant and Catholic, who informed my understanding of Angola, I will cite only three. Henry Curtis McDowell, who took the black American experience back to Angola for a distinguished missionary career of forty years, encouraged my appreciation of African culture. Gladwyn Murray Childs, by his pioneering work *Umbundu Kinship and Character,* challenged me to recognize the importance of kinship relations and proverbs in Angolan life. F. Ian Gilchrist, combining the personal experience of being African in sentiment, language, and commitment with the skills and perspective of a person trained in scientific medicine and African history, warned against letting my emotional involvement with Angola impede my rational analysis.

Undoubtedly my understanding of Angola was greatly enhanced by my knowledge of Portuguese and Umbundu. Therefore, I must acknowledge my debt to António Pinto Ribeiro and Antónino Hei, who, among other tutors, taught me their languages not as an academic exercise but with the enthusiasm that makes language an instrument of pleasant and profitable communication.

LAWRENCE W. HENDERSON

Leisure City, Florida

Acronyms

ABCFM	American Board of Commissioners for Foreign Missions
ALIAZO	Alliance des Ressortissants de Zombo: Alliance of Zombo Natives
AREC	Association des Ressortissants de l'Enclave de Cabinda: Association of the Natives of the Enclave of Cabinda
ASSOMIZO	Association Mutuelle des Ressortissants de Zombo: Mutual Association of the Natives of Zombo
CFB	Caminho de Ferro de Benguela: Benguela Railway
CONCP	Conferência das Organizações Nacionalistas das Colônias Portuguesas: Conference of Nationalist Organizations of the Portuguese Colonies
CTT	Direcção dos Serviços de Correios, Telégrafos e Telefones: Directory of Mail, Telegraph, and Telephone Services
DGS	Direcção Geral de Segurança: General Directory of Security
DPRA	Democratic People's Republic of Angola
DTA	Divisão dos Transportes Aéreos: Division of Air Transport
ELNA	Exército de Libertação Nacional de Angola: Army for the National Liberation of Angola
EPLA	Exército Popular de Libertação de Angola: Popular Army for the Liberation of Angola
FALA	Fôrças Armadas de Libertação de Angola: Armed Forces for the Liberation of Angola
FCPPA	Front Commun des Partis Politiques de l'Angola: Common Front of the Political Parties of Angola
FLEC	Frente para a Libertação do Enclave de Cabinda: Front for the Liberation of the Enclave of Cabinda
FNLA	Frente Nacional de Libertação de Angola: National Front for the Liberation of Angola
FPLN	Frente Patriótica de Libertação Nacional: Patriotic Front for National Liberation

FRELIMO	Frente de Libertação de Moçambique: Front for the Liberation of Mozambique
GRAE	Govêrno Revolucionário de Angola no Exílio: Revolutionary Government of Angola in Exile
LSM	Liberation Support Movement
MAC	Movimento Anti-Colonialista: Anti-Colonial Movement
MFA	Movimento das Forças Armadas: Movement of the Armed Forces
MLEC	Mouvement de Libération de l'Enclave de Cabinda: Movement for the Liberation of the Enclave of Cabinda
MPLA	Movimento Popular de Libertação de Angola: Popular Movement for the Liberation of Angola
MUD	Movimento de Unidade Democrática: Movement of Democratic Unity
MUDJ	Movimento de Unidade Democrática—Juvenil: Movement of Democratic Unity—Youth
OAU	Organization of African Unity
OPVDC	Organização Provincial de Voluntários e Defesa Civil: Provincial Organization of Volunteers and Civil Defense
PAIGC	Partido Africano de Independência da Guiné e Cabo Verde: African Party for the Independence of Guinea and Cape Verde
PCA	Partido Comunista de Angola: Communist Party of Angola
PDA	Partido Democrático de Angola: Democratic Party of Angola
PIDE	Polícia Internacional e de Defesa do Estado: International and State Security Police
PLUA	Partido da Luta Unida dos Africanos de Angola: Party of the United Struggle of Angolan Africans
PRA	People's Republic of Angola
PSP	Polícia de Segurança Publica: Public Security Police
UNEA	União Nacional dos Estudantes Angolanos: National Union of Angolan Students
UNITA	União Nacional de Independência Total de Angola: National Union for the Total Independence of Angola
UPA	União das Populações de Angola: Union of the Peoples of Angola
UPNA	União das Populações do Norte de Angola: Union of the Peoples of the North of Angola

ANGOLA

Five Centuries of Conflict

Introduction

When Angola became independent, on November 11, 1975, it had no legal government to receive power from the Portuguese, who had held it for five centuries. The High Commissioner in Luanda lowered the Portuguese flag and formally recognized Angolan independence without transferring authority to any of the contending nationalist movements. Such an anomaly would have raised questions anyplace in the world. However, this was just one more puzzle compounding the mystery which has surrounded Angola in the minds of outsiders. In 1953, a journalist commented that "Portuguese Africa is generally thought of as being nothing but a backwoods wilderness, inexpressibly remote, forlorn and primitive."[1] When the Portuguese presence was withdrawn, Angola, while certainly not a remote and primitive wilderness, still presented an enigmatic image to the world.

Angola, the seventh largest nation in Africa, was lost in the vague classification "Portuguese Africa" and could scarcely be distinguished from the other colonies: Mozambique, Guinea, Cape Verde, São Tomé, Príncipe, and São João de Ajudá. The Salazar-Caetano regime which ruled Portugal for half a century had tried to keep the colonies out of sight, and succeeded in part because of Portugal's own obscurity after the seventeenth century. The poorest nation in Western Europe, Portugal played out its role on the world stage in the shadow not only of the great powers, Spain, France, and Great Britain, but also of the lesser, Holland and Belgium.

Suddenly, in 1961, both Portugal and Angola attracted world attention. Portuguese and Spanish exiles, protesting dictatorship in their homelands, hijacked the Portuguese luxury liner *Santa Maria* off the coast of Venezuela, with the intention of sailing to Africa and liberating Angola. The plan aborted, but foreign

1. John Gunther, *Inside Africa* (New York: Harper, 1955), p. 585.

journalists attracted to Luanda found that this quixotic Iberian
venture had coincided with an African revolt against Portuguese
colonialism. Before dawn on February 4, 1961, a hundred or
more men with knives and clubs attacked two prisons and a
police station to free political prisoners in the capital. The attack
failed, but news reports of it reinforced the request that had
been made by African and Asian states a month earlier, that the
United Nations Security Council hold a special meeting on Angola. As the United Nations was debating Angolan self-
determination, the armed revolt against colonialism leapfrogged
from the capital to the coffee-producing region in the north.
There, beginning March 15, 1961, Angolans attacked towns,
administrative posts, and coffee plantations. Altogether,
perhaps 2,000 whites and 50,000 blacks were killed during the
six months of attacks and reprisals before the Portuguese, with
the help of troop reinforcements from the metropole, reestab-
lished their military control of the north. By the end of 1961,
Portugal had demonstrated both the will and ability to maintain
its colonial empire in the face of guerrilla attacks from within
and the tide of anticolonialism sweeping the world.

The conflicts of 1961 brought Angola to world attention and
raised certain questions we will try to answer by looking at five
centuries of conflict in Angola.

Where exactly was Angola located? How was the territorial
identity of Angola defined? Could Angola's resources compensate for the cost of the wars in Angola, Mozambique, and
Guinea? These geographical questions lead us in Chapter 1 to
look at the scene of the conflict.

From 1961 to 1965, the Angolan people directly involved in
the war of liberation were Kongo or Kimbundu. After the mid-
sixties, names of other Angolan peoples appeared in the news
stories: Chokwe, Ganguela, Umbundu, Kwanyama. Observers
faced a new set of questions about Angola: Who were the Angolans? Did they identify themselves as Angolans or as members of
distinct ethnolinguistic groups? A related question was raised
about the white population: Did they identify themselves as Portuguese or as Angolans? In Chapter 2 our attention will be
turned to these combatants in the conflict.

The thirteen-year war waged by the Portuguese against Angolan independence raised the question why Portugal was so determined to retain power over Angola. What was the relationship between the Portuguese and the Angolans over the centuries? What was the legacy of the slave trade to Angola in the modern world? Chapter 3, a historical sketch, illustrates how the slave trade dominated the conflicts from the fifteenth through the nineteenth century. The transition from slavery to colonialism, the period from 1885 to 1920, is covered in Chapter 4. The colonial period will be defined in Chapter 5 as the period from 1921 to 1960, during which time Portugal exercised direct control over the whole territory of Angola.

On January 15, 1975, the Portuguese Government signed an independence agreement with the three Angolan nationalist movements: the Popular Movement for the Liberation of Angola (MPLA), the National Front for the Liberation of Angola (FNLA), and the National Union for the Total Independence of Angola (UNITA). The agreement pledged the three movements to work together with Portugal in a coalition Transitional Government during a ten-month period prior to independence. The inauguration of the Transitional Government in Luanda on January 31, 1975, raised new questions: Why were there three movements? How did they differ? What was the background of the three leaders, Agostinho Neto, Holden Roberto, and Jonas Savimbi? Chapter 6 recounts the formation of the Angolan nationalist movements and their struggle against Portuguese nationalism from 1961 through 1965.

In the early 1970s, Portuguese colonialism seemed more firmly entrenched than ever in Angola. Foreign investments were stimulating economic growth; the nationalist forces were restricted to remote rural areas; and public criticism of colonial policy was prohibited by government decree. Then in February 1974 this illusion of colonial strength was shattered by the enthusiasm which made a book about colonial policy into an all-time best seller in Portugal. *Portugal e o futuro,* by General António de Spínola, challenged the official policy that the colonial question could only be solved by military means and advocated a sociopolitical solution. Spínola, the most charismatic figure in Portugal, could publish the book because he was only articulating in public the conclusions reached privately by those elements of society—business, the church, and the military—which had been the main supporters of the Salazar-Caetano regime. Portuguese business had perceived that its future was in Europe, not in Africa; Portuguese Catholicism saw that it could not maintain the myth of its Christian civilizing mission in the colonies after the Church had passed through the reforming experiences of Vatican II; and the Portuguese military had organized the Movement of the Armed Forces in opposition to the colonial wars.

Decolonization was the concluding plank in the platform of the Movement of the Armed Forces as it overthrew the Salazar-Caetano regime in a bloodless coup on April 25, 1974. The world was confused and asked why the very officers who fought for thirteen years in Angola, eleven years in Guinea, and ten years in Mozambique had now overthrown Portuguese fascism and colonialism. The peoples of the three colonies and the leaders of their liberation movements were not so much confused as incredulous. Had Portugal really changed its colonial policy, or was this just another ruse like changing the name from "colony" to "province" or "province" to "state"? Chapter 7 traces the conflicts within Portuguese and Angolan nationalisms and responds to other questions.

In 1965, under the military and economic pressure of its three colonial wars, Portugal shifted its colonial policy and invited foreign investors into Angola. One of the costs to Portugal of this change was the exposure of its colonies to more international scrutiny. For example, Gulf Oil Corporation and its subcontractors brought Americans into Luanda and Cabinda. Meanwhile, concerned citizens in the United States mounted a "Boycott Gulf" campaign to protest American economic support for the Portuguese war effort. Germans, South Africans, and French also responded to Portugal's invitation to invest in its largest colony. The United Nations made studies to explore such questions as the effect of foreign investments on the population of Angola and on international politics.

On the day Huambo fell, February 11, 1976, the Council of Ministers of the Organization of African Unity (OAU) decided by a simple majority to recognize the People's Republic of Angola. What role did the OAU play in the liberation struggle against Portugal and in the conflict between the movements? The United Nations received Angola into membership December 1, 1976. Since 1960 the question of the Portuguese colonies, especially Angola, had occupied an important place on the agenda of the United Nations. How significant was UN pressure on Portugal? What part did the United Nations take in strengthening Angolan nationalism?

For arms and munitions each movement depended upon outside sources of supply, among them Zaïre, the USSR, the United States, Yugoslavia, East Germany, and Algeria. By October 1975 not only was foreign material significantly influencing the balance of power between the rival nationalist movements, but foreign troops were playing decisive roles in the military conflict. Charges and countercharges by the movements against foreign intervention raised new questions: Who had supplied arms and munitions to the movements during the years of the anticolonial war? How did foreign troops come to intervene? At whose invitation?

Within two weeks after the inauguration of the Transitional Government, fighting started between the movements. The violence escalated until the leaders of the movements sat down together in Nakuru, Kenya, in June 1975 to "solemnly pledge to renounce the use of force as a means of solving problems and to honour all commitments." The ink was hardly dry on the agreement before shooting broke out again among the movements.

When the MPLA declared the independence of the People's Republic of Angola (PRA) in Luanda on November 11, 1975, the excluded parties, FNLA and UNITA, made separate declarations of independence, then formed a coalition government of the Democratic People's Republic of Angola (DPRA) with its capital in Huambo. Cuban troops equipped with Russian materiel, which had secured control of Luanda for MPLA before Independence, began to clear the remaining FNLA forces out of the north and to move south. Exactly three months after Independence Day, the MPLA captured Huambo. Holden Roberto and Jonas Savimbi threatened to continue the struggle and resist the military and political power of the MPLA. To substantiate these threats, what internal support could they rely on? Could they continue to resist without foreign aid? For the first three years of independence, opposition to the recognized MPLA government reached a high level of intensity. UNITA's experience of fighting against the Portuguese from 1966 to 1974 inside Angola, without a foreign base, prepared it to continue both active and passive resistance throughout the period 1976–1978. FNLA, deprived officially of its traditional base of operations in Zaïre, slowly regrouped and continued sporadically to challenge the MPLA. The Front for the Liberation of the Enclave of Cabinda (FLEC) used both forest areas of the Enclave and refuges in Zaïre and the Congo from which to attack government forces. It met stiff resistance because Cuban troops were concentrated in the enclave to protect the oil wells and pipelines so necessary to the Angolan economy. The Luanda government faced two serious questions three years after Independence. Could it incapacitate the guerrilla opposition? And could it win the political loyalty of the majority of Angolans? The final chapter will respond to these questions.

CHAPTER 1

The Scene of the Struggle:
The Angolan Natural Environment

The separation of Angola's natural and human environments into two chapters in this book is more than just a useful literary device. In some ways, it reflects one of the basic differences between the European industrial and the African peasant perspectives which has led to conflict. Some foreigners were attracted to Angola by its mineral wealth, fertile plateaus, and natural harbors without considering that the land was an inheritance of peoples. Other foreigners came to wrench men, women, and children from their lands and ship them as slaves to a new world where they had no roots.

"Etu tua tunga vovipembe viovopakulu" (We have roots in the fields of our ancestors) goes an Umbundu proverb that indicates the strength of the Angolan peoples' identification with the land. Individuals belong to communities and communities have roots in the land, a symbiotic relationship that includes not only the land but its flora and fauna as well. Even such stresses as colonialism, urbanization, migratory labor, refugee flights, and civil war have not destroyed this identification between the people and their natural environment. Therefore, Angolans may rightly take umbrage at this chapter which describes their land as though it were a vast, uninhabited territory.

Borders

We speak about Angola as though it had been a clearly identified territory for 500 years, but its present borders were legally defined and recognized only in the twentieth century. As in most of Africa, the frontiers were shaped by European powers as they resolved their military, political, and commercial conflicts. The negotiators ignored the human-ethnic concerns of the local populations and arbitrarily chose natural boundaries acceptable to the competing foreign parties. All but 810 miles (1,296 kilometers) of the 3,800-mile (6,080-kilometer) border of Angola are defined by water—either rivers or the Atlantic Ocean. The Congo forms the most obvious natural frontier, and the northern border was the first one definitely set by international treaty. During most of the nineteenth century, Portugal, Great Britain, and France attempted to establish their rights to trade in the Congo basin. Portugal built forts at several points, but was forced to abandon them by French threats and British gunboat diplomacy. In 1884/85 at the Berlin West African Conference, the European colonial powers that had gathered to discuss the issue of free trade in the Congo basin considered the rival territorial claims to the area over which Portugal would eventually establish sovereignty. The frontiers at the mouth of the Congo were fixed by a treaty signed by Portugal and the Congo Free State on May 25, 1891.

The northern frontier of Angola runs up the middle of the Congo River to the Livingstone Falls and then cuts east across nine affluents of the Kasai River. The Kasai forms the eastern border of Angola and Zaïre to the ridge which divides the tributaries of the Congo, like the Kasai flowing north and west, from those of the Zambezi flowing south and east. For 130 miles the frontier tops the ridge which is a continental divide where the borders of Zaïre, Zambia, and Angola converge. A traveler through the area 100 years ago noted that by cutting a 20-mile canal the Congo and Zambezi could be connected and internal navigation be established from the west to east coast.

The frontier between Angola and Zambia is a compromise between the rival claims of Portugal and Great Britain in the scramble for central Africa. Following the Berlin Conference, as part of direct negotiations with France and Germany, Portugal drew a map, which has become famous as the "pink map" (*mapa côr-de-rosa*), uniting Angola and Mozambique. France and Germany agreed to Portugal's grand plan to control a strip of land right across central Africa; however, Portugal had not negotiated with Britain, its principal rival for this territory. The British challenged a Portuguese expedition into the disputed territory and in 1890 presented an ultimatum to the Portuguese minister for foreign affairs. The Portuguese had no alternative but to accept an eastern frontier for Angola which is 750 miles (1,200 kilometers) from Mozambique, allowing Britain to establish its colonies—Malawi, Northern and Southern Rhodesia—between the two Portuguese colonies.

From the point of convergence of Zaïre, Zambia, and Angola, the border follows affluents of the Zambezi south to Namibia. Although the interests and rights of Africans did not figure significantly in the competition between European powers to settle Angola's borders, at times colonial nations used treaties they had signed with African leaders to establish their own territorial claims. In defining the Anglo-Zambia border, for example, Great Britain made use of a treaty it had signed with the kingdom of Barotse to reinforce its territorial claims.

The southern border of Angola was negotiated out of the conflicting interests of Portugal and another of its European rivals, Germany, which had established a protectorate over South-West Africa in 1890. In the south, the border of Namibia connects major rivers until it reaches the Ruacana Falls of the Cunene River. As the northern frontier started up the Congo River from the Atlantic, so the border in the south ends by following the Cunene River 200 miles (320 kilometers) through some of the driest stretches of land in southern Africa until it empties into the Atlantic. The final demarcation of this border was approved by Portugal and South Africa in 1931.[1]

The western border is formed by the Atlantic Ocean between the Cunene and the Congo. Outside of these borders, on the Atlantic coast north of the Congo River, is the enclave of Cabinda. This territory occupied an ambiguous position in the Portuguese colonial framework. The Portuguese constitution listed Cabinda as a separate territory rather than as an integral part of Angola, but administratively the enclave was simply one district of the colony of Angola, ruled as all the others were from Luanda. Portugal had claimed an extensive territory north of the mouth of the Congo, but was left with an irregularly

1. Luís de Matos, "*A fixação das fronteiras de Angola,*" in *Angola: Curso de extensão universitária ano lectivo de 1963-64* (Lisbon: Instituto Superior de Ciências Sociais e Política Ultramarina), p. 83.

shaped piece of land running about fifty miles along the Atlantic and seventy-five miles into the interior. Cabinda is surrounded by the Republic of the Congo on the north and east and by Zaïre on the south. As presently defined territorially, Angola is less than 100 years old. Its borders were fixed as a result of political and commercial conflicts between Portugal and its colonial competitors, with no regard for the boundaries of the peoples of Angola and no participation by their leaders.

Topography

The topography of Africa resembles an upturned plate, the center being a large plateau surrounded by a narrow coastal plain. The plateau and plain are linked by a transitional strip which in some places is a steep escarpment and in others is a gentle slope. Angola follows this same configuration. Most of Angola stands within the central African plateau with elevations above 3,250 feet (1,000 meters). The transitional strip or sub-plateau varies in height from 1,300 feet (400 meters) to 3,250 feet (1,000 meters), and is cut by ravines and steep valleys except in the Cuanza basin where the slope is more gentle. The coastal plain ranges from a maximum of 125 miles (200 kilometers) at the mouth of the Cuanza to a minimum of ten miles (16 kilometers) at Benguela.

Geography and history facilitated the penetration of the interior by European explorers and settlers in the north of Angola. The Portuguese landed first at the mouths of the Congo and Cuanza rivers, where the slope from the coastal plain to the plateau is gentle. Farther south, where the Portuguese arrived a century later, the steep escarpment makes travel inland by boat impossible and on foot very difficult.

Angola conforms to the characteristics of the continent with its high central plateau, but it has a more favorable coastline than most of Africa. Instead of the usual African coast without deep bays or gulfs penetrating inland and comparatively few rocky headlands to afford shelter to adjoining bays, Angola has four natural harbors: Luanda, Lobito, Moçâmedes and Porto Alexandre. With the exception of Moçâmedes, the Benguela Current has formed these bays as it runs up the Angolan coast

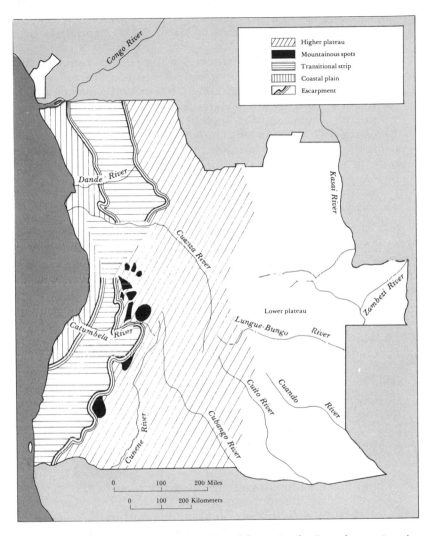

Topography and rivers of Angola. Adapted from *Angola: Curso de extensão universitária ano lectivo de 1963–1964* (Lisbon: Instituto Superior de Ciências Sociais e Política Ultramarina), p. 18.

and deposits the sand carried by the Cuanza, Catumbela, and Cunene rivers.

The sailing vessels of the fifteenth to nineteenth centuries did not require deepwater ports, so Mpinda was as useful as Luanda, and Benguela as efficient as Lobito, for unloading trinkets and cloth and loading slaves. The development of steamships in the twentieth century, and the need to load heavy mineral cargoes, gave Angola a strategic advantage which allowed Lobito to become the main port of transit for the copper and other minerals on which the economies of Zambia and Zaïre depend.

These natural geographic advantages also increased the potential for conflict because the Angolan coastal ports control access to central Africa and are strategic points on the southern Atlantic sea routes.

Climate

The Benguela Current has formed the valuable harbors of Angola. It also brings cold water from the Antarctic which, together with the high altitudes of the central plateau, moderates the temperature of Angola. Although it is within the tropical zone, the climate of Angola ranges from temperate to subtropical. Most of Angola falls within the zone of central Africa which experiences only a 5 to 15 degree range in temperature from the coldest to the warmest months. Temperatures are constant also between different areas of Angola. For example, the mean annual temperature of São Salvador do Congo on the northern plateau is 72.5° F. and at Caconda on the central highlands, 67.2°.

The seasons in Angola as in all of central Africa are distinguished by precipitation rather than temperature. The wet season in most of the country begins in October and ends in April, with no precipitation during the other five months. The narrow coastal strip also has two seasons, but there is a difference. The coast is blanketed with low clouds and fog during the dry season instead of enjoying the cloudless blue sky of the central highlands.

The climate of the central plateau is healthful for human habitation and propitious for a variety of types of agriculture from semitropical coffee, pineapples, and bananas to temperate wheat, corn, and peaches. The competition for land to cultivate in this favorable climate contributed directly to the outbreak of the war of liberation in 1961.

Rain not only defines the seasons but also sustains agriculture, the basis of the Angolan economy. The Umbundu proverb which corresponds to "for everything there is a season and a time for every matter under heaven" (Ecclesiastes 3:1) says, literally, "The matters of the wet season are discussed in the dry season and the matters of the dry season are discussed in the wet season" (*"Ondaka yondombo yi vanguiwa vokuenye; ondaka yokuenye yi vanguiwa vondombo"*). For most Angolans, rain is more than a necessity for agriculture. According to the Nhaneca-Humbe, "Rain belongs to God." The most sacred power that the king may exercise is to make rain (*okulokesa*). Whatever the source, the distribution of rain is uneven in Angola. It ranges from a yearly low of five inches in the Namib desert to an average of ten to twenty inches in the coastal plain and forty to sixty inches on the central plateau.

Rivers

In spite of the unevenness of the rainfall, a hydrographic map of Angola reveals a network of rivers and streams which waters all sectors of the country. More than fifteen rivers run along the borders of Angola and many others with a permanent flow have their sources in the highlands and empty into the Atlantic. The largest of these internal rivers is the Cuanza, which rises in the central highlands and flows north and west into the ocean forty miles south of Luanda. This network of rivers not only provides water for human consumption and agriculture, but also is a major source of energy. Hydroelectric plants are located on four rivers: Mabubas on the Dande River and Cambambe on the Cuanza River provide energy for the capital and much of the north. Biópio and Lomaum on the Catumbela River supply hydroelectric power to Lobito and Benguela at the coast as well as to industries in the Cubal-Ganda area. On the Cunene River, the dam at Matala provides a regular flow of water and more energy than southern Angola has required to date. The tremendous potential of the Cunene River to supply water and power to the desert areas of Angola and Namibia has been long recognized.

The German emperor and the king of Portugal reached an agreement in 1886 over water rights on the Cunene.[2] After World War I, Portugal continued to negotiate with South Africa, which had been entrusted with the mandate for South-West Africa, over the use of the Cunene River to guarantee Namibia's water supply. The final agreement projecting the construction of twenty-seven dams for irrigation and energy on the Cunene River was reached in 1969.

Access to water and its power will continue to be a focus of conflict in the arid region of southern Angola and northern Namibia, as it was in the last stages of the independence struggle (1975–1976), when South African troops invaded Angola in part to protect the Calueque Dam on the Cunene River.

Soil

The prosperity expected of such a vast, well-watered plateau with its favorable climate is impaired by the many factors which conspire to impoverish the soil of Angola. First of all, the particles that compose the soil are formed from the basement of metamorphic rock seamed by quartz veins. When this underlying rock is shattered it forms tiny "sand"grains which are sharply angular and of varying sizes, in contrast to vast areas of Europe and North America where the underlying rocks are sedimentary in origin and the tiny mineral fragments are more or less rounded. The angular rock fragments common in Africa can be compacted by simple pressure; even raindrops in a tropical downpour are sufficient to consolidate the surface.

High temperatures and abundant rainfall favor bacterial decay so that in the areas of Angola with these climatic conditions, wastes are quickly decomposed and little humus accumulates in the soil. Torrential rains leach soils of minerals, leaving behind a dense clay of low nutrient value. In the dry season evaporation is rapid, which deposits salts in the soil. Finally, the common practice of clearing land by burning the vegetation bakes the surface soil and destroys its organic matter.

In spite of the precarious state of the soils, however, Africans developed both agricultural and pastoral ecosystems which

2. *The Cunene Dam Scheme and the Struggle for the Liberation of Southern Africa* (Geneva: World Council of Churches, 1971), p. 3.

maintained an acceptable level of soil fertility in most parts of Angola.

Flora

Tropical grassland or savanna covers most of Angola. The system of shifting cultivation accounts for the elimination of much of the forest from the plateau and the vast spreading of the savanna. The farmer clears a plot of land by cutting down the trees and burning them; he then uses the ash as fertilizer. When the soil is depleted, after the plot has been cultivated for a few years, the farmer abandons the field and starts over again clearing a new area. However, since the clearing is not done thoroughly or consistently, the savanna is still partially wooded.

Only two small areas of Angola, Maiombe in Cabinda and the Dembos in Cuanza North, sustain rich equatorial forests. The Maiombe forest is precarious because it must maintain itself through four months of drought per year. Nevertheless, rivers, protection from dry winds, and soil that can accumulate humidity make possible a very heterogenous stand of trees. Among the most valued are white and pink mahogany. In the Dembos forest the principal trees are African teak, barwood, and a variety of mahoganies—swamp, white, cedar, and sapele. The encroachment of coffee plantations into the Dembos has greatly reduced the forest area.

The third vegetal zone in Angola is the subdesertic steppe which lies between the savanna and the desert. The grotesque baobab tree that flourishes in this zone seems to substantiate the Arabian legend that "the devil plucked up the baobab, thrust its branches into the earth, and left its roots in air."[3] In the more argillic soil, sandalwood and ironwood are commonly found as well as the fanpalm; these make even the desert look like a tropical park. The subdesertic steppe extends along the coastal strip as far north as Luanda.

Fauna

Angola's savannas, steppes, and desert still have a rich variety of animal life even though the numbers have been reduced by

3. *Encyclopaedia Britannica*, 1969 edition, III, 138.

the penetration of new highways to the four corners of the country and by the spread of firearms to the most remote areas of Angola since 1961. The mammals found extensively in Angola include the elephant, rhinoceros, giraffe, hippopotamus, buffalo, zebra, lion, leopard, cheeta, hyena, jackal, lynx, wild pig, gorilla, and chimpanzee. Angola has a great variety of antelopes, from the large kudu and eland to the tiny pygmy, including the almost extinct great sable, which is found only in the fork of the Cuanza and Luando rivers.

The birds of Angola include an equally exciting variety: ostrich, pelican, flamingo, ducks, Guinea fowl, pheasant, doves, parrots, hornbill, and wild turkey. In humid areas, Angolans cut the grass and bushes back from their homes to protect themselves against snakes, including pythons, black mamba, and vipers.

Fish are more important economically than mammals, birds, or reptiles. Angola has the best fishing grounds of southern Africa, where the Benguela Current mixes its cold water with the warm Agulhas Current, giving temperatures and upsurges favorable to plankton. The sea off Angola is relatively calm, which also facilitates fishing. In addition to African species, most of the fish common on the Atlantic coast of Europe are found in or near Angolan waters. The most abundant are stickleback, tuna, shark, mackerel, anchovy, sardine, and whiting. Angola is also wealthy in river fish, which contribute an important part of the food supply to many Angolans.

Minerals

Minerals have played an important role in the struggles for military, territorial, commercial, and political control of Angola. In the sixteenth and seventeenth centuries, the Portuguese were attracted by legends of silver and gold. In the twentieth century, North American, British, Belgian, French, German, and South African interests participated with the Portuguese in the exploitation of copper, iron, diamonds, mica, manganese, and petroleum. Exploration indicates that other minerals, including uranium, are present in exploitable quantity and quality.

The search for silver was one of the principal motives for the military occupation of parts of Angola by the Portuguese in the sixteenth century.[4] In 1530, Afonso I, the king of Kongo, sent two silver bracelets to the Portuguese king, John III, which prompted him to send several expeditions from Lisbon to find the fabled mines of Cambambe. Only in 1604 did an expedition under the leadership of Manuel Cerveira Pereira verify that there was no silver in Cambambe.[5] To the present, no commercially exploitable deposits of silver have been found in Angola.

Iron has played a more ancient and practical role in the history of Angola. Ironworking—mining, smelting, and forging—was one of the characteristics of the Bantu as they moved down from West Africa and entered Angola. Angolans are literally the "People of Ngola," a blacksmith hunter who, according to oral tradition,[6] invaded the territory between the Cuanza and Dande rivers and established a Kimbundu monarchy. Present knowledge of these oral traditions does not allow us to identify a particular man or date his arrival, but one constant strand in the traditions is that ironworking technology was an essential element in the forming of the Angolan peoples. The Umbundu proverb, "The hoes of Ngola are recognized by their quality" ("*Atemo a Ngola a limbukila vulengo*"), has brought the fame of Ngola's iron-making skill down to the present generation. From the Bakongo in the north to the Ovambo in the south, Angolans have had access to iron through all of their history and have elevated the ironworker to a superior economic and religious position in their societies. The king of the Kongo used the title *Nangula a Kongo*, "Blacksmith of the Kongo."[7]

Angolans have also known and worked copper for centuries, but this metal has not been as easily accessible and does not play as important a role in Angolan cultures.

Diamonds were thought to be confined to Lunda District until

4. Ralph Delgado, *História de Angola* (Dafundo, Portugal: Edição do Banco de Angola), I, 176.

5. James Duffy, *Portuguese Africa* (Cambridge, Mass.: Harvard University Press, 1959), p. 59.

6. David Birmingham, *Trade and Conflict in Angola: The Mbundu and Their Neighbors under the Influence of the Portuguese 1483–1790* (Oxford: Clarendon Press, 1966), p. 20.

7. George Balandier, *Daily Life in the Kingdom of the Kongo from the Sixteenth to the Eighteenth Century* (New York: World, 1969), p. 41.

the exclusive contract of the Angola Diamond Company, Diamang, expired in April, 1971. Since then, commercially exploitable deposits of diamonds have been found in Moxico, Bié, and Cuando-Cubango.

Petroleum was discovered in Angola before the end of the eighteenth century and samples were sent to Lisbon,[8] but the first commercial discovery was made in Benfica, near Luanda, in 1955. By 1974 the Cabinda oil field was considered one of 105 giant fields in the world.[9] Petroleum has been the center of economic rivalry between competing companies as well as the focus of political conflict.

Angola is attractive because of its full range of natural resources. The generally well-watered land sustains a rich flora and fauna. Even the semidesert areas in the south and along the coast are crossed by rivers which potentially could make the deserts bloom. Although the soil suffers most of the debilitating effect common to central and southern Africa, it is capable of sustaining both subsistence and market agriculture. The subsoil of Angola contains mineral wealth that has been only partially explored and scarcely exploited. Energy, the essential element for economic development, is available both through hydroelectric potential and substantial oil reserves.

With a population of only 12 persons per square mile (4.8 per square kilometer), Angola's struggles in the past and present are not due to lack of space or of natural resources. Rather, the competition among the various peoples of Angola and the added rivalry with foreign interests for control and exploitation of the human and natural resources have produced five centuries of conflict.

8. Douglas L. Wheeler and René Pélissier, *Angola* (New York: Praeger, 1971), p. 142.

9. It was calculated to have proved petroleum reserves of 1.2 billion barrels, over the minimum (1 billion barrels) for the category of giant field (*Africa Report,* March–April 1975, pp. 50–54).

CHAPTER 2

The Angolans: The
Human Environment

The combatants in the struggle for the vast and wealthy land
of Angola included the peoples living in Angola, those of surrounding African countries, and even Europeans, Americans,
and Asians. This chapter confines itself to a description of the
peoples of Angola as they were in 1920, by which date Portugal
had established effective occupation of the whole colony. We do
not imply that before 1920 Angolans lived within traditional,
static cultures and that after that date, change was initiated by
the arrival of Europeans. Constant transformation characterizes
all known cultures. In certain features of Angolan life—
agricultural methods, social relations, linguistic forms—the
change from 1920 to the present may be imperceptible, but for
consistency the past tense will be used to describe the peoples of
Angola in 1920 even though many features of these cultures
may still prevail.

Ethnolinguistic Groups

To avoid either lumping all Angolans into one category or
attempting to describe every locally identifiable group, I have
chosen the middle course of dividing Angolans into their major
ethnolinguistic groupings. Not only is this classification well established academically, but even more important, these groups
have been the principal combatants in the conflicts that have
characterized Angola's history.

The word *tribe* is not used to describe the Angolans, since it
has a pejorative meaning for most Americans and Europeans.
People will be employed for the unit which in other writing might
be called "tribe." A people occupies a more or less defined territory, usually to the exclusion of others by virtue of its common

possession of and adherence to a particular way of life and by its involvement in a coherent social system. This common way of life (or culture) includes institutional modes of behavior, accepted values and ideas, and artifacts. Such a way of life, together with the corpus of myth and tradition which informs and supports it, is considered by the people to be its heritage.[1] A people speaks a dialect of a language which is mutually understood by other peoples, together with whom it forms an ethnolinguistic group.

The basic ethnolinguistic division in Angola is between Bantu and non-Bantu. Wilhelm Bleek, a German linguist in South Africa, proposed the term *Bantu* in 1856 to refer to a family of languages which uses the root *-ntu* for "person": *muntu,* singular, and *bantu,* plural. The Bantu, who now occupy most of central and southern Africa, migrated slowly and in small groups for the past 2,000 years. Our knowledge of the origins and migrations of the Bantu and particularly of the Bantu peoples of Angola is still very sketchy.

The homeland of the original Bantu was probably the Benue Valley, along the present Nigeria-Cameroon border, from which through a process still unknown the Bantu-speaking people dispersed over a subcontinent, the whole of Africa south of a line from the Bight of Benin to southern Somalia. Scholars differ as to the causes of this vast human migration. Oliver and Fage contend that an economic revolution produced the expansion of the Bantu population,[2] while Vansina offers the explanation that it was probably triggered by the great population growth in Nigeria, caused by large numbers of people gradually driven out of the increasingly arid Sahara desert after 2500 B.C.[3]

The Bantu who arrived in Angola, perhaps as early as the thirteenth century, were technologically different from those who started from the Benue Valley in the pre-Christian era. They had learned to smelt and work iron, and it is a sign of

1. P. H. Gulliver, "Anthropology," in *African World; A Survey of Social Research,* ed. Robert A. Lystad (New York: Praeger, 1965), p. 65.
2. Roland Oliver and J. D. Fage, *A Short History of Africa* (Baltimore: Penguin, 1962), pp. 30–32.
3. *The Horizon History of Africa,* ed. Alvin M. Josephy, Jr. (New York: American Heritage, 1971), p. 263.

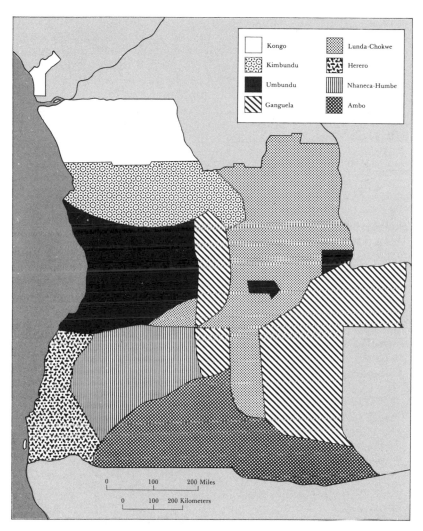

Legend:

- Kongo
- Kimbundu
- Umbundu
- Ganguela
- Lunda-Chokwe
- Herero
- Nhaneca-Humbe
- Ambo

0   100   200 Miles

0   100   200 Kilometers

Ethnolinguistic groups of Angola. Drawn by the author and published in *Angola* (Rome, IDOC International, 1975), facing page 1.

cohesion of the Bantu world that their metallurgical terminology developed homogeneously over the whole area occupied by Bantu speakers.[4] The second technological change was the cultivation of banana and taro, which were introduced from Southeast Asia through East Africa early in the Christian era. One of the most extraordinary facts of botanical distribution is that practically none of the important forest foodcrops of the world is indigenous to Africa.[5] The acquisition of cattle was the third technological change which affected the eastern and southern Bantu. From the cattle-herding stream of the Bantu migration came the peoples who populated southern Angola. One migratory route seems to have come down the Congo River and then moved eastward and south on the Kasai along the present eastern frontier of Angola to the headwaters of the Zambezi. Exact dates are impossible to determine, but by about A.D. 1200 the Bantu had established a variety of regional cultures in Central Africa which are the direct forerunners of the ethnic cultures that will be identified in this chapter.

The ethnolinguistic groups will be presented in an order that follows both the geography and the history of the conflict from north to south. Starting in the north we find the Kongo, who occupied the center of the Euro-African historical stage of west-central Africa when our five centuries begins. South of the Dande River the several peoples forming the Kimbundu ethnolinguistic group moved to the fore in the sixteenth and seventeenth centuries. By the end of the eighteenth century the Umbundu, who were concentrated on the Benguela highlands, participated more actively in the conflict. The southern Nhaneca-Humbe, Ambo, and Herero confronted other groups principally in the ninteenth and twentieth centuries. The eastern groups, Lunda-Chokwe and Ganguelas, were farther from the coast, where most violence was initiated and registered. The Portuguese, the last major ethnolinguistic group, have resided principally at the coast, but their impact has been felt throughout Angola during the entire five centuries. The other non-

4. Ibid., p. 264.
5. Oliver and Fage, p. 28.

Bantu group, the Bushmen-Hottentot, were victims of cultural violence and have been practically eliminated from Angola.

The space and data available do not permit a systematic analysis here of each ethnolinguistic group. Rather, the discussion will focus on some feature of each group that is characteristic but in most cases not exclusive to the particular group. Then certain common characteristics shared by the vast majority of Angolans who are Bantu will be noted. In the case of the Bantu ethnolinguistic groups, I have followed the convention in English transliterations of dropping the prefixes except in the cases of the two largest groups which have a common root name— *mbundu.* Consequently, the adjectival prefix serves to distinguish the Kimbundu, who occupy the districts of Luanda, Cuanza North, Cuanza South, and Malange, from the Umbundu, who are concentrated in the districts of Benguela, Huambo, Huíla, and Bié.

The Kongo Group—from Kingdom to Clan

The Kongo ethnolinguistic group, with about 13 percent of the population, was the third largest in Angola. It included eight related peoples who occupied Cabinda and the current administrative districts of Zaïre and Uíge. Although two-thirds of the Kongo lived in Brazzaville (Congo) and Zaïre, the Angolan Kongo are privileged because the ancient capital of the kingdom was in Angola. The Xikongo, the largest people in this group, occupied the area around the capital, Mbanza Kongo, or São Salvador, about 80 miles (128 kilometers) south of the Congo River. The Xikongo, together with seven other peoples—Susso, Zombo, Sorongo, Iacas, Congo, Pombo, and Suco—formed the Kongo ethnolinguistic group.

Persons of this area identified themselves most frequently as members of one of the eight peoples. However, their identity with the whole Kongo ethnolinguistic group was strengthened by the fact that the Kongo region had the only centralized monarchy in Angola. Therefore, in the major conflicts in which Kongo participated, they did so as subjects of the Kingdom of the Kongo, the most prestigious kingdom of Angola. The historical sketch in the next chapter will indicate that during two of the

five centuries the Kingdom of the Kongo was unified and powerful. For the past three centuries the kingdom has provided
mainly proud memories and hope for restoration. Nevertheless,
the memories and hopes were strong enough to give the kingdom a key role in the development of Angolan nationalism and
also in the Portuguese efforts to combat this nationalism.

SOCIAL ORGANIZATION

The strongest social cohesion among the Kongo was provided
by the matrilinear clan. A Kongo proverb stated that the person
who left his clan was like a "locust who has lost his wings"; he has
crossed the boundaries beyond which security, solidarity, and
affection are no longer guaranteed in all circumstances.[6] The
clan consisted of the descendants of a common line, "whether
they lived underneath (the dead) or above (the living) the
ground," who were bound together by a community of blood.
Only women of free status carried this blood, which conferred
membership in the clan. The mother and son were of the same
clan, but the father remained a stranger in the clan sense even
if he did provide access to a paternal kinship or *kitata*. The clan,
which was represented and administered by an elder, regulated
most social relations. It defined incestuous sexual relations, for
the blood community forbade relations between a man and a
woman who bore the same clan name, and guaranteed access
to the clan territory of which the ancestors, founders of the
first settlements, remained the "owners." The transmission of
land rights and the line of descent operated from maternal uncle
to nephew. The clan created the conditions for security and
solidarity.

Not only was the social organization of the Kongo society
based on female descent, but the daily existence of the Kongo,
which resembles patterns common to most peoples of Angola,
was dependent upon female labor. Women went to the field
early each morning with baskets, calabashes, and hoes on their
heads. On their backs some of the women carried babies; others
led toddling children by the hand. When they arrived at their

6. George Balandier, *Daily Life in the Kingdom of the Kongo from the Sixteenth to the
Eighteenth Century* (New York: World, 1969), p. 181.

fields, the women hoed the mounds of manioc, corn, or pumpkins or planted the manioc stems. They also split pumpkins and dried the seeds in the sun or grubbed up the peanuts and spread them to dry, according to the season of the year. In late afternoon the women returned from their fields, their baskets piled high with food, bundles of firewood, and calabashes of water. They and the young girls then prepared the main meal of the day for the family. Although palm kernels, peanuts, plantains, bananas, sweet potatoes, yams, and maize might have been eaten as snacks through the day, the Kongo had not really eaten until they had *luku,* manioc or cassava mush.

While women provided vegetable foods for the family, men supplied the meat or fish. In addition to caring for the domesticated goats, sheep, pigs, and fowls, hunting was an important male occupation. At the beginning of this century the men also collected goats, pigs, sheep, various kinds of farm produce, palm wine, slaves, and manufactured goods and took them to any of four markets: konzo, nkenge, nsona, and nkandu. These have given their names to the four days that make up the Kongo week; markets held on a certain day all over the Lower Congo are called konzo, and the markets held the next day are named nkenge. Every village had within reasonable walking distance at least one weekly market where goods could be bartered.

The forge and the palm were symbols of daily life in the Kingdom of the Kongo during the sixteenth to the eighteenth century.[7] The palm represented the abundance of nature and the forge the most notable human skill. Among artisans—who were especially honored by Kongo society—the blacksmith was the most noble. Iron metallurgy spread through the region around the fourteenth century, or at about the time the kingdom was forming, which helps explain the myth that the sovereign who created the Kongo was a blacksmith king. By the beginning of the twentieth century the introduction of European trade knives, hoes, and guns had practically eliminated smithing as one of the skilled arts of the people. However, the palm still stood, and in the 1920s, as two centuries before, "the gifts of the

7. Ibid., pp. 89–138.

palm tree are found everywhere: in the walls and roofs of the houses, in game traps and fisherman's snares, in the public treasury as well as in clothing, cosmetics, therapeutics, nourishment and finally in the system of symbols uniting man with his fellows and with his gods."[8]

WORLD VIEW

As with most Bantu, the Kongo lived in a world in which the visible and the invisible, the secular and the sacred, the human and the divine, overlapped. Each person was composed of four elements: body (*nitu*); two souls, the spiritual soul (*moyo*) and the perceptible soul (*mfumu kutu*); and the name (*zina*). Human beings inhabited a universe with the spirits (*bisimbi*), those who had passed through death. All these Kongo beings were creatures of Nzambi Mpungu, the supreme God of both traditional religion and the Christian faith. In religious ritual the Kongo did not worship Nzambi Mpungu, but appealed to the ancestors (*bakulu*) for aid and protection.

Magic was a dimension of the Kongo universe which did not deal directly with God or the ancestors. The common Kongo magical practice was *loka e nkisi,* cursing with the aid of a charm. Although anyone with the proper charm and appropriate incantation could employ magic, certain persons were trained as specialists. There were many varieties of magic specialists (*nganga*), such as the *nganga a ngombe,* or witchfinder; the *nganga a zumbi,* or luck-giving medicine man; the *nganga a nazji,* or fetish medicine man; and the *nganga a mbambi,* or ulcer curer.

As was pointed out above, there are no static, traditional cultures since all human life is constantly changing. Still, certain dimensions of culture are more stable than others, and the social structure and world view of the Kongo people seem to be examples of such relative stability. As one scholar put it, "It appears that the essential processes of Kongo social life and the symbols associated with them, have remained much the same through the recorded phases of Kongo history."[9]

8. Ibid., p. 90.
9. Wyatt MacGaffey, *Custom and Government in the Lower Congo* (Berkeley: University of California Press, 1970), p. 306.

The Kimbundu Group—the Heart of Assimilation

The Kongo's immediate neighbors to the south, between the Dande and Cuanza rivers, belonged to the Kimbundu ethnolinguistic group, which had nearly twice the population of the Kongo. The Kimbundu spread from Luanda at the coast to the Cassange basin in the eastern part of the district of Malange. Twenty peoples were listed in the Kimbundu group: Ambundu, Luanda, Luango, Ntemo, Puna, Dembo, Bangala, Holo, Cari, Chinje, Minungo, Bambeiro, Quibala, Haco, Sende, Ngola or Jinga, Bondo, Songo, Quissama, and Libolo.

ASSIMILATION

The Portuguese influence, which was more extensive and intensive in the Kimbundu area than in any other region of Angola, diminished the importance of the Kimbundu peoples as social or political units. Héli Chatelain, a Swiss-American missionary linguist, studied the Kimbundu language at the end of the nineteenth century and divided it into two main dialects: Luanda, used in the capital and the coastal plain, and Ambaca, used on the plateau. This linguistic division coincided with political and social rivalries which have affected the Kimbundu group and the history of that part of Angola to the present.

Ambaquistas were proud of their long association with the Portuguese and their role in the subjection of Angola. A young Ambaquista writing an autobiographical sketch in 1953 proudly recalled his past:

[My grandfather] was born in 1861 in the region of Lucamba, Ambaca. He was a mestizo; it is known that in the region of Ambaca the Europeans first established their residence—after Luanda; it was the Ambaquista people who fought side by side with the European soldiers to fight and subject almost all of Angola, principally in the areas of Cassambo, Bondo, Bangala, Luando and the South. Therefore, this was the first Angolan people to learn to read and write, even using a banana leaf as paper, sap from the tomato leaf as ink and chicken feather as a pen. They were the secretaries of many Angolan kings. . . . [My father] studied reading and writing in an old official school in Malanje where he learned enough to be a trader for the rest of his life. He was recruited to serve in the Portuguese army, fighting and subjecting the natives of the Cassamba and Ngola regions and killing any chiefs who revolted or rebelled against Portuguese rule. . . . Having finished his duty to defend the Fatherland fighting against his brothers of the same race, whether because of heroism or whatever reason.[10]

Chatelain also witnessed to the important colonial role of the Ambaquistas by affirming that "it is not the Portuguese nor the Germans or Belgians, but the black Ambaca people who have opened up the Kwangu, Kuilu and Kassai basins."[11] Another sign of the assimilation of the Ambaca people is that the term *mundele,* which means white person, is used by surrounding peoples to refer to the Ambaquistas. In the interior, *mundele* may mean not only a European, but *um preto de sapatos,* a black wearing or owning shoes.[12] However, the same Kimbundu peoples who spoke of the Ambaquistas as *andele* would also say when an Ambaca person approached: "It is no one, just an Ambaquista."

ECONOMY

The Kimbundu economy was primarily agricultural and, like the Kongo, the Kimbundu peoples cultivated cassava as their principal subsistence crop. For both groups, cassava mush (*fungi*) was the staff of life. The Kimbundu farmers were the first in Angola to cultivate rice and by the end of the nineteenth century were producing coffee for the export market. As among most Angolans, the Kimbundu expected women to have certain skills in tilling, cooking, washing, sewing, trading, and midwifery, while men should have learned something about building a house, hunting, cooking, trading, and medicine. In addition to this general knowledge expected of all adults, the Kimbundu recognized certain special crafts and trades: medicine and divining, hunting, fishing, wood carving, spinning and weaving, smelting and smithing, and basket, mat, rope, and pottery making. By 1920 certain European trades were becoming common in the Kimbundu area: tailoring, shoemaking, carpentry, cooperage, and masonry.

10. Sequeira João Lourenço, "Apontamentos da minha vida" (unpublished autobiographical manuscript, Lobito, October 15, 1953), p. 3.
11. Heli Chatelain, *Folk Tales of Angola* (Boston: Houghton Mifflin, 1894), p. 14.
12. Ibid., p. 259.

Kimbundu commerce was carried on by barter, through the exchange of salt, wax, and honey for guns, powder, or cloth. Rubber, game, cattle, and agricultural produce were bartered for rum, blankets, and trinkets. Labor was also valued as an item of barter as Songo men carried loads between Malange and Dondo for guns, rum, or cloth. In 1894 Chatelain reported that slaves were still an important item of trade in Angola: "Slavery and its unavoidable concomitant, the slave trade, are practiced all over Angola [referring to the Kimbundu area]. It is based on three facts: the right of the uncle to dispose of his nephews and nieces as merchandise, the absence of penitentiaries, and war."[13]

The *kimbanda*, or medicine man, used both medicines and rites to protect the health of the Kimbundu peoples against such common Angolan diseases as malaria, intestinal parasites, recurrent fever, and pneumonia, as well as against the regional disease of sleeping sickness, which affected the whole northern part of the country, and the syphilis common near white settlements. We have few reports to help us know the state of the people's health, but there is evidence that the Kissama population was reduced by smallpox from over 30,000 in about 1900 to 10,000 in 1929.[14]

The Kimbundu not only learned to speak Portuguese as they became assimilated, but also produced the first Angolan written literature. All the peoples of Angola had a rich oral literature—folktales, proverbs, poetry, and songs—but it was among the "Africans" who were located mostly in Luanda at the end of the nineteenth century that creative writing appeared. The word "Africans" referred in that context to a distinct cultural group of blacks and mestizos who were in close contact with Europeans. This Angolan elite, working mostly in commerce and public service in the capital, found journalism a vehicle for the expression of their literary talents. The first periodical edited by "Africans," *O Echo de Angola*, appeared in 1881, and during the next ten years several other periodicals using Kimbundu and Portuguese circulated in the capital.

13. Ibid., p. 9.
14. George Peter Murdock, *Africa: Its Peoples and Their Culture History* (New York: McGraw-Hill, 1959), p. 292.

Joaquim Dias Cordeiro da Matta, born in 1857 in Incolo-e-Bengo, was the most distinguished and prolific of the first generation of African writers. He expressed himself through poetry, novels, chronicles, history, and journalism. Inspired by and in collaboration with Chatelain, Cordeiro da Matta also published pedagogical, philological, and ethnographic studies.

The Umbundu Group—Villagers and Traders

With about 36 percent of all Angolans speaking Umbundu, this was the largest ethnolinguistic group. In spite of being the largest, they were the most homogeneous group in Angola; in fact, it was possible to classify the Umbundu as a people rather than a group of peoples.

The Umbundu were concentrated south of the Cuanza River on the central highlands in the most populous districts of Angola: Huambo, Benguela, and Bié. From this population center the Umbundu scattered to every district so that this most homogeneous group was also paradoxically the most wide-ranging of all linguistic groups.

AGRICULTURE

Most Umbundu, like most Angolans in 1920, lived in rural areas and depended on subsistence agriculture for their basic food supply. The importance of cash crops was already on the increase, but, whether for subsistence or cash, the main crop was corn and the basic rhythm of Umbundu life was determined by its cultivation. The word for year, *ulima,* comes from *okulima,* to cultivate. Cultivation began just before the first rains in September and, depending on the date of the rains and their consistency, planting spread from early October to well into December. The Umbundu farmers spent the next three months hoeing the corn; they harvested it after the rains ended in April or early May. The *ulima,* or yearly cycle, moved inside a larger twenty- to forty-year cycle made up of six to fifteen years of cultivation, two to four years of grass fallow, and sixteen to twenty years for the regeneration of shrubs and small miombo trees.

These cycles applied to the *epia* (plural *ovapia*), the upland field. Since the last quarter of the nineteenth century, the Ovimbundu had also cultivated river bottoms, *olonaka* (singular *onaka*). They planted the river gardens at the end of the dry season and the crops were ready to harvest in January during the little dry spell which was also the traditional time of hunger. A third type of field was the *ocumbo* (plural *oviumbo*), literally the encircled space near the house, where such vegetables as cabbage, kale, tomato, okra, and peppers were grown.

The Umbundu economy passed through a variety of phases in the nineteenth and early twentieth centuries, but during this period the Umbundu always cultivated corn to sustain life. Farming had never been considered a profession (*ocipinduko*) by the Umbundu, whether it produced crops for subsistence or sale. In the mid-nineteenth century subsistence agriculture was a relatively small part of the Umbundu economy. Hunting and gathering, beekeeping, trade and war, crafts, fishing, small livestock and poultry, provided greater wealth. The rubber trade dominated the Umbundu economy from 1874 to 1900. In 1920 the effective occupation of the central highlands by the Portuguese authorities and traders eliminated trade and war from the Umbundu economy and left the people with subsistence agriculture. However, the Portuguese traders were encouraging cash crops so they could profit from the peoples' efforts by trading cloth, salt, sugar, palm oil, and hoes for corn and beans.

THE VILLAGE

The most distinctive unit in Umbundu society was the village, *imbo* (plural *ovaimbo*) which was composed of ten to fifty households, and included 100 to 1,000 people. The village commonly bore the name of the founder, of whom the current elder would probably have been a descendant. Only the village elder, *sekulu*, could speak of "my village" (*imbo liange*); for everyone else it was "our village" (*imbo lietu*). Childs quotes a village elder as saying, "In our Umbundu country [we] people do not build together [i.e., in the same village] unless we are blood relations."[15] The

15. Gladwyn Murray Childs, *Umbundu Kinship and Culture; Being a description of the social structure and individual development of the Ovimbundu of Angola, with observations concerning the bearing on the enterprise of Christian Missions of certain phases of the life and culture described* (London: Oxford University Press, 1949), p. 28.

Umbundu distinguished themselves from their neighbors to the north, the Kimbundu, and to the east and south, the Ganguelas or Ambo, emphasizing that they were village-dwelling people. For them, the real values of village life seemed to be the sociability and mutual help that a man living among his kind could enjoy. Umbundu villages could not be distinguished absolutely from those of neighboring groups, but they were relatively larger and more firmly united by kinship ties.

In the village, wattle-and-daub houses were scattered haphazardly in household clusters. The living houses, which may have been of two or three rooms, were usually rectangular. Specialized houses were commonly circular: the granary (*osila*), the spirit hut (*etambo*), the men's clubhouse (*onjango*), and the kitchen (*ociwo*).

The word for family, *epata,* came from *okupata,* meaning to tie or braid. According to Umbundu culture, those bound together extended beyond the nuclear family to include two lineages: the paternal *oluse* and the maternal *oluina.* The chief function of the *oluse* was to bind together the local residence group. The *oluina* was not a local group, but when an Ocimbundu spoke of his family, *epata,* in the sense of an extended kinship association with a known elder as head, he or she was usually referring to the *oluina.* Property was also inherited through the *oluina,* from mother's brother to sister's son.

MONARCHY

In 1920 the Umbundu were organized politically into a dozen kingdoms, the most powerful being Bailundo, Bié, Huambo, Chiyaka, Galangue, and Andulo. The kings exercised three principal functions: communicating with the spirit world, relating to other peoples, and dispensing justice.

The king was high priest for his people since the spirits of the king's ancestors were the principal communal deities. He and his medicine men sacrificed at the royal shrine to control the elements and ensure fertility and success in hunting. Closely related to these religious functions of the king was the use of magic, witchcraft, and divination to protect himself and his people. Fulfilling his second or diplomatic function, the king made agreements with other kings to promote trade, and to make war on neighboring peoples to provide his court with tribute and his warriors with plunder.

Although religious and diplomatic functions might have been regarded as his primary responsibilities, the Umbundu king actually spent more time dispensing justice than in any other activity. Proverbs appropriate for the judgement of cases at court were more numerous than any other category, except perhaps those used for the education of the young. The trials were usually lengthy and only came to a close when the king gave his judgment. "The advocate speaks; the king concludes or decides" (*"O popia onganji, o malapo osoma"*). The king was generally not arbitrary in his decisions, but was bound by the customs of his people as well as by the opinions of his councillors. To strengthen his argument that the king, though a divine representative, was also a democratically chosen leader, an observer from the early nineteenth century comments: "The government of Bailundo is democratic. These heathen mix with the infamous humiliations of the orientals the unabridged coarseness of the English people at election times in England. The kings defer to and flatter their counsellors; these are they who elevate a king to the throne and also who cast him down."[16]

Each Umbundu king held authority over a number of subkingdoms or *atumbu*. The largest kingdom, Bailundo, had about 200 *atumbu,* and each *etumbu* ruled over three to 300 villages. (The word *ombala* was used for the capital of the kingdom and subkingdoms.) After the Bailundo War of 1902 and the effective occupation of central Angola by Portuguese authorities during the first quarter of the twentieth century, the kingdoms were eliminated as functioning political units and the terms *king* and *capital* referred to the subkingdoms.

UMBUNDU INFLUENCE

The populous, homogenous, but scattered Umbundu exercised a cultural imperialism among their neighbors of other ethnolinguistic groups. Umbundu is the African trade language from the coast into Katanga. The Umbundu have the tradition of being traders, not only in Angola, but of Central Africa, and

16. Ibid., p. 22.

have learned to adapt to a variety of peoples and cultures on their trading caravans. They also were the first group in central and southern Angola to adapt to Portuguese civilization. Some Angolans considered this adaptability a virtue, but others considered it a sign of weakness and lack of character. The Umbundu were to occupy an important position in the Portuguese exploitation of Angola, not only because they were centrally located and the most populous group, but because they were the most tractable.

The Kongo, Kimbundu, and Umbundu accounted for about 70 percent of the population of Angola. The other nine groups composed the remaining 30 percent.

The Ambo Group—Herders and Farmers

Few peoples have named themselves. The Hereros of Namibia gave the name Ambo to their neighbors to the north who straddled the border between Angola and Namibia.[17] In Angola the term has been applied to the ethnolinguistic group which includes the Cuanhama, Cuamatui, Evale, and Cafima in the area from the 16° latitude to the frontier. The Ambo, who composed less than 3 percent of the population, had most of Angola's cattle and were the principal suppliers of beef steers and of young animals for the central highlands. The economy should be called agropastoral for the Ambo depended on both agriculture and cattle raising equally; however, the possession of cattle gave more status than successful cultivation.

The two main crops were sorghum and millet. The latter was dignified with the name *oilia* (food) since it had a threefold advantage over sorghum: it grew in poorer soil, resisted long dry spells, and could be stored for two to three years.[18]

ECONOMY

The agricultural year began at the end of the dry season with the cleaning of the fields, the gathering of the stubble in small

17. Carlos Estermann, *Etnografia do sudoeste de Angola,* Vol. I, *Os povos Não-Bantos e o grupo étnico dos Ambos* (Lisbon: Junta de Investigações do Ultramar, 1960), p. 77.
18. Ibid., p. 167.

mounds with the straw that the cattle had left, and then the burning of the mounds. In October, when the first signs of rain appeared, cultivation (*okulima*) began. The affinity of the Ambo and Umbundu cultures was revealed by the similarity of their agricultural vocabulary. The women, who did the cultivating, used a hoe (*etemo*), which was not heavy, but the short handle required the women to bend double to use it. In a normal year the millet seed was planted by the end of November, but the rains in the extreme south of Angola might be irregular, in which case the seed was planted at intervals as the signs of rain appeared. A few of the more fertile patches were saved for sorghum. In small quantities, beans, squash, and melons were planted among the millet. With the first rains, the weeds began to grow and the more intense work of hoeing began.

To move fertilizer from the corral, which was an integral part of the household enclosure, to the area of the cultivation outside of the enclosure was taboo, but with the frequent shifting of the household within that area, by the end of a twenty- to thirty-year cycle there was no spot which had not been a corral at some time. Nevertheless, the very poor, sandy soil was still deficient in nitrogen.

The millet matured at the end of March or beginning of April and the harvest, *eteyo*, began. After the grain was dried, thrashed, and sifted, it was placed in the huge elevated baskets, *oma-anda,* which served as storage bins. The old year was "broken," *oku totola omudo,* and the new year began with the tasting of mush made with new grain.

The pastoral year was related to the agricultural year, with the family herd staying at the farmstead after the harvest to eat the stubble of the harvest. In August or September the cattle could begin to graze in the alluvial plain, *evanda,* of the Cunene River.[19] In December or January the river rose and flooded the plain, so the herds were pastured closer to the settlement. When

19. Eduardo Cruz de Carvalho, "'Traditional' and 'Modern' Patterns of Cattle-raising in Southwest Angola: Critical Evaluation of Change from Pastoralism to Ranching" (paper presented at the annual meeting of the Africa Studies Association, Denver, Colo., November 1971, revised and abridged), p. 16.

the stubble was mostly consumed, the majority of the cattle, with the exception of a few head remaining in the settlement to supply the family's milk, were moved to the communal pasture-lands in the interior, on the high sandy plain, *etunda*. Here the herds were gathered in the areas with some water supply, often very far from the permanent settlement.

The herds were mixed on the basis of a complex socioeconomic relationship between ownership and holding of cattle. The cattleowners, for technical as well as sociocultural reasons, distributed their cattle among various relatives and friends, with the result that each herd included cattle belonging to different owners. Thus the Ambo provided insurance against epidemics and kept the herd within manageable size. The system also served sociocultural purposes by hiding the number of cattle owned by any one person to avoid the envy of kin or pressures from government authorities to sell more cattle. In addition to acting as a leveling mechanism, the distribution of cattle served to extend and strengthen social relationships.[20]

SOCIAL ORGANIZATION

The Ambo did not live in villages as did the Umbundu. The rural population was divided into communities or districts, *mukunda,* with each community consisting of 100 to 300 family units and laying claim to a loosely defined area, *chilongo*. An individual family unit occupied its own farmstead, *ongubo,* which was one large enclosure averaging from fifteen to fifty acres, surrounded by entwined branches of thorn shrubs. The farmstead was composed of the dwelling or kraal complex (*ehumbo*), the farming plots (*tchikove*), and the area of private pastureland (*ongole*). The *ehumbo* was a stockaded dwelling divided into compounds containing sleeping and storage huts, corrals and pens, and space for social life. Over the years the respective position of the *ongubo*'s components was rotated, but the total farm complex was permanent.

The Ambo family was matrilinear and the children belonged to the family of the mother. At times the father, *tate,* said that his children were *ovana vovanu,* "children of other people." The fam-

20. Ibid., p. 6.

ily relations were based on maternal descent, but the holder of authority was usually a man.[21]

The Ambo were not only united in extended matrilinear families, as were the majority of Angolans, but were the only group with well-defined totemic clans. Such clans had a totem, an animal or plant by which the members were identified and which was considered their common ancestor; a taboo against eating the meat or fruit of the totem; and exogamous rules between members of clans.[22] Among the twenty-odd clans were such totems as ox, dog, lion, hyena, and millet.

The Ambo did not have a centralized monarchy, but each people had its king. Among the Ambo in Angola, the kings of the Kwanyama played a dominant role. The last king with real authority, Mandume, was defeated by the Portuguese in September 1915 and the traditional capital, Onjiva, near the border of Namibia was given the name of the conquering general, Pereira d'Eça. At independence the town again was called by the traditional name, Onjiva.

The Ambo, a proud people, when pressed by Portuguese colonialism, were able to go over the border of South-West Africa to seek economic or educational opportunities. They knew more English, Afrikaans, or German than Portuguese.

The Nhaneca-Humbe Group—the Conservatives

The Nhaneca-Humbe, lying geographically and culturally between the Umbundu and the Ambo, accounted for about 5 percent of the Angolan population.[23] They spread across the districts of Huíla and Cunene from the towns of Chongoroi and Quilengues in the north to the border of Namibia in the south. The Nhaneca-Humbe are bound on the west by the Chela escarpment and on the east by the Cunene Valley. Ten peoples compose this group: Muilas, Gambos, Humbes, Donguenas, Hingas, Cuancuas, Handas of Quipungo, Quipungos, Quilengues-Humbes, and Quilengues-Musos. The traditions of

21. Estermann, I, 136.
22. Ibid., pp. 141–49.
23. Estermann, *Etnografia*, Vol. II, *O grupo étnico Nhaneca-Humbe* (Lisbon: Junta de Investigações do Ultramar, 1960), pp. 15–17.

the peoples of this group tell through typical legends how pastoralists, agriculturalists, and hunters combined to form their various societies.

The economy of the Nhaneca-Humbe was based on a combination of farming and animal husbandry. Showing its close relation to Umbundu and Ambo culture, the word meaning "to cultivate" is *okulima* and the crops are a combination of the Umbundu's corn and the Ambo's millet and sorghum. In the well-watered fields in the north of the area, the Nhaneca-Humbe follow the agricultural patterns described above for the Umbundu. In the semidesert region of the south, Ambo practices are used.

The Nhaneca-Humbe man shared with his Ambo neighbors the ambition to own a herd of cattle, but success in achieving this goal varied greatly. Some men had very large herds, others moderate-sized, and many had only one or two head of cattle. In the 1920s a moderate-sized herd would have had about 100 head.[24] Hunting and fishing were also important means of supplying food among some of the Nhaneca-Humbe peoples.

Political and religious authority among the Nhaneca-Humbe resided in the king. However, this ethnolinguistic group did not have the tradition of a centralized monarchy. The various peoples which composed the group have never been united in one kingdom like the Kongo or even in a federation like the Umbundu. In fact, even at the level of the individual peoples there was marked social disunity. For example, the Humbes were divided into four political units of which two considered themselves completely autonomous. Under the Portuguese colonial system of direct rule the African rulers were deprived of any real political power, but they maintained some religious authority.

The ruler was considered sacred because his subjects believed that the spirits of his ancestors dwelt in him and that they were responsible for protecting the people against such calamities as drought, hunger, sickness, and death. One of the powers entrusted to the ruler by the ancestors was that of making rain, *okulokesa*.[25]

24. Ibid., p. 182.
25. Ibid., p. 164.

The Nhaneca-Humbe was the most conservative group of peoples in Angola. They had been less influenced than others by European culture even though a relatively large settlement of Portuguese invaded their territory in the middle of the nineteenth century. This conservatism which resisted urbanization caused Sá da Bandeira, in the center of the Nhaneca-Humbe territory, to be the only city in Angola with a white majority.

The Herero—True Herders

The Herero group could dispute the classification of "most conservative" with the Nhaneca-Humbe, but the Herero peoples were so few in number that their place in the Angolan scene was less significant. The few thousand Dimbas, Chimbas, Chavicuas, Hacavonas, Cuvales, Dombes, Cuanhocas, and Guendelengos occupied the territory in the districts of Benguela, Moçâmedes, and Huíla, reaching inland from the Namib Desert.

The Herero in southwestern Angola were related to the Herero in Damaraland, Namibia. Legend tells us that this Bantu group moved down from the great lakes in Central Africa to the upper Zambezi Valley. From what is now the eastern border of Angola they moved west until some of them reached the coastal strip, approximately four centuries ago. As a continuation of this migration or as a separate move, some of the Herero pushed south into Namibia.

Economically, the Herero are the most exclusively pastoralist of all Angolans. Neighboring groups, the Ovambo and Nhaneca-Humbe, may value their pastoral more than their agricultural wealth, but they have long agricultural traditions. As recently as 1958, the oldest Herero could still remember the time before agriculture had entered their economy. An observer who arried in Damaraland in 1869 described the Herero devotion to their cattle in these terms:

The Herero dedicate themselves passionately to raising cattle. For them this activity means everything. Their imagination is filled day and night with their herds, just as a devotee of the stock market thinks about the fluctuations which his stocks might suffer. He lives and dies for his cattle. He sings about their qualities. A true empathy exists between the owner and animals for which he will sacrifice all his time. . . . The Herero does not shrink from work as he tries to increase the number of his cattle, and at this he is a master.[26]

The Lunda-Chokwe Group—Proud Hunters

The peoples belonging to the Lunda-Chokwe group include the Lunda, Lunda-lua-Chindes, Lunda-Ndembo, Mataba, Cacongo, Mai, and Chokwe. In the hyphenated name of this ethnolinguistic group, "Lunda" refers to the great empire of Central Africa which sent political chiefs from Katanga/Shaba to the most populous areas of eastern Angola in the seventeenth century. Among the peoples found by the Lunda chiefs were the Chokwe, who lived astride the watershed of the Kasai, Cuango, Zambezi, and Cuanza rivers in east-central Angola. The Chokwe sociopolitical organization was built around twelve matrilineal clans ruled by petty lineage chiefs. The Lunda imposed themselves as political chiefs over the local lineage heads and founded kingdoms on the model of the Lunda empire.

Most Lunda chiefs who established political control in northeastern Angola continued to recognize the suzerainty of the Lunda empire, but the Chokwe refused to send tribute to the Lunda emperor.[27] Until the middle of the nineteenth century the Chokwe remained a small, obscure, and independent people. About 1850 they began to expand and by 1920 they had spread east beyond the Kasai River, which formed the boundary with the Belgian Congo, and west to the Cubango River, which runs between the Cuando-Cubango and Huíla districts.[28] From an area about 100 miles in diameter they exploded to occupy a territory four times that size. In 1920 the Chokwe, who were only about 8 percent of the Angolan population, were scattered across the districts of Lunda, Moxico, Bié, and Cuando-Cubango.

EXPANSION

The Chokwe expanded by four principal means: small hunting parties, merchant caravans, raiding parties, and mass migra-

26. Estermann, *Etnografia*, Vol. III, *O grupo étnico Herero* (Lisbon: Junta de Investigações do Ultramar, 1961), p. 125.
27. Joseph Calder Miller, "Chokwe Expansion, 1850–1900" (M.A. thesis, University of Wisconsin, 1967).
28. Ibid., pp. 4–5.

tion.[29] The end of the slave trade in the mid-nineteenth century opened the door for the economic exploitation of ivory, beeswax, and rubber, in which the Chokwe were wealthy. The Chokwe, who were good hunters, had accumulated firearms. When ivory could be freely traded, they sent out hunting parties in ever-widening circles to kill elephants and sell the tusks. After ivory, beeswax was the second article to replace the slave trade in the Angolan economy. Apiculture reinforced agriculture and hunting. The Chokwe and the Luchaze were responsible for the production of most of the wax received at Luanda and Benguela. By 1851 the Chokwe wax enjoyed a reputation as the best in southern Africa, and in 1855 it was a major export of the region.

The Chokwe were also in a position to profit from the rubber boom in the last third of the nineteenth century since their forests produced most of the early rubber exports and rubber gathering fitted into the Chokwe economic pattern of hunting and agriculture.

This sudden wealth from ivory, wax, and rubber allowed the Chokwe to overcome the forces which had kept Angolan population levels stagnant: poor health conditions, limited food supply, and the human drain from the slave trade. They acquired by trade or raid a large number of women slaves, or pawns, who not only added to the Chokwe population by their own considerable number but were of child-bearing age. The Chokwe social structure facilitated integration of the foreign women, with a resulting dramatic increase in population which produced the only mass migration in modern Angolan history.[30]

During this expansive period the Chokwe attracted the attention and epithets of neighboring peoples and outside observers. "The gypsies of Angola" and "Bohemians of Central Africa"[31] are two phrases used to describe the Chokwe. David Livingstone, after crossing Africa from the Cape to Luanda, classified the Chokwe as the most savage and least hospitable people he had met. These characterizations reflect the determination of the

29. Ibid., p. 49.
30. Ibid., pp. 15–16.
31. Eduardo dos Santos, *Sobre a religião dos Quiocos* (Lisbon: Agência Geral do Ultramar, 1956), p. 16.

Chokwe to guard their own traditions and repel the domination of European culture.[32]

HUNTING

Hunting played a larger role in the economic life of the Lunda-Chokwe than in that of any other ethnolinguistic group in Angola. Commonly in the African division of labor hunting was a male activity, but among these peoples everyone participated in the hunt, although it is true that the larger wild game was the special responsibility of the men. The women's role was not less important in hunting, however, since more of the meat consumed was from small game such as rabbits and rodents. The Lunda-Chokwe used four methods of hunting, varying them according to what was appropriate to the season, the number of hunters, and the type of game: pursuit, ambush, encircling with fire, or trapping.

AGRICULTURE

Lunda-Chokwe agriculture was based upon cassava. The importance of this crop in the culture is shown by the fact that they distinguished thirteen varieties of bitter cassava and five of sweet. Sorghum had been the main crop and food of these peoples before the introduction of cassava, and several varieties of sorghum were still cultivated, as were beans, peanuts, sweet potatoes, squash, and peppers and other condiments. In the Moxico district the cultivation of corn had been increasing because of favorable climatic conditions and contacts with Umbundu and Ganguela, for whom this was the principal crop. The common system of shifting agriculture had reduced the once heavy forests of the area, but since the fields seldom exceeded one hectare per farmer, the trees had not been systematically cleared.

The Chokwe were known as proud, independent hunter-warriors. They were also famous as artists. Chokwe sculptors carved fine human figures and ritual masks. Mural painting was another art at which the Chokwe excelled.

---

32. Thomas Louttit, *Trial and Triumph in Chokweland, Central African Jubilee or Fifty Years with the Gospel in "The Beloved Strip"* (London: Pickering and Ingles, n.d.), p. 31.

The Ganguela Group—Fisher Men and Women

The remaining twenty Bantu peoples in Angola were gathered together into the Ganguela ethnolinguistic group which accounted for perhaps 7 percent of Angolans. Redinha classified the Luimbe, Luena, Lovale, Lutchazi, Bunda, Ganguila, Ambuela, Ambuila-Mambumba, Econjeiro, Ngonoielo, Mbande, Cangala, Iahuma, Gengista, Ncoia, Camachi, Ndungo, Nhengo, Nhemba, and Avico, all as Ganguela.[33] Murdock included most of these people in a Lunda cluster together with the Chokwe.[34]

The economy of the Ganguelas was based upon agriculture, hunting, and fishing. Since agriculture and hunting were discussed in more detail earlier in the description of other peoples, this section refers especially to fishing, using as a model the Luvale, a Ganguela people who were the most expert fishermen in Angola. The Luvale were extraordinary in organizing not only their economic but also their social and religious life around fishing, but many of the Ganguela peoples followed practices similar to those of the Luvale. Located in the eastern salient of Angola, the Luvale area is watered by two perennial rivers, the Zambezi and the Lungwebungu.[35] Rainfall occurs from mid-October to early April; the average precipitation during this period is about forty-five inches.

Fishing

Luvale fishing activities formed an annual cycle correlated with the environment, and, except at the height of the flood, fish were caught throughout the year. The Luvale regarded their fishing cycle as beginning at the end of the year after the rain started but before the water table had risen high enough to start filling the draining depressions. About the end of November or early December, preparations were made for the spawning run of the mud barbel. A fence of reeds was built across a small affluent of a larger stream, leaving a passage in the middle; from

33. José Redinha, *Distribuição étnica de Angola* (Luanda: Centro de Informação Turismo de Angola, 1962), pp. 17–18.
34. Murdock, p. 293.
35. C. M. N. White, "The Role of Hunting and Fishing in Luvale Society" in Elliott P. Skinner, ed., *Peoples and Cultures of Africa: An Anthropological Reader* (Garden City, N.Y.: Doubleday, 1973), pp. 122–42.

the latter on the upstream side a circular fence, *malela,* was constructed into which the fish passed and from which they could not escape. As the water rose, the fish came upstream to spawn in the flooded drainage depressions; when the circular enclosure was found full of fish, the men entered and killed the fish with spears and axes. The fish were split and dried and for the next two months, January and February, fishing was at a standstill.

The second stage of the fishing cycle began when the flood receded. Fish weirs were then built across seepage streams on plains feeding into larger streams. These weirs, called *makalila,* consisted of a sod dam to block the flow; holes were left in them and on the downstream side pocket-shaped traps of matting called *vikanga* were placed, into which the fish from upstream fell as they descended with the receding flood. Fishing in *makalila* went on in March and April. By May these seepage streams had become dry and it was necessary to repeat the process on the larger streams. From May to July the Luvale fished at the large dams, which were constructed with poles and branches as well as sod. Cylindrical basket traps big enough to catch a crocodile were placed on the downstream side. During this period great numbers of people camped along the rivers and streams in temporary shelters.

By August the flood had fallen so far that the weirs and dams were no longer productive, but numerous pools remained. A man and his wife would fish the small pools by bailing out the water with baskets. The larger pools could not be bailed and these were treated with fish poison. In addition to their activities in this annual cycle, the Luvale fished with hook and line, traps, nets, drag baskets, and flares at other times not regulated by the annual cycle.

All major economic activities of Bantu peoples were accompanied by ritual practices. The most important of the special observances among the Luvale were those connected with fish poisoning. Sexual intercourse was forbidden between the participants on a fish-poisoning expedition; this was significant because men and women participated together in fish poisoning so that the taboo had to be observed throughout the period of the expedition. A senior member of the party struck a blow with a hoe at the fish-poison plant, whereupon the rest of the party lay down on their backs and writhed as a symbol of the dying and wriggling fish. A variety of magical charms were used to ensure good fishing, as were certain rituals to show respect to the fisherman's guardian ancestral spirit, *mukulu.*

The Ganguela group was the most heterogeneous in Angola. Each of the twenty peoples was so small and isolated that neither the peoples individually nor the group as a whole played a major role in the conflicts of Angola.

The Non-Bantu

The eight ethnolinguistic groups already described, which formed perhaps 99 percent of the population of Angola in 1920, were all Bantu. The remaining peoples were non-Bantu: the Khiosan, representatives of the peoples who lived in Angola before the Bantu invasion; and the Portuguese, who succeeded in dominating the Bantu for about a century, but have now largely withdrawn.

Khoisan—the Native Angolans

The Kung Bushmen in southern Angola call themselves *zhu twa si,* "the harmless people."[36] They call non-Bushmen *zo si,* which means "animals without hooves" because, they say, non-Bushmen are angry and dangerous like lions and hyenas. When the Bantu "animals without hooves" entered Angola four to ten centuries ago, they found hunting-gathering populations who were so harmless that they were soon dominated, and by the beginning of the century were represented only by a few thousand Khoisan and Vatua.

"Khoisan" is a compound of the Hottentots' name for themselves, Khoikhoi, and their name for Bushmen, San.[37] If there were ever Hottentots in Angola they have been eliminated or removed. By the first two decades of the twentieth century a few thousand Bushmen in small family bands wandered across southern Angola and into the Kalahari Desert. The slightly built,

36. Elizabeth Marshall Thomas, *The Harmless People* (New York: Knopf, 1959), p. 24.
37. Jean Hiernaux, *The Peoples of Africa* (New York: Scribners, 1974), p. 98.

yellow-skinned Bushmen lived a nomadic life with no permanent settlements. They built simple windbreaks of a semicircle of saplings stuck in the ground and tied together at the top, covered with grass. The Bushmen practiced no agriculture and owned no domesticated animals, except perhaps a dog. The division of labor by sex follows a single pattern, with men doing the hunting and fishing and women the gathering.

The Bushman social organization was simply the nuclear family. A band, which seldom surpassed twenty people, may have consisted of an old man and his wife, their daughters, the daughters' husbands and children, and perhaps an unmarried son or two. Custom allowed polygamy, but few men were successful enough at hunting to support more than one wife.

As combatants in the violent history of Angola, the Bushmen have followed a strategy of retreat and flight. "Bushmen deplore and misunderstand bravery. The heroes of their legends are always little jackals who trick, lie, and narrowly escape, rather than larger, bolder animals such as lions. . . . In the Bushmen's stories, lions are always being scalded, duped, cuckolded, or killed."[38] Bushmen not only avoided a fight with their fierce white and Bantu neighbors; to survive in their inhospitable desert without more effective tools, cattle, or agriculture, Bushmen had to cooperate with each other. Their culture insisted that they share their most prized personal possessions, such as a sharp knife or strong bow, to avoid making other Bushmen jealous.

In the conflict between the Khoisan and the Bantu who invaded their territory, the Khoisan first retreated geographically to isolated, unoccupied areas in southern Angola or across the border into Namibia or Botswana. In the twentieth century the Bushmen have found no more open spaces into which they could flee so they have retreated culturally. They have exchanged the game or fruits from their hunting and gathering for the agricultural products of the Bantu and more recently have cultivated their own small plots and raised cattle. The Khoisan have been victims of "culturocide" at the hands of the Bantu and so have played no part in the other conflicts of An-

38. Thomas, p. 22.

gola, although in the 1960s the Portuguese did try to use them to fight against the nationalist guerrillas.

The Portuguese—Colonizers and Settlers

The African combatants shared a traditional culture based on kinship relations, subsistence economy, and spiritual-symbolic worldview. Among themselves the African peoples of Angola fought over land, cattle, slaves, and political hegemony, but the conflicts were brief, sporadic, and localized. The most aggressive, consistent, and wide-ranging combatants have been the Portuguese. Other peoples have straddled the border, having kinsmen in neighboring territories, but only the Portuguese had their homeland and capital outside of Angola. Consequently, a description of the Portuguese must include not only the few who resided in Angola, but also some observations on the European nation and its culture which participated in the conflicts in Angola during five centuries.

Looked at economically and politically, Portugal in 1920 did not qualify as a colonial power. Economically, Portugal was as much colony as colonizer. It depended on capital from other western European countries, in particular England, to which Portugal sent 70 percent of its exports.[39] The Industrial Revolution of the eighteenth and nineteenth centuries had hardly touched Portugal, which in 1920 was still 80 percent rural. It had a few profitable agricultural products—wine, cork, and fruit—but was dependent on imports for such staples as wheat, sugar, and codfish as well as for basic industrial materials—coal, iron, steel, and machinery. Portugal's industrial underdevelopment is illustrated by the fact that it used only one-seventh the amount of energy in its factories as Belgium did.[40] Occupying such a dependent position, Portugal was unable to provide the capital necessary to develop Angola, which was fourteen times larger than the metropole.

In 1920, Portugal suffered such severe political instability that it was not able to administer its colonies effectively. It was

39. A. H. de Oliveira Marques, *História de Portugal*, Vol. II, *Desde os tempos mais Antigos até ao governo do Sr. Pinheiro de Azevedo* (Lisbon: Palas Editores, 1974), p. 197.
40. Ibid., p. 193.

struggling to maintain its first Republic, which began on October 5, 1910, with the overthrow of the monarchy. During the sixteen years of the Republic the government changed forty-five times; in 1920 alone, seven ministries passed in procession. Political unrest and serious economic problems were exacerbated by the impact of World War I, in which Portugal fought on the side of the Allies from 1916 to 1918.

How could such a poor and unstable nation as Portugal maintain a colonial empire longer than Belgium, France, and Great Britain? Three factors, at least, qualified Portugal as a colonial nation, if not a colonial power.

NATIONALISM

First, nationalism gave Portugal a pride which to foreigners seemed unjustified. Portuguese tradition held that of all the ethnic, linguistic, and regional communities of the Iberian Peninsula, only Lusitania established and maintained its national identity. Catalonia, Valencia, Murcia, Andalusia, New Castile, Old Castile, Aragon, Navarro, the Basque Provinces, Estremadura, León, Asturias, and Galicia were united into one nation-state, Spain, while Lusitania secured its own national independence.

A thousand years before Portugal achieved political nationhood, the Greek geographer Strabo recognized the strength of Portuguese nationalism: "And yet the country north of the Tagus, Lusitania, is the greatest of the Iberian nations and is the nation against which the Romans waged war for the longest time."[41]

ROMAN CULTURE

Second, Roman culture—law, language, and religion— endowed Portugal with self-confidence and even a sense of superiority. Rome dominated Lusitania for five centuries and although the number of Romans who actually settled there was small, Roman influence was pervasive and enduring. The Portuguese language descended directly from Latin, and neither

41. *The Geography of Strabo,* English trans. Horace L. Jones, 8 vols. (London: Loeb Classical Library, 1917-23), Vol. II, p. 65.

the pre-Roman Iberian cultures nor the Germanic languages of the Visigoth period (sixth to eighth centuries) exercised much influence on it.[42] Portuguese also maintained its Latin structure and vocabulary through the period of Moorish influence. Arabic provided about 600 words, mainly names for clothes, furniture, agricultural and scientific instruments, and equipment introduced into Portugal by the Moors during the centuries (eighth to twelfth) of Arab domination. Most of these words have since been replaced by French, Italian, or English words. The Portuguese nation has also been a strong defender of the Roman form of Christianity, not having passed through the Reformation which was common to most of the rest of western Europe. So Portugal felt a responsibility to a civilizing mission which originated in Rome even before its own nationhood.

CLASS STRUCTURE

Finally, the particular class structure of Portugal encouraged the perpetuation of colonialism. The Portuguese were divided into four classes in the early twentieth century.[43] The wealthy bourgeoisie ruled Portugal, basing their power on banking, major commerce, and large landholdings. They reinforced their wealth by ties with foreign capital and the exploitation of the colonies. The monarchy was their symbol of order and privilege. The wealthy bourgeoisie supported the Catholic Church and were in turn supported by it. The upper-echelon officers in the armed forces could be counted on the defend the wealthy bourgeoisie even though they did not all come from that class.

The principal enemy of the wealthy bourgeoisie was not the workers and peasants, who were powerless, but the lesser bourgeoisie—the middle class. They were concentrated in the principal urban centers—Lisbon and Oporto—working in commerce, industry, and the professions, and were middle- and lower-level government employees, university students, middle- and lower-level military officers, and a few small landholders. They sought economic power and were concerned about the

42. Oliveira Marques, *História de Portugal,* Vol. I: *Desde os tempos mais antigos até ao governo do Sr. Palma Carlos* (Lisbon, Palas Editores, 1974), pp. 18–24.
43. Oliveira Marques, II, 209–11.

backwardness of the country and the future of the colonies. The lesser bourgeoisie were antimonarchic, anticlerical, and nationalistic, in contrast to the wealthy bourgeoisie.

The working class, also concentrated in the two principal cities, was very small in 1920. The estimated 100,000 Portuguese working in the factories of Lisbon and Oporto were mostly illiterate and not class conscious. However, by 1920 a small nucleus of socialists, a slightly larger anarchist group, and a few communists existed in Portugal.[44]

The peasants—the vast majority of Portugal's population— were an amorphous mass. Almost all were illiterate, living frugally when not miserably. Fishermen and their families lived in similarly deprived conditions.

The wealthy bourgeoisie, the church, and the armed forces were the three pillars of Portuguese colonialism. During the short-lived First Republic (1910–1926) the lesser bourgeoisie gained some power and began to question the injustices of the colonial regime. António Salazar, however, who came to power in 1932, constructed his New State on the same three pillars. He also ended the republican experiment in parliamentary democracy, which had opened the door to representation from the colonies. British, French, and Belgian colonialism came to an end when the anticolonial pressures within the metropoles reinforced pressures from the colonies. The hierarchical class structure in Portugal impeded these internal metropolitan pressures. As we will see, however, Portuguese colonialism followed the same pattern as in other countries and finally collapsed under the combined pressure of the Movement of the Armed Forces in Lisbon and military and political attacks of the liberation movements in the colonies.

WHITE SETTLERS

This chapter describes the population of Angola as it was in 1920 after Portugal had established "effective control" but before modernization had been felt by most Angolans. The very phrase "effective control" is called into question by the fact that in 1920 there were only 20,700 whites in Angola and they

44. Ibid., p. 210.

formed a mere 0.48 percent of the total population.[45] The number is significant compared to the white population in other African colonies in the second decade of the twentieth century, but it hardly measured up to Portugal's pretentions. Not only colonial rhetoric, but the basic colonial statute affirms that "it is the organic essence of the Portuguese Nation to carry out the function of possessing and colonizing overseas domains and of civilizing the indigenous populations."[46]

Even more notable than the small quantity of white settlers was their poor quality. Most of the whites in Angola were soldiers or exiled criminals, *degredados,* who were sent to Angola to serve their sentences rather than being put in jail in Portugal. In 1881, of the 1,450 European residents of Luanda, half (721) were civil or military criminals, whereas only 394 were free men outside of the army.[47] A stable, growing white population would require an equal number of men and women, but in 1902 little more than 100 European women were found in Angola, all but eight to ten of whom were *degredadas.*

Few Portuguese came to Angola voluntarily before 1920 because of the negative image of Africa held by Europeans. The government promoted planned settlement schemes, but the free transportation, land, housing, animals, seed, and subsidies only attracted a few Portuguese who had been unable to succeed at home. Even as late as the decade from 1911 to 1920 the government turned again to *degredados* and established agricultural penal colonies in the southern district of Huíla.

In 1912, Portuguese officials described the white settlers as "generally poor, ignorant and illiterate and, for those very reasons, without much ambition, withdrawn and lacking initiative."[48] In 1950 almost half of the white population over five years of age had never attended school and another 40 percent had only completed the four years of primary school.

45. Gerald J. Bender and P. Stanley Yoder, "Whites in Angola on the Eve of Independence: The Politics of Numbers," *Africa Today,* 21 (Fall 1974), 26.

46. 1933 Colonial Act, Article II.

47. Michael Anthony Samuels, *Education in Angola, 1878–1914: A History of Culture Transfer and Administration* (New York: Teachers College Press, 1970), p. 10.

48. Gerald J. Bender, "Planned Rural Settlements in Angola, 1900–1968" (unpublished research study), p. 6.

Few, poor, and uneducated, the Portuguese population was not distributed evenly across Angola but was concentrated at the coast. For white settlers to be the principal means of the Portuguese "civilizing" mission in Angola would have required their equitable distribution all across the colony. In 1930, 56 percent of the Europeans lived in the cities and three-quarters of the urban population was concentrated in the coastal cities of Luanda, Lobito, Benguela, and Moçâmedes. In a total population that was 90 percent rural and agricultural, only 2,746 whites (less than 10 percent of the active white male population) were working in agriculture.

The conflicts between the Portuguese and Angolans were essentially economic or political, but white racism always exacerbated them. The inferiority complex of the uneducated, criminal settler population contributed to a virulent form of white racism among the Portuguese which infected all classes from top to bottom. No disease is more dangerous than that which is undiagnosed. The Portuguese always considered themselves free from racial prejudice and so were unable to see that white racism contaminated even the positive programs which they projected or executed.

Mestizos

Paradigmatic of Portugal's mythology that it had been endowed with a special, nonracial, colonial attitude was the adage "God created the whites and the blacks, and the Portuguese created the mestizo." Surveys made in Africa, North and South America, and the Caribbean show that the degree of miscegenation in colonial situations is directly related to the ratio between the number of white men and white women, rather than to nationality, colonial policy, or morality.[49] In 1846 there were almost 11 white men for every white woman in Angola.[50] By 1920 that had dropped to 187 to 100 as had the frequency of miscegenation. This change was also reflected in the total population ratio between whites and mestizos. In the mid- nineteenth

49. Gerald J. Bender, *Angola under the Portuguese: The Myth and the Reality* (Berkeley and Los Angeles; University of California Press, 1978), pp. 19–58.
50. Ibid., pp. 51–53.

century there were more than three mestizos for every white in the colony; by 1920 that ratio was reversed.

In the eighteenth and nineteenth centuries, when the mestizo population was equal to or larger than the white, the mestizos performed important roles as middlemen in the slave trade and occupied key posts in business, the civil service, journalism, the military, and politics. "They seldom, if ever, identified with the Africans because for all practical purposes they were Portuguese in nearly every way except color."[51] In the period 1912–1925 at least two mestizos were mayors of Luanda and several were city councillors. The white population doubled between 1900 and 1920 and outnumbered the mestizos who therefore lost their privileged position. Nevertheless the mestizos continued to identify with the Portuguese in the struggles between Europeans and Africans. Even though they were second-class citizens, they clearly ranked above the blacks, who were not citizens but "natives."

Boers

In 1920 the 18,000 Portuguese in Angola were reinforced by approximately 2,000 Boers. The Portuguese had been hopeful that these white settlers from South Africa would strengthen their hold on the black populations. About 600 Boers, "the Thirstland Trekkers" under the leadership of Jakobus Botha, left from Mafeking, South Africa, in 1875 to escape British rule. They spent five and a half years journeying across the desert of Bechuanaland and South-West Africa with their wagons and cattle. In 1880 the remaining 300 Boers arrived on the Huíla highlands and were given extensive tracts of land at Humpata.

The Portuguese were suspicious of the Boers, as they were of all foreigners, but they hoped that these rugged Protestant pioneers would help subdue the rebellious Africans and also develop the rural economy by agriculture and cattle raising. Lisbon supported these hopes by giving Portuguese citizenship to the Boers in 1882, with freedom from taxation for ten years, the right to use their own language, and their own municipal representation.

51. Ibid., p. 53.

For the first two decades the Boers did not disappoint the Portuguese. They did help "pacify" the Umbundu at the turn of the century. Soon, however, tension grew as the Boers followed their nomadic ways, leaving their good land uncultivated, exterminating game by their reckless hunting, and causing complaints to authorities because of cruelty to Africans. To aggravate these differences, the Boers refused to become Catholics or to send their children to Portuguese schools.

The population of Angola in 1920, approximately 3,150,000, was divided into nine major ethnolinguistic groups, seven Bantu—Kongo, Kimbundu, Umbundu, Ambo, Nhaneca-Humbe, Lunda-Chokwe, and Ganguelas—and two non-Bantu—Khoisan and Portuguese. The nine groups included at least eighty peoples.

The non-Bantu groups are small in population, but important as representatives of the past and the future. The Khoisan remind Angolans of the peoples that occupied their land before the Bantu arrived. The Portuguese introduced Angola to the new international, industrial, and secular society into which it has entered as an independent nation.

The seven Bantu groups differ from one another as regards their internal unity. They occupy an extended spectrum from extreme homogeneity to extreme heterogeneity:

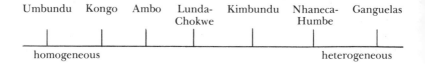

At one extreme is the Umbundu group, which is so united culturally that it could actually be classified as one people rather than a group. The Umbundu language is spoken by the whole people and the only dialects which could be included in the group would be those of such marginal peoples as the Hanya and Chisanji.

At the other extreme is the Ganguela group. Probably some of the peoples in this group should themselves be considered as distinct ethnic groups and not combined with others. By definition, each people in an ethnolinguistic group speaks a dialect of one mutually comprehensible language. On the basis of intelligibility, several of the Ganguela dialects could legitimately be considered languages in their own right. However, the Ganguela ethnolinguistic group acquires its classification more by outside pressures than by self-identification. The larger and more aggressive Lunda-Chokwe on the north and east and the Umbundu on the west, both of whom have limited the territory occupied by the Ganguelas, consider them one group.

Between the extremes, the Kongo are next to the Umbundu on the side of homogeneity, in part because they were the only group with a centralized monarchy. The Ambo group is relatively homogenous because only four of its peoples are in Angola. If we were including other peoples of the group residing in Namibia, it would be more heterogenous. The Lunda-Chokwe occupy the middle position on the spectrum as a result of their rapid expansion from 1850 to 1920. The Kimbundu is on the side of heterogeneity because it contains peoples who were mostly thoroughly assimilated into Portuguese culture as well as others who were the last dominated by colonial military might. Next to the Ganguelas on the extreme of heterogeneity is the Nhaneca-Humbe group, which has been in the process of fragmentation so that even some peoples, such as the Humbes, are being fractured into smaller units.

The seven Bantu ethnolinguistic groups shared common social, economic, political, and religious characteristics. Thus, in 1920, all Bantu peoples in Angola respected similar patterns of social unity based on kinship ties. Although the importance of matrilinear and patrilinear relations differed from group to group and even from people to people, in all cases the kinship ties were decisive in establishing marriage patterns, economic responsibilities, access to land, local political authority, and spiritual well-being. As European influence increased in Angola, the communal, kinship-based society clashed more openly with the invading individualistic, commercial civilization.

Similarly, most Angolans were in the process of transition from a subsistence to a market economy in 1920. They could be classified economically as peasants since their economic security lay in their having certain rights in land and in the labor of family members on the land, but they were also involved in a wider economic system which included the participation of non-peasants. From 1920 the economic conflict was not so much between the subsistence and market economies as between the status of peasant and proletarian. In becoming proletarians, the Angolans would lose their land rights.

As Portugal established effective occupation in Angola by 1920 it reduced traditional political authorities to the status of powerless intermediaries between the people and the colonial administration. The rules of subkingdoms or clusters of villages, however, continued to perform important ceremonial and judicial functions. As Angolans were excluded from participation in the dominant political process, they sought ways to express and realize some of their aspirations in voluntary associations such as churches or cultural organizations. Finally, they created illegal political associations as instruments to regain their voice in governing their own nation.

The African peoples of Angola also shared a worldview—a coherent set of nonverbalized assumptions about reality—in which persons, as spirits, lived in a kinship community not only with the present but with past generations. Persons were essentially spiritual beings and their welfare depended not only on the satisfaction of material needs but also on maintaining the right relations with other spirits. Such right relations determined standards of moral conduct and required the fulfillment of religious rites and magical techniques. Symbols utilized in religion and magic not only represented reality, but were charged with power to affect reality.

This communal, spiritual, symbolic world view contrasted sharply with the individualistic, materialistic, secular world view of the Europeans. Such nonverbalized assumptions are usually unconscious and therefore unexamined, so world views do not clash openly. However, as traditionalism and modernism vie for dominance over Angolans in the twentieth century, some comprehension of the conflicting world views helps us understand how Angolans evaluate even those struggles which may appear to outsiders to be simply social, political, or economic.

CHAPTER 3

The Slave Trade: Four Centuries of Conflict, 1482–1884

One theme serves as the key to understanding not only the history of Angola but Angola in the modern world. From our historical perspective, we can see that the dominant historical fact which affected all aspects of life in Angola, from its penetration by Europeans in the fifteenth century to the transition to colonialism in the nineteenth, was the slave trade.

The Aims of Portuguese Exploration

In 1415 when Prince Henry the Navigator (1394–1460) envisioned the Age of Discovery, he included commerce as only one of five goals. Of these the first was scientific—to penetrate the unknown. There was the immediate objective of reaching out beyond the Canary Island and Cape Bojador and the master objective of finding a sea route to India. Commerce came second: Should a Christian population perchance be found, trade profitable to both parties might be carried on and "many kinds of merchandise might be brought to this realm." The third goal was military—to discover the real strength of the national and religious enemy, the Muslim Moors, and what territory they occupied, "because every wise man is obliged by natural prudence to wish for a knowledge of the power of his enemy." As the fourth, political goal, Henry "sought to know if there were in those parts any Christian princes in whom charity and the love of Christ was so ingrained that they would aid him against those enemies of the faith." And last came the missionary—"his great desire to make increase in the faith of our Lord Jesus Christ and to bring him all the souls that should be saved."[1]

1. Gomes Eanes de Zurara, *The Chronicles of the Discovery and Conquest of Guinea,* trans and ed. Charles R. Beazely and Edgar Prestage (London: Hakluyt Society, 1896), Vol. I, No. 95, pp. 27–29.

The prince and his successors took significant steps toward all these goals, but it soon became clear that the commercial interest surpassed all others as the Portuguese did in fact find "many kinds of merchandise" to be traded.

As the Portuguese explorers passed Cape Bojador (1434) and entered the fishing grounds of the Guinea coast, they shipped dried fish back to Europe. The Cape Verde Islands, Fernando Po, and São Tomé produced sugar, which became a main article of commerce. Ivory was another prized commodity obtained from the area known as the Ivory Coast. Pepper, wax, hides, amber, and indigo supplemented the major items of commerce in the fifteenth century. By the end of the fifteenth century, gold and slaves had superseded all other exports. Portugal during this period was the principal trader of gold, carrying £100,000 of the precious metal per year from West Africa to Europe. However, for Portugal the slave trade dominated all other commerce by 1600.

Even so, in 1482 when John II, who had taken over the responsibility for overseas expansion after the death of Prince Henry, sent his first expedition of discovery to Africa under the command of the squire Diogo Cão, he did not foresee that Angola would play such a key role in the slave trade.

Cão spent eighteen months on his first voyage and explored the coast of what is now Gabon, Zaïre, and most of Angola. Since Cão was under instructions to investigate any possible passage across Africa, he was attracted by the muddy discharge of the Congo River sixty miles from the coast, and went ashore to place a monument with this inscription: "In the 6681st year of the creation of the world and the 1482nd year of the birth of Our Lord Jesus Christ, the very high, excellent and powerful ruler, King John II of Portugal ordered that this land be discovered and these monuments placed by Diogo Cão, squire of his house."[2]

The Portuguese intended to discover new lands, as the monument indicated, but they had no intention of conquering

2. Ralph Delgado, *História de Angola, primeiro período e parte do segundo 1482 a 1607,* 2 vols. (Dafundo, Portugal: Edição do Banco de Angola), Vol. I, p. 62, trans. L. W. H.

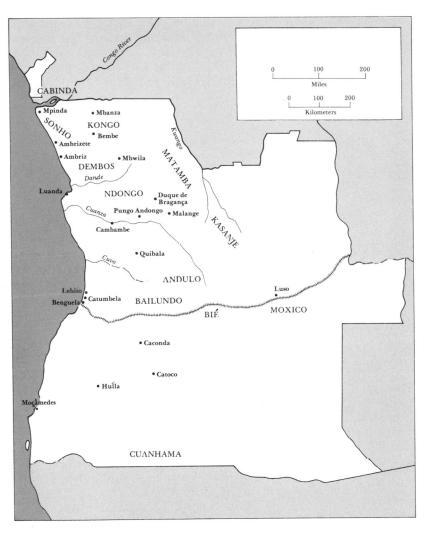

Historical map of Angola, 1482–1920. Political and geographic areas are shown in larger type.

lands or peoples. Portugal carried on the slave trade principally from uninhabited West African islands such as Arguin (Mauritania), Santiago (Cape Verde), and São Tomé. A thousand slaves a year on their way to Lisbon are reputed to have passed through Arguin, the leading Portuguese slave port of the fifteenth century.[3]

Brother Kings

The early contacts between Portuguese and Angolans were peaceful. The king of Sonho and his people were the first Angolans to see these strange white visitors and, although he could not speak Portuguese, the king was able to communicate to Cão and his men that he owed allegiance to the king of the Kongo, who lived farther inland. Cão left four (Franciscan) monks in Sonho as he continued south beyond modern Lobito. Returning from the south to find the monks gone from the coast, Cão seized four hostages and took them back to Lisbon.[4]

In Lisbon the Kongo hostages found many Africans in the Portuguese capital. Slavery had been practiced by the Moors in the Iberian Peninsula, and the Christians continued to use slaves. Portugal's North African campaigns in the first half of the fifteenth century gave new impetus to the institution. These slaves were being integrated into Portuguese society when West African captives began to reach the country in considerable numbers. A census of 1554 fixed the number of slaves in Lisbon at about 10 percent of the population. However, King John II and his court received the Kongolese not as slaves or even as hostages, but as representatives of another noble court, entrusting them to a monastery where they were instructed in the Christian faith and baptized.

On their return to Africa the Kongolese Christians were welcomed joyously by family and friends, and the Portuguese were invited to accompany them to Mbanza, the capital of the Kingdom of the Kongo, to meet the king, the Mani-Kongo. The meeting of Mbanza was one of mutual discovery. Cão presented gifts from the king of Portugal to the Mani-Kongo, which the

3. Oliveira Marques, I, 354.
4. Delgado, I, 64.

impressive African ruler received seated on a royal stool of ivory, surrounded by his councillors and men-at-arms. The Kongolese hostages described the court in Lisbon, the capital of the expanding Portuguese empire, while the four Franciscan monks related their experiences of two years in the court of the strongest ruler of west-central Africa. In terms of population, political centralization, and industrial development, the two kingdoms exchanging gifts and experiences were not that different.

The friendship and mutual respect which characterized this first official contact between an Angolan king and the king of Portugal grew over the next half century. More Kongolese were sent to learn Portuguese and the knowledge and skills which the language put at their disposal. From Portugal, priests, craftsmen, agriculturalists, and technicians were sent to work in the court of the Mani Kongo. The period of "royal brotherhood" reached its apogee during the reigns of King Manuel I of Portugal (1495–1521) and his remarkable Kongolese contemporary, the Mani-Kongo Nzinga Mbemba (1506–1543?), who was baptized Afonso. King Manuel addressed King Afonso as "Most powerful and excellent king of Manycongo," and the Mani-Kongo generally began his letters with the salutation "Most high and powerful prince and king my brother."[5]

Yet the hero of this era of royal brotherhood, the king of the Kongo, was rent between two ways of life. He had two names—Nzinga Mbemba and Afonso—one Kongo and one Portuguese. In his efforts to win the crown, Afonso was supported by the European and Christian interests; his rival, Mpanza, was supported by the *nganga*, the representatives of ancestral religious beliefs and practices. Sources of our knowledge of King Afonso are mostly missionary and border on hagiography. They do not describe the bitter struggle in the life of the Angolan ruler, but we have some glimpses of the conflict between rival cultures. For example, Pope Leo X, in a letter addressed to King Afonso's son Henrique, who was the first black African bishop, states that this clerical office was not revocable even if it appeared that Afonso's

5. Basil Davidson, *The African Slave Trade: Precolonial History 1450–1850* (Boston: Little, Brown, 1961), p. 122.

son was born of "an adulterous king and an unmarried mother."[6] Polygamy was, of course, legal in Kongo society, but adulterous relations were as rigorously condemned by traditional mores as by Christian. Although the pope evidently envisioned a simple conflict between Christian morality and traditional immorality, Afonso was in the far more agonizing position of having to choose between two ways of life, each with its own compelling moral code. The tension between African and European ways of life has run through the past five centuries of Angolan history.

A second conflict in the life of King Afonso was between his zealous, first-generation, Christian faith and the corruption, avarice, and greed of the Portuguese Christians. Portuguese admitted to plundering, cheating, and robbing the Kongolese. Even the missionaries who were supposed to be the king's Christian mentors found buying and selling slaves more attractive than educating and evangelizing the people. Instead of living together in the large residence prepared for them, the thirteen or fifteen priests who arrived in 1508 each set himself up in private quarters, one with an African mistress by whom he had a child. King Manuel of Portugal recognized the immorality of the clergy and included a special section on abuses of the clergy in the *regimento* or instructions which he sent to the Kongo in 1512. At one point, King Afonso directed a long letter to King Manuel of Portugal to review the plots and disturbances caused in his kingdom by unruly Portuguese profiteers and slave trade agents. In his final lines he wrote: " . . . and we beg your Highness not to leave us unprotected or allow the Christian work done in our kingdom to be lost, for we alone can do no more."[7] Afonso felt keenly the conflict between his own commitment and the faithlessness of the Portuguese "Christians."

After the death of King Afonso, the Kingdom of the Kongo fell into a series of struggles for succession. It never again regained the position which it held over neighboring kingdoms. The first conflict between European and African cultures,

6. António da Silva Rego, *Curso de missiologia* (Lisbon: Agência Geral do Ultramar, 1956), p. 268.
7. Duffy, *Portuguese Africa,* p. 16.

centering in the Kingdom of the Kongo, was nonmilitary. Although the European culture had the support of two powerful kings, Manuel of Portugal and Afonso of the Kongo, African culture won: "By 1615 most traces of Christian life had disappeared; the white population (which had only been about 200 at the greatest) had died, fled or been absorbed. . . . São Salvador was a deserted city in 1690, its twelve churches in ruins, its walls and fortress in ruins. [Henry M.] Stanley who explored the area in 1874–79 professed that he could find no trace of Portuguese civilization, no mark of their sovereignty."[8]

From Contact to Conflict

The relatively peaceful confrontation between European and African cultures in the period of the "brother kings" was followed by the more violent clashes of a period of military conquest. South of the Bakongo peoples, but still tributary to the Mani-Kongo, lived the Kimbundu-speaking peoples. The Ngola,[9] a legendary warrior from the west, established control over the Ndongo, a Kimbundu-language people, and the kingdom of Ngola began to compete with the kingdom of the Kongo to which it owed allegiance. Seeing that the presence of the Portuguese gave the Kongo certain advantages, the Ngola in 1519 asked King Afonso to intercede on his behalf for an embassy of Portuguese merchants and priests. Perhaps because the request was accompanied by silver, allegedly from Ngola, the Portuguese sent their first official expedition to this Kimbundu kingdom in 1520 under the leadership of Balthasar de Castro. However, the Ngola was not satisfied with the benefits offered by the expedition and kept Castro captive in his court for six years, only releasing him through the intervention of the Mani-Kongo.[10]

Tension between the kingdoms of Kongo and Ngola increased because of the competition for profits from the slave trade. The

8. Ibid., p. 22.

9. Joseph C. Miller, *Kings and Kinsmen: Early Mbundu States in Angola* (Oxford: Clarendon Press, 1976), pp. 63–70. *Ngola*, which means "small piece of iron," became the title of a leader who was able to unite Mbundu kinship groups into larger, more flexible political units.

10. Duffy, *Portuguese Africa*, pp. 50–51.

Portuguese presence in the Kongo stimulated the demand for slaves and the favorite campaigning ground of the Kongolese was among the populous Kimbundu, south of the Dande River. The Kimbundu not only were the victims of trade, but also profited from it by their role as intermediaries in furnishing slaves to the north and selling slaves through the illegal port of Luanda. Portuguese from the island settlement of São Tomé encouraged the Kimbundu traders to sell slaves through Luanda since they wished to break the monopoly which Lisbon and Mbanza enjoyed in forcing all slaves to be exported through Mpinda, the official port at the mouth of the Congo where they could be taxed.

To reassert its authority, the Kingdom of the Kongo attacked a force of the tributary Kingdom of Ndongo in 1556. Each side had the support of Portuguese soldiers; however, the Kongo army was defeated in the battle of the Dande. Recognizing that this victory might cut his kingdom off from the advantages of Portuguese commercial contacts which had come mainly through the Kongo, Ngola Inene, King of Ndongo, sent an ambassador to Lisbon requesting official Portuguese representatives at his court. Before such an arrangement could be completed, both kings, Ngola Inene of Ndongo and John III of Portugal, died. The Kingdom of Kongo also sent an ambassador to Lisbon to explain its loss of the battle of the Dande and to defend the traditional sovereignty of the Mani-Kongo over Ndongo. In a compromise solution, the queen regent, Dona Catarina, agreed to send Ndongo an ecclesiastical expedition composed of four Jesuits, two priests and two lay brothers. In 1560, the Jesuits set sail with Paulo Dias de Novais, the grandson of Bartolomeu Dias, who had reached the Cape of Good Hope seventy years before. Ngola Ndambi, who succeeded Inene, kept the expedition waiting at the mouth of the Cuanza and after various delays finally received this second expedition to Ndongo, accepting the gifts sent from Lisbon but refusing to allow any evangelization. The thirty-odd members of the expedition were sent back to their ship and the Ngola held Paulo Dias, Father Francisco de Gouveia, and two other men. Dias was detained for five years and Father Gouveia remained a prisoner in the capital of Ndongo until his death in 1575, fifteen years later.

Kabasa, the capital city, which contained 5,000 to 6,000 houses surrounded by a post fence, was compared by Father Gouveia to the Portuguese city of Évora.[11]

The captivity of Dias de Novais and Father Gouveia produced influential spokesmen for a new policy of military conquest. Several factors convinced Portugal that it could not depend on diplomatic arrangements with "brother kings" or its own commercial resources to compete in the world slave market. First, Portugal produced little cloth, or at least little that could compete in price and quality with the indigenous palm cloth,[12] while England and Holland manufactured good-quality cloth and metalware to exchange for slaves. Second, some unidentified invaders[13] from the east, whom the Portuguese called Jagas, forced the king of Kongo and the Portuguese from Mbanza into exile on an island in the Congo River, convincing the Portuguese that they needed some territory where they were masters and did not depend upon an African sovereign. In addition, the reports of mineral wealth in Angola were persistent and had created a legend of a fabulous silver mine in Cambambe which could only be found and exploited if Portugal ruled the area. Also, the Jesuits had become convinced that only preaching by the sword would succeed in tropical Africa.[14] "Almost all have verified that the conversion of these barbarians will not be attained by love."[15] Finally, the ignorance of African geography led many to believe that the Congo or Cuanza rivers would provide the shortest route to Mozambique and India, but this exploration also depended upon military conquest.

As a result, in 1571 King Sebastian gave the experienced Paulo Dias de Novais the charter for the military conquest of Ngola. By means of a *donatária*, a territorial proprietorship patterned after the system used in Brazil, Lisbon hoped to bring about the conquest, colonization, and evangelization of Angola

11. Delgado, I, 253.

12. David Birmingham, *The Portuguese Conquest of Angola* (London: Oxford University Press, 1965), p. 2.

13. Joseph C. Miller, "Requiem for the Jaga," *Cahiers d'Etudes Africaines XIII* (1973), 149.

14. Birmingham, *Portuguese Conquest*, p. 10.

15. Bender, *Angola under the Portuguese*, p. 137.

at an inconsequential cost.[16] The title given to Paulo Dias by the charter, "Governor and Captain General of the Kingdom of Sebastião in the Conquest of Ethiopia," greatly surpassed his accomplishments. Dias spent three years in Lisbon gathering the resources to fulfill the demanding charter, which required him to explore the coastline all the way to the Cape of Good Hope; to garrison his captaincy with 400 men; to build three fortresses between the Dande and the Cuanza; to build a church; and to bring into Angola some 100 families, to whom he was to give seed and implements.

Military Conquest in the North

Dias de Novais's arrival in Luanda in 1575, which marks the beginning of a century of military conquest, was almost as discouraging as his first arrival at the mouth of the Cuanza fifteen years before. This time he found forty or fifty Portuguese already settled on Luanda island, trading with the Ngola, but they feared Dias with his new powers, which authorized him to regulate and tax their lucrative business. The Portuguese traders "leaked" to the Ngola the purpose of Dias's expedition—to conquer and colonize Ndongo—and this precipitated armed resistance to the Portuguese plans of conquest.[17] In 1579, the Ngola had thirty or forty Portuguese at his court killed. He confiscated their trade goods and then moved on with a huge army to attack the fort of Nzele where Dias was encamped, thirty miles inland from Luanda. The sixty Europeans and 200 African troops held out at Nzele, initiating a decade of indecisive battles. Terrorist tactics rather than pitched battle were used, as indicated in a report by a Catholic priest in 1583 that 619 noses were cut off by the Portuguese and sent to the coast as trophies.[18]

From 1575 to 1605, the first stage of the military conquest, the principal goal was to reach Cambambe, the site of the legendary silver mines. Finally, under Manuel Cerveira Pereira, the Portuguese reached Cambambe and established a fort manned with

16. Duffy, *Portuguese Africa,* p. 53.
17. Birmingham, *Portuguese Conquest,* pp. 14–23.
18. David Birmingham, *Trade and Conflict in Angola: The Mbundu and Their Neighbors under the Influence of the Portuguese 1483–1790* (Oxford: Clarendon Press, 1966) p. 54.

250 soldiers to serve as a base camp for those who would explore for silver.[19] This small military accomplishment in no way compensated the Portuguese for their final disillusionment when they discovered that there were neither mines nor silver in Cambambe.

During the second period of the conquest, from 1605 to 1641, the Portuguese concentrated on using the military to promote the slave trade. During the four centuries of the trade, slaves were obtained in three ways: subject chiefs paid slaves as tribute to their masters who were African rulers or Portuguese traders and officials; slaves were purchased at markets established in the interior by African rulers; and slaves were acquired by direct warfare. Pursuing this third method, the Portuguese succeeded in increasing the slave trade, but at the expense of destroying the kingdom of Ndongo and decimating the people. Many who were not captured or killed fled eastward, with the result that the kingdoms of Kasanje and Matamba in the Kwango River valley developed politically and economically. This period of militant slave trading illustrates the "common effect of the slave trade to undermine the states with which Europeans had direct contact, while causing those who indirectly supplied slaves to prosper."[20] During the era of the "brother-kings," the Kongo had declined while Ndongo was remote enough to benefit from receiving European goods without losing its traditional identity and sovereignty. In the period of conquest, the Kingdom of Ndongo was ruined and Kasanje and Matamba were strengthened.

In the third stage of the conquest, 1641 to 1683, Portugal realized that it could not achieve the specific aims of its colonial policy without direct confrontation of its principal enemies: Holland, Kongo, Ndongo, and Matamba.

The Dutch Role

Holland's role in the conflict that followed was based on two separate motivations: to control the sea lanes and slave trade and to express hostility to Spain, from which the Netherlands had just become independent. Angola and Brazil were appropriate

19. Delgado, I, 399.
20. Birmingham, *Portuguese Conquest,* p. 14.

objects of Holland's aggression because they had been part of
the Spanish empire since 1580, when Portugal was united to
Spain under Hapsburg domination. The Dutch fleet, in the pursuit of these economic and political aims, captured strategic Portuguese ports—Bahia (1624) and Pernambuco (1630) in Brazil,
and Luanda (1641) and Benguela (1641) in Angola.

Therefore, in 1644 when the Overseas Council in Lisbon
called upon Brazil to help in the campaign against the Dutch, the
American colonists were willing to answer, since the loss of Angola had caused more hardships in Brazil than in the metropole.[21] After two unsuccessful expeditions to Angola, Lisbon
called upon its most distinguished colonial leader, Salvador Correia de Sá e Benavides, a wealthy Brazilian landowner, former
governor of Rio de Janeiro and general of the Brazilian fleets in
the campaign against the Dutch in Pernambuco. In 1647, Salvador Correia was appointed governor of Angola with instructions to restore the colony to Portuguese control. His prestige
was such—and the need for slaves for American sugar plantations so great—that he was able to raise funds and men in Rio de
Janeiro for the third Brazilian armada, for which the Portuguese
crown furnished only five ships. In May 1648, fifteen ships and
1,500 men departed from Rio. The Brazilians made an unsuccessful assault on the fortress of São Miguel in Luanda. Salvador
Correia then faced the prospect of confronting the Dutch forces
which were already in Luanda, reinforced by European and
African soldiers returning from an expedition to the interior.
To his great surprise, the Dutch commander that same morning
agreed to a conference on the surrender of Luanda. The reasons for his eagerness to capitulate are not clear; overestimation
of the Brazilian army, reluctance to suffer a long siege, shortage
of munitions, all must have contributed to the decision. Under
the terms of the settlement the Dutch were permitted to withdraw with their slaves and property, the Portuguese supplying
sufficient transportation to evacuate them. Shortly after the fall
of Luanda, the Dutch relinquished Benguela and São Tomé.

From the restoration of Portuguese control over Angola in

21. Duffy, *Portuguese Africa*, p. 66.

1648 until the abolition of slavery in 1836, Angola was practically a colony of Brazil.[22] This dependence had a solid economic base as the contemporary saying indicated: "Without sugar there is no Brazil and without Angola there is no sugar." The independence of Brazil in 1822 inspired visions of a new kind of relationship between Angola and Brazil, so that in 1823 soldiers and settlers in Benguela banded together in a separatist revolt against Portugal, proposing to join with newly independent Brazil in the so-called Confederação Brasílica.

For the history of Angola, the conflict between the Dutch and Portuguese was not as significant as the role which the Dutch played in stimulating and supporting conflict between various African rulers and the Portuguese. At the beginning of the seventeenth century the Dutch had set up a factory at Mpinda for the export of slaves. The Portuguese requested the king of the Kongo to expel the foreigners, but in spite of proddings from the Portuguese bishop in São Salvador, the Mani-Kongo dragged his heels, apparently preferring to let the enterprising Flemings share the monopoly held by the Portuguese. With the return of the Portuguese to Luanda in 1648, the conquering general and governor, Salvador Correia, drew up a peace treaty with the Kongo. The harsh conditions imposed by the Portuguese required the king of the Kongo to prohibit Portugal's enemies from entering his kingdom, to come to Portugal's aid in case of war, to indemnify Portugal for losses during the Dutch war, to give the Portuguese free passage up the Congo River, and to cede to the Portuguese crown the mountains which were reputed to contain gold and silver.[23]

The treaty did not end the hostility between the Kongo and the Portuguese. The battle which marked the end of Kongo as a power was fought at Mbwila on October 29, 1665. The Portuguese force consisted of 200 European troops and 150 settlers, 100 African musketeers, and 3,000 African bowmen. They confronted a massive Kongolese army of bowmen and 190 musketeers led by twenty-nine Portuguese who lived in Kongo.

22. Delgado, II, 399.
23. Delgado, II, 397–98.

Superior Portuguese firepower accounted for the defeat of the larger Kongolese force. The Portuguese celebrated their victory by carrying the head of the king of the Kongo to Luanda. Portugal did not keep control of the kingdom, but found that the disunity and lack of effective government made it a good field for slave recruiting.

On the path to the conquest of Ngola, Portugal had driven the Dutch from Luanda in 1648 and conquered the Kongo in 1665. In the 1620s the Portuguese had placed a puppet, Ari Kiluanji, the chief of Pungu-a-Ndongo, on the throne of the kingdom of Ndongo. During the Dutch occupation Ndongo had been loyal to the Portuguese. After the expulsion of the Dutch the Ngolas were dissatisfied with the treatment they were receiving from the Portuguese and decided to establish their independence from Portugal. When the Ngola attacked a chief living near the Portuguese fort of Mbaka, the Portuguese recognized that their attempt to rule Ndongo indirectly through an amenable king had failed. The Ngola Ari attacked caravans going to the interior and then retired to his capital at Pungu-a-Ndongo, where he thought himself adequately defended by its huge black boulders. After a siege of several months the stronghold was taken in 1671 and the Portuguese established a new fort on the site, thus marking the end of Ndongo as even a semi-independent kingdom.

Queen Nzinga

The Angolan heroine in the period of Portuguese conquest was Queen Nzinga, who was monarch successively of Ndongo and Matamba. This colorful, dynamic queen, who captured the imagination of Portuguese historians, ruled in one part or another of the Kimbundu territory from 1624 to 1663. Nzinga made her dramatic entry into Angolan history as an emissary of her brother Ngola Mbandi, King of Ndongo, to negotiate with the Portuguese governor in Luanda. When a Portuguese official received an African ruler or diplomat in an audience he did not furnish a chair for his black counterpart; the black was expected to stand. Nzinga, realizing that this custom was to be followed in the palace of the governor where she was being received, ordered one of her female servants to kneel down on all fours so that she could sit on the servant's back. This incident, showing

Nzinga's personal pride and ingenuity, was memorialized in several drawings.[24]

Her political skill and acumen were demonstrated by her success in persuading the governor to recognize Ndongo as an independent monarchy owing no allegiance to Portugal even though her brother had been defeated in battle. She also made him promise to help the Ngola to expel the Imbangala, invaders from the east who were causing serious trouble in Ndongo. Nzinga succeeded to the throne of Ndongo after her brother Ngola Mbandi died under suspicious circumstances. Recent historical research has increased respect for Queen Nzinga's ability by revealing that she did not possess the usual kinship requirements of a Ngola and that Mbundu women were strongly discouraged from assuming political titles and strictly prohibited from assuming the position of *ngola a kiluanji*.[25]

Nzinga was baptized as Ana de Sousa and agreed to allow slave traders, missionaries, and Portuguese officials at the central marketplace near her capital if the Portuguese would withdraw from a fortress constructed near the historic capital of her kingdom during the wars of the previous decade. The next Portuguese governor reneged on his predecessor's promise to remove the fortress from her lands, and her relations with Luanda worsened after she began to offer asylum to slaves fleeing Portuguese plantations near the coast. The Portuguese forced her off the throne and replaced her by a puppet. Nzinga made alliances with bands of Imbangala warriors from the east, but this proved an unstable political base from which to operate. She then headed east for the kingdom of Matamba, which had two advantages for her: it had an exceptional precedent among the southern Kongo and northern Kimbundu for rule by females; and with the disintegration of the Kongo and Ndongo kingdoms, Matamba had become the principal African slave-trading state in the Luanda hinterland. Nzinga built a strong alliance with the Dutch, and during that period Matamba dominated the whole Kimbundu area. With the defeat of the Dutch, Nzinga was

24. Delgado, II, 72.
25. Joseph C. Miller, "Nzinga of Matamba in a New Perspective," *Journal of African History* XVI, 2 (1975), 206.

forced into another period of alliance with the Portuguese in order to export the slaves she captured or received from vassals. By manipulating her powerful neighbors, the Portuguese, Imbangala, and Dutch, Nzinga dominated Kimbundu politics and diplomacy for forty years, until her death in 1663.

The period of conquest, which had begun with the arrival of Paulo Dias de Novais at Luanda in 1575, ended in 1683 with the Treaty of Matamba. Kongo and Ndongo, previously strong monarchies, were not so much conquered as shattered. Portugal did not rule those kingdoms, but they were incapable of interfering with its trade through their territories. At the same time the kingdoms of Matamba and Kasanje in the Kwango basin were strengthened and their trade relations with Portugal were regulated by the treaty.

Military Conquest in Central Angola

Portugal, a kingdom, tended to identify each society with which it successively dealt as a kingdom. This identification was correct in the case of the Kingdom of the Kongo, which was comparable in size and political structure to Portugal at the end of the fifteenth century. In the case of the Kimbundu, Portugal generalized to the whole area between the Dande and the Cuanza the name of the Kingdom of Ngola, from *ngola,* the title of the Ndongo king, although the territory was never united under one kingdom. In 1615, Portugal identified the third part of the territory which was going to form its colony of Portuguese West Africa by "separating the kingdom of Benguela from the kingdom of Angola."[26] Actually there was no kingdom of Benguela. Portugal conjured up the kingdom of Benguela with no basis in fact except a vast territory south of the Cuanza River which was exciting Portugal's interest as another source of wealth.

Manuel Cerveira Pereira, who had been named Conquistador do Sul, wrote to King Philip II of Spain and Portugal giving his first impressions of Benguela as having healthful air, fertile soil, abundant fish in the bay, and being near two rivers with excellent running water. The new governor and his party soon dis-

26. Delgado, II, 42.

covered that they were on a swampy, unhealthy, and inhospitable coastal strip, but Cerveira Pereira still named the settlement São Filipe de Benguela after his patron.

If the natural setting of the port of Benguela was not hospitable, the name evoked dreams of wealth. Ships stopping along the southern coast of Angola in the sixteenth century had seen Africans with copper objects. The same Cerveira Pereira who had been disillusioned to find no silver in Cambambe when he arrived there in 1604 now nourished the dream of copper in Benguela. Rumor had it that the peoples of Benguela made copper bells and bracelets and even exported considerable quantities to Brazil. Pereira dug some rocks from the Cuvo River and sent them to Lisbon, but the king wrote to say that the samples proved that the legend of Benguela's copper was no better founded than the legend of the silver of Cambambe.[27]

As a result of geography, Benguela did not play as great a role in the conflicts of the first three centuries of this period of Angolan history as did the Kongo or Ngola. The peoples of central and southern Angola were not as accessible to the coast because of the steep escarpment which separates the coastal plain from the interior highlands.

Continuous contact between the Portuguese and the population centers of central Angola did not begin until the end of the eighteenth century. Benguela had been founded at the coast in 1617 and a fortress was built in the hinterland at Caconda, almost four or five days' journey from Benguela in 1680. However, only under Francisco de Sousa Coutinho, a farsighted governor of Angola, the first one convinced of the immense superiority of the Benguela highland, was the Caconda *presídio* moved to the present site on the plateau in 1769. Five years later the Portuguese started a military campaign, which lasted from 1774 to 1776, against the Umbundu kingdoms. The kings of Bailundo and Andulo, who were captured at this time, seem to have decided that it was safer and more profitable to trade with the Europeans than to raid their establishments.[28]

At the end of the eighteenth century, Caconda, the first per-

27. Ibid., p. 64.
28. Childs, p. 197.

manent settlement on the Umbundu plateau, had a population
of about 250 Portuguese men with as many as 15,000 Africans
residing in the vicinity.[29]

The Slave Trade

Slavery in a variety of forms had existed in African societies
quite independently of the international slave trade. Clientage,
pawnship, serfdom, debt bondage, apprenticeship, and household slavery differed fundamentally from the slavery which became integrated into the slave trade. Household slavery was
common among all the peoples of Angola and was not considered a great evil.[30]

The distinctive characteristic of the slavery which became integrated into the slave trade was marketability. Household slavery was useful in a subsistence economy. The slave trade was
only possible in a market economy, and, in fact, in a world market economy. Africa participated in this incipient world economy by furnishing slaves, and Angola became a point on the

29. Duffy, *Portuguese Africa*, p. 98.

30. Maria Chela Chikueka, an Umbundu woman, explained the meaning of
slavery from her own experience in an unpublished paper in 1975: "In the
African society the slaves were considered as members of the family. They were
called sons, daughters, uncles and aunts, cousins, brothers and sisters. They lived
and ate from the same dish with their master. They intermarried with the
families of their masters. Even today when referring to a slave, it is not unusual
to hear in a village this expression, *omola okuokuo*, 'the child I bore with my arms.'
Slaves in African societies were not strangers; they were members of the
families . . .

"The quarters of the kings were sanctuaries for slaves. The ethic [sic] law
allowed any slave who was mistreated by his master freedom to flee to seek
sanctuary in the king's quarter, he automatically became the king's child. He or
she was not considered to be a slave anymore. He was now called *ocilitumbike,*
"child by goodwill," and he was given a sign to indicate that he was a free person;
one of his ears was pierced. From then on this person had all the privileges of a
king's child; he or she married in the royal family and took his place as one of the
king's heirs. In African society, all of the slaves integrated into the communities.
As Portuguese slave trading continued, however, the entire African dignity was
lost. People became articles of the market."

For a comprehensive examination, see Suzanne Miers and Igor Kopytoff, eds.
Slavery in Africa: Historical and Anthropological Perspectives (Madison: University of
Wisconsin Press, 1977).

triangle which bound together Old World capital, New World land, and African labor.

The slave trade played a negative role in Portugal's own economic history. At the end of the Middle Ages, Portugal had a strong commercial class which seemed to give it an advantage as Europe entered the age of international commerce. Portugal's early lead in the slave trade profited the commercial interests, but did not move it to develop industry or wage labor. England, France, and Holland exploited the slave trade to transform feudalism into industrial capitalism, which demanded raw materials and markets more than slave labor or plantations. Therefore, by the middle of the eighteenth century, when they found the slave trade to be a brake on their economic development, they proceeded to abolish it. Portugal, on the other hand, resisted the abolition because the plantation-slave trade economy was compatible with its feudal system. By depending on the slave trade so long, its economy stagnated, and only now, after being freed of its colonies, is Portugal facing the possibility of participating directly in the world industrial economy.

Since slaves were the main item of Angola's trade from the fifteenth through the nineteenth centuries, it is not surprising that the major conflicts of Angola centered around the slave trade. The real and potential profits of the slave trade encouraged the Portuguese monarchy to maintain fraternal relations with the Kingdom of the Kongo. Portugal's desire to dominate the slave trade was a principal motive for the sending of the expedition under Paulo Dias de Novais with instructions to subdue the Kingdom of Ndongo. The ambition to control the sources of supply of the trade was at the root of the conflicts between the kingdoms of Kongo, Ndongo, Matamba, Kasanje, and others. The Dutch fleet which captured Luanda and was finally driven from the Angolan coast was part of the European struggle to monopolize the slave trade. São Tomé, São Salvador, and Luanda competed for a greater share in the Portuguese trade. The slave trade caused internal strife in each kingdom as the monarch sought to strengthen his or her rule and profit politically and economically from the trade while tributary kings attempted to trade independently. Such strife fractured the

major kingdoms and created instability and violence as increasing numbers of rulers had a direct supply of arms and munitions.

THE EXTENT OF THE TRADE

How large was the slave trade which dominated Angola from
1500 to 1850?[31] Four million slaves exported from Angola is a
reasonable estimate, or an average of 11,000 per year for 350
years. The records are neither complete nor accurate, but
enough studies have been made of various parts of Africa and
also of each country to which the slaves were shipped to make
present estimates fairly reliable. The total number of slaves
landed in the Americas from all parts of Africa is estimated at
about 10 million. Angola would seem to have been the largest
supplier of slaves in the world. Perhaps 30 percent of the slaves
in the trade for the whole period of three and a half centuries
came from Angola. The records do not supply information as to
how many of the estimated 4 million who embarked in Mpinda,
Luanda, or Benguela actually came from the territory which is
now known as Angola. Undoubtedly some came from the area
north of the present boundary and also farther inland than the
present eastern frontier. In the 1780s and 1790s, for example, a
great Angola slave rush pushed the Kimbundu and Umbundu
traders to lengthen their reach into the interior.

Because Portugal imposed a tax on all slaves exported, it had a
vested interest in keeping records of those slaves who actually
embarked. However, there are no records and little reliable information from which calculations can be made as to the relation
between the number of persons who were originally captured
and those who actually embarked. One observer of conditions
during the 1780s used as a working estimate death rates of 50
percent during the slaves' march to the coast and 40 percent of
the remainder in Luanda.[32] If this estimate can be taken seriously, it means that 13 million persons were captured in the
hinterland of Angola to supply 4 million slaves to the ships sail-

31. Philip D. Curtin, *The Atlantic Slave Trade: A Census* (Madison: University of
Wisconsin Press, 1969), pp. 3–13.

32. Joseph C. Miller, paper written at University of California at Los Angeles
1976.

ing for the Americas. If the loss in the "middle passage" from Africa to the Americas is added to the loss from capture to embarcation, Basil Davidson's estimate of a total of 50 million Africans lost in the slave trade may not be extreme.[33]

THE IMPACT OF THE TRADE

Even more difficult than estimating numbers of slaves exported is evaluating the impact of the slave trade on Angola during these four centuries. The personal suffering caused by the slave trade can never be calculated. From Angolans we do not even have the sketchy autobiographies which are available from a few West Africans.[34] Perhaps only 25 percent of the slaves captured in the hinterland of Angola arrived at their destinations at a sugar plantation in Bahia, Brazil, or at a mine in Mexico.[35] The serious wounds and violent death inflicted at the time of capture, the separation from family and friends, the hunger and thirst along bush trails, the cruel punishments by agents or guards, the diseases and injuries sustained without medical assistance, and the month-long voyage huddled in the cramped, filthy hold of a sailing vessel are aspects of the personal impact of the slave trade of which we cannot even conceive.

When we try to make an evaluation of the social impact of the slave trade we are again faced with a statistical problem. The 4 million slaves who embarked from Angolan ports were what proportion of the population of the territory from which they were taken? We have no reasonable census figures for Angola before 1940, when the total was registered as 3,738,010. An estimate made in 1897 gave a total of 18,551,037.[36] The great

33. Davidson, *African Slave Trade,* pp. 80–81.

34. Philip D. Curtin, ed., *Africa Remembered: Narratives by West Africans from the Era of the Slave Trade* (Madison: University of Wisconsin Press, 1967).

35. A more cautious estimate states that "the violence of capture and the dangers along the way surely meant that at least as many were killed as were delivered to the plantations." Philip Curtin, Steven Feierman, Leonard Thompson, and Jan Vansina, *African History* (Boston: Little, Brown, 1978), p. 247.

36. Óscar Soares Barata, "Aspectos das condições demográficas de Angola," *Angola: Curso de extensão universitária, ano lectivo de 1963-64,* p. 123.

discrepancy between these two totals only illustrates the problem of arriving at even rough figures for the population from which the slaves came. Without such a calculation, we cannot make a useful assessment of the social impact of the slave trade on Angola.

Politically the slave trade created great instability. The kingdoms of the Kongo and Ndongo were subverted or conquered in the struggle to control parts of the slave trade. New kingdoms or autarkies were formed to take advantage of the presence and greed of slave traders, but they were based on the foundation of disobedience to traditional authorities. Such fragmentation and competition for profits created political tension and military conflict.

Economically, Angola suffered inestimable loss from the slave trade. The strongest men and some women (in Brazil one out of four slaves was a woman)[37] were drained off from an economy which depended primarily upon the physical energy of hunters, warriors, traders, and farmers. Articles bartered for slaves were nonproductive: trinkets, textiles, tobacco, brandy, wine, firearms, powder, and lead shot. Force and violence were necessary for the capture of many of the slaves, but at some point in the process from the original acquisition in the hinterland to the embarkation at one of the ports, the slave was exchanged for articles highly prized by Angolans. Very early in the slave period, King Afonso of the Kongo recognized the importance of the "voracious appetite" of the Africans for goods coming from Europe. He wrote to the king of Portugal in a letter dated October 18, 1526:

Moreover, Sir, in our Kingdoms there is another great inconvenience which is of little service to God, and this is that many of our people, keenly desirous as they are of the wares and things of your Kingdoms, which are brought here by your people, and in order to satisfy their voracious appetite, seize many of our people, freed and exempt men; and very often it happens that they kidnap even noblemen and the sons of noblemen and our relatives, and take them to be sold to the white men who are in our Kingdoms; and for this purpose they have con-

37. Leslie Bethell, *The Abolition of the Brazilian Slave Trade: Britain, Brazil and the Slave Trade Question 1807–1869* (Cambridge: Cambridge University Press 1970), p. 4.

cealed them; and others are brought during the night so that they might not be recognized.[38]

If this appetite had been satisfied with productive articles, the slave trade might have included some redeeming economic value, but each article of trade either undermined some local Angolan industry or introduced destructive or disruptive commodities. Therefore the slave trade was doubly pernicious economically—it diverted human energy from productive enterprises and fed nonproductive items into the economy.

New crops and diseases which were introduced at the time of the slave trade are sometimes included in the calculation of the impact of the slave trade. Manioc and maize were imported into Africa by the end of the fifteenth century. These cultigens, because they were more efficient than the foods they replaced, promoted population growth. The slave trade statistician Curtin speculated that population growth resulting from the new food crops probably exceeded population losses through the slave trade.[39]

Another factor affecting Angola during the slave trade was the importation of diseases new to this part of the continent. Our knowledge of epidemiological history is even less developed than that of demographic history. However, again it is inaccurate to relate the introduction of diseases directly to the slave trade since any other kind of contact could have transmitted them.

During the fifteenth to the nineteenth centuries, the Catholic Church argued that the impact of the slave trade in Angola was spiritually positive. The King of Portugal responded as a good Catholic upon being presented with some fifty-four slaves: "I have much joy in them, because of their salvation, who otherwise would have been destined to perdition."[40] Both Church and state required that slaves be baptized before being exported:

On the wharfs at Luanda as late as 1870, there could still be seen a marble chair in which the bishop had sat and baptized by boatloads the

38. *The Horizon History of Africa,* ed. Alvin M. Josephy, Jr. (New York: American Heritage, 1971), p. 334.
39. Curtin, *Atlantic Slave Trade,* pp. 270–71.
40. John T. Tucker, *Angola: Land of the Blacksmith Prince* (London: World Dominion Press, 1933), p. 16.

poor wretches as they were rowed alongside the ship. The Government collected its tax, the pious ecclesiastic received his fee, and the slaves had their first introduction into the white man's religion.[41]

We lack both data and instruments to measure accurately the full impact of the slave trade on Angola. We can conclude, however, that the slave trade was the single most important cause of conflict during 400 years of Angola's history.

It is customary to see Angola as the product of Portugal's colonial ambitions or as the creation of Angolan nationalism, both of which will be discussed in later chapters. However, these forces came to shape modern Angola after the slave trade had transformed Ngola, which was not even a kingdom but the title of the ruler of the Kingdom of Ndongo, into Angola. The peoples of this vast territory had been divided into autonomous kingdoms or regionally defined ethnolinguistic groups. The slave trade paradoxically prepared the way for the formation of Angola in two ways. First, it shattered the isolated but proud kingdoms of the territory, depriving the ravaged peoples of their traditional political identities. Second, the trade defined a new territory based on the limits of Portuguese commercial contacts. The map of Angola conformed roughly to the area from which the Portuguese had drawn slaves over the centuries.

41. Ibid., pp. 16–17.

CHAPTER 4

The Transition from Slave Trade to Colonialism, 1884–1920

Portugal began the slave trade in the fifteenth century and reluctantly closed that chapter of world history in the mid-nineteenth century. The Industrial Revolution, the Enlightenment, and religious-philanthropic movements of the eighteenth century had generated pressure in Europe to end the slave trade. Denmark banned the traffic to its citizens in 1792; England and France followed with similar prohibitions in 1807 and 1818. Portugal was not under the same direct economic and intellectual pressures, but its western European neighbors exerted diplomatic and military pressure so that in 1836 Portugal issued a royal decree abolishing the slave trade on Portuguese vessels in Portuguese Africa. Trade statistics for the last decade of the eighteenth century had indicated that the export tax on slaves accounted for 88.1 percent of the income of Angola.[1] In 1843, seven years after the official abolition of the trade, Angola still derived 66 percent of its revenue from the slave duties imposed at ports of embarkation.[2] The Angolan slave trade was effectively ended not by royal decree in Lisbon or action taken in Luanda, but by international coercion in the form of a British naval squadron operating along the coast of Brazil in 1850–51. By 1852 the Brazilian branch of the trans-atlantic slave trade had been completely crushed.[3] This development was immediately reflected in the drying up of the Angolan trade and the flowing of lawful commerce in ivory,

---

1. Jan Vansina, *Kingdoms of the Savanna* (Madison: University of Wisconsin Press, 1966), pp. 184–85.
2. Wheeler and Pélissier, *Angola*, p. 52.
3. Bethell, p. 359.

beeswax, and rubber, which produced greater revenue than slaves.[4]

Many Portuguese and some African chiefs protested that the end of the slave trade would ruin Angola economically,[5] but other articles of trade increased in importance. In 1834, the royal treasury's monopoly in ivory was ended, which stimulated that trade and opened a door for perpetuating slavery. Ivory had always been brought to the coast on the backs of Africans and they could now be called carriers instead of slaves.[6] As the British naval commander and explorer Verney Lovett Cameron wrote in the 1870s, "In the countries where ivory is cheapest and most plentiful none of the inhabitants willingly engage themselves as carriers, and traders are obliged to buy slaves to enable them to transport their ivory to a profitable market."[7] Beeswax was such an important item of commerce as the slave trade declined that the balls of wax, weighing about two pounds, were a standard of exchange. These balls were made into larger cakes for foreign export.

By 1869 the first experimental export of raw rubber was made and by 1887 it was the leading export product of Angola. The brief period of the rubber trade can be divided into three phases: from 1874 until 1886, during which only "first-class" rubber, from the plants themselves, was exported; from 1886, when the discovery of "second-class" or "red rubber" from a root caused a boom which lasted until 1900; and finally, the period of decline until the rubber export stopped in 1916 due to the deterioration of quality and the drop in price. The rubber trade was essentially an African venture, whereas the slave and ivory trades were capitalized by Europeans. Cameron's description of the slaves carrying ivory contrasts sharply with Child's summary of the popular rubber caravans:

Everyone who was able to carry a load joined a caravan. It had always been the custom to take boys on trading expeditions, as young as they

4. James Duffy, *A Question of Slavery* (Cambridge, Mass: Harvard University Press, 1967), p. 5.
5. Wheeler and Pélissier, p. 91.
6. Childs, p. 200.
7. Verney Lovett Cameron, *Across Africa*, Vol. II (London: Daldy, Isbister, 1877), p. 322.

could go—say, from their tenth year—as a part of their education. Now girls were also taken and hardly any but the women stayed at home to raise the crops and provide rations for the caravans. European residents experienced great difficulty in securing necessary porters, and this was one reason for finally putting through the wagon-road.[8]

The rubber trade changed the agricultural pattern in the central highlands. The large caravans required a greater supply of food for rations on the long journey and the increased trading at the coast provided a greater market for foodstuffs. The Umbundu therefore changed from seasonal subsistence agriculture to intensive, cash or barter cultivation.

Angolans promoted the ivory, beeswax, and rubber trade when slaves could no longer serve as the main article of international commerce. Sá da Bandeira, the liberal Portuguese statesman, and the Conselho Ultramarino in Lisbon had other plans to replace the slave-trading economy. New revenues were sought from two sources: increased taxation of the African population and increased customs from ports and harbors. Such plans required greater military control of both the coast and the hinterland. Sá da Bandeira ordered the occupation and annexation of the ports of Ambriz and Cabinda in 1838, but the Portuguese only succeeded in executing the plan in Ambriz in 1855 and Cabinda in 1883. Inland, the Portuguese army occupied Duque de Bragança (1838), Quibala (1856), Bembe (1856), and São Salvador (1859–60). But the Angolan resistance to Portuguese military occupation was so strong that Lisbon in 1860 had to send a special expeditionary force of 700 troops to quell the African rebellions prompted by Portuguese expansionist activities. The fact that the Portuguese had to fight to reconquer the capital of the Kingdom of the Kongo, and that they were able to hold it for only ten years before the tiny Portuguese garrison was forced to evacuate in 1870, gives the lie to the common phrase "five centuries of Portuguese colonialism in Angola."

In addition to alternate commerce and taxation based on military occupation, the Portuguese tried a third method of economic development of Angola to replace the slave trade econ-

8. Childs, p. 209.

omy: white colonization. The port settlement of Moçâmedes was founded in 1840 about 200 miles (320 kilometers) south of Benguela. In a curious manner the ties between Brazil and Angola provided reinforcements for this new settlement in 1849. The year before, an antislavery nativist revolt in the Brazilian city of Pernambuco had made recent Portuguese immigrants fearful of their future, and they petitioned the Lisbon government for assistance in finding a salubrious area of Africa to which they could go. Since the overseas ministry had been seeking unsuccessfully to promote the settling of Africa, it responded promptly, suggesting the area of Moçâmedes and promising financial aid. One hundred and seventy Pernambucanos sailed for Angola in 1849 and the next year another 130 Portuguese followed. In spite of the best efforts of the governor general, who was on hand personally to arrange for their reception, drought and the failure of the cane crop made some of the families decide to move to Luanda. Others moved inland to the Huíla highland, thus starting a new settlement which was to become the main city in southern Angola, named after the minister in Lisbon who banned the slave trade, Sá da Bandeira.[9]

The abolition of the slave trade, the search for substitute articles of trade, the cessation of the crown monopoly in ivory, and white colonization focused attention of the economic potential of the central highlands. Portuguese merchants were attracted to the highland, and the Umbundu came into their own as the most important African traders below the equator.

One of the first merchants to penetrate into the center of Angola was Francisco da Silva, known as Silva Porto. He had sailed at the age of twelve for Brazil, where he served a merchant apprenticeship in Rio de Janeiro and Bahia. In 1839 he arrived in Luanda and traded in the backcountry of the capital for two years before moving to Benguela. From the coast city, Silva Porto moved 390 miles (624 kilometers) inland to the center of the Viye kingdom, which the Portuguese called Bié, and there he built his home and stockade, Belmonte, less than a mile from the modern town which bore his name. Silva Porto became the chief advocate for colonization of the central highlands and the

9. Duffy, *Portuguese Africa,* p. 98.

expansion of the Portuguese presence into the whole of central Africa. Therefore when several Swahili traders appeared in Benguela in 1852, after an overland trek from Zanzibar on the east coast, and the provincial governor sought someone to return with the merchants to carry messages to the governor of Mozambique, Silva Porto agreed. He departed the same year, but illness and local wars impeded his journey in Barotseland and caused him to doubt whether he could go the whole way. Some of his *pombeiros* did continue with the Swahili across the continent to the southern tip of Lake Nyasa and the Rovuma River; one of these *pombeiros*, Domingos Cakahanga, an Umbundu, kept a diary which was later edited by Silva Porto.[10]

In Barotseland, Silva Porto met David Livingstone and gave him valuable information about the country through which the missionary would have to travel on his way to Luanda. This encounter with Britain's foremost promoter of trade in central Africa strengthened Silva Porto's conviction that the Portuguese government should do more to promote its own trade and development in the interior. He advocated railroads to the centers of Angolan commerce in Bié, Bailundo, and Caconda and warned that the neglect of Angola's richest district could only lead to infiltration by foreign agents and the increasing disrespect of the African for Portuguese authority. In 1863, when a provincial governor gave his opinion that domination of the coast was sufficient, Silva Porto scornfully disagreed, saying: "This is how it is in Portugal, where the only things that matter are pointless rivalries, while the foreigner mocks us and even, in his audacity, spits in our faces. Oh, misfortune! Damn the indifferent ones."[11]

The Scramble for Africa

Portugal could not remain indifferent as the end of the slave trade caused the "scramble for Africa."[12] Industrial capitalism

---

10. Childs, p. 204.
11. Duffy, *Portuguese Africa*, p. 194.
12. Eric Axelson, *Portugal and the Scramble for Africa 1875–1891* (Johannesburg: Witwatersrand University Press, 1967), p. 1 n. "Scramble for Africa" became a popular phrase after *The Times* of London used it in a leading article, September 19, 1884.

needed workers in Africa to produce the raw materials for the
European and American factories, to build roads and railroads,
and to provide a market for European production more than it
needed slaves to cultivate sugar, cotton, or tobacco in the
Americas. The phrase "scramble for Africa" is misleading in that
it seems to make Africa the object of European ambitions.
Rather, the European nations only began scrambling for Africa
when they came into conflict with their European rivals in Africa. The principal aim of the Europeans was to maintain a balance of power with their European competitors while they
sought their own aggrandizement through freedom of trade
and unimpeded access to raw materials.

Angola was one of the vortexes of the scramble as Portuguese,
French, Belgian, and British interests clashed at the mouth of
the Congo. Germany, seeking to assert its imperial prestige, announced a protectorate just south of Angola—South-West Africa. The Berlin West African Conference, called jointly by
France and Germany, gave international dignity to the scramble.
Every nation in Europe except Switzerland, plus the International Association of the Congo and the United States of
America, met in Berlin from November 1884 to February 1885.
No African nation was represented, although the announced
concern of the conference was, first, to clarify the status of international trade on the Congo and of navigation on the Niger
and, second, to define conditions under which future territorial
annexations in Africa might be recognized.

Portugal's lengthy and frustrating negotiations with Great
Britain over territorial occupation and definition of borders illustrates the overriding importance of European interests in the
scramble for Africa. Great Britain resisted signing any treaty
recognizing Portuguese sovereignty in Angola until the French
explorer Pierre Savorgnan de Brazza and King Leopold II's
International Association of the Congo staked out claims to territory in the Congo basin for France and Belguim. After more
than a year of negotiations, Portugal and Great Britain signed a
treaty recognizing Portuguese sovereignty from Cabinda south
of Ambriz and up the Congo River to Nóqui. Portugal assumed
that its claim to the whole mouth of the Congo was recognized by
international treaty. However, again European interests inter-

vened as France, Germany, and the International Association of the Congo as well as English public opinion protested, and the new treaty was never ratified. The Berlin Conference did not enter into the details of border definitions but accepted two principles in response to the concerns expressed in the call to the conference: first, there would be freedom of trade and navigation in the Congo basin and freedom of navigation along the Niger; and, second, any power henceforward annexing territory or instituting a protectorate would notify all the signatories and recognize the "obligation to insure the establishment of authority in the regions occupied by them on the coasts of the African Continent sufficient to protect existing rights, and . . . freedom of trade and of transit under the conditions agreed upon."[13] This second principle of the Berlin Conference became Portugal's agenda in Angola from 1885 to 1920: to establish "effective occupation."

Pacification

"Pacification," or military conquest, was one dimension of the establishment of authority. The difference between the military campaigns of 1885 to 1920 leading to effective occupation and those so common during the whole period of the slave trade was in the result, not in the means. Earlier Portuguese military actions usually ended in the retreat of the "victorious" force and the return to the *status quo ante bellum* after achieving some immediate objective, such as the recovery of debt or damages, intimidation of the enemy, establishment of local leadership, or the gaining of an advantage in negotiations. In the few cases where a fort or customs post was built at the end of a military campaign, the effect was local or temporary. In contrast to the earlier pattern, the military campaigns of the first two decades of the twentieth century resulted in continuing administrative control of the whole area by the Portuguese.

Even at the mouth of the Congo, where the Portuguese had arrived in 1482, they did not exercise control at the end of the

13. R. J. Gavin and J. A. Betley, eds., *The Scramble for Africa: Documents on the Berlin West Africa Conference and Related Subjects 1884/1885* (Ibadan: Ibadan University Press, 1973), p. 300.

nineteenth century. The governor of the district of the Congo in 1912–13 confessed that Portugal only ruled a narrow strip of land along the coast and as recently as 1902 Africans who lived less than a kilometer from the coast had imposed taxes and fines on the Portuguese traders.[14] In 1908 the Portuguese had to organize a mobile military column to quell a revolt against the payment of the hut tax by the Mussorongos. A revolt against contract labor challenged Portuguese rule among the Bakongo in 1913–15, but by this time it could be handled by police rather than military action.

The Dembos

The Dembos, a people of the Kimbundu group, proved one of the most difficult for the Portuguese to subdue. Although the Dembos lived within a 100-mile (160-kilometer) radius northeast of Luanda and occupied strategic points on one of the most frequented slave routes, the Portuguese did not establish effective occupation of the Dembo area until 1920. A Portuguese historian has catalogued fifteen military actions or campaigns in the Dembos from 1631 to 1919.[15] In the "first campaign," the *dembo,* or king, of Ambuila-Andua fought a force consisting of 150 Portuguese soldiers and 50,000 Kongolese sent by King Alvaro IV of the Kongo. The Portuguese accounts exaggerate the size of the enemy forces to impress readers with the bravery and valor of their own troops. Such is the account of the fourth campaign in the Dembos, which was called the greatest battle fought in Africa in which the enemy, according to the same historian, had 100,000 troops. He justified his undoubtedly extreme estimate by quoting an Italian traveler through the area who reported 900,000 enemy troops.

The Dembos were in a constant state of rebellion from 1877 to 1919, when the fifteenth military campaign ended with a Portuguese victory. This victory permitted the Portuguese to estab-

14. Relatório do Governador José Cardoso, *No Congo Português: Viagem ao Bembe e Damba—considerações relacionadas. Sept. a Out. 1912, Luanda, 1911* (Imprensa Nacional, 1944), pp. 42–43.
15. António de Almeida, *Relações com os Dembos: Das cartas do dembado de Cakulu-Kahenda* (Lisbon, 1958), p. 7.

lish administrative occupation lasting forty-two years, until the outbreak of the war of liberation in 1961. The Dembos was the scene of some of the earliest nationalist attacks and was one of the few areas that the Portuguese did not succeed in completely reconquering before April 25, 1974.

The three stages of the occupation of the district of Moxico illustrate the history of Portuguese colonialism in Angola.[16] In 1894 a penal colony was created similar to those established in Bengo (1867), Malange (1883), and Caconda (1885). The Major Captaincy of Moxico took the place of the penal colony in 1902 and in turn this was combined with the captaincies of Alto Cuito, Alto Zambeze, and Luchases to form the Military District of Moxico in 1917. The process of occupation reached its goal when the military district became the Distrito Administrativo do Moxico in 1922 and the capital, Vila Luso, was built on the left bank of the Luena River. The transformation of Moxico through the stages of penal colony, captaincy, military and administrative district from 1894 to 1922 was typical of the Portuguese effort to establish effective occupation of Angola.

The Bailundo War

The most important war of "pacification" was the Bailundo War of 1902.[17] The importance does not stem from the duration or ferocity of this war since it only lasted four and a half months and the casualties probably did not exceed 2,000. Rather, the Bailundo War is crucial in the history of Angola because it symbolized Portugal's complete domination of the most populous region of Angola. This decisive conflict grew out of the celebration of the inauguration of King Kalandula of Bailundo, the ceremonial "seating on the stool" which was the principal symbol of African authority. A councillor of the king, Chief Mutu ya Kevela, received two jugs of rum on credit from a Portuguese

16. D. Gabriel de Sousa, *A Portugalização do sudoeste de Angola* (Lisbon: Agência Geral do Ultramar, 1967), p. 21.

17. C. Diane Christensen and Douglas L. Wheeler, "To Rise with One Mind: The Bailundo War of 1902, an Introductory Analysis" (draft paper, 1971); and Fola Soremekun, "The Bailundo Revolt, 1902," *African Social Research*, 16 (December 1973), pp. 447–73.

trader and when the creditor pressed for payment the chief did not respond. The trader complained to the local Portuguese official, who gave Mutu ya Kevela ten days to pay. He lived up to his name, meaning "hard squash," by refusing to be intimidated either by the trader or by the official. King Kalandula and other chiefs encouraged Mutu ya Kevela, perhaps because of exhilaration over the "stooling" celebration but certainly because of the resentment which had been simmering against Portuguese traders for some time.

Several factors coincided at the end of the nineteenth century to heighten the hostility of the Ovimbundu toward the Portuguese. The Portuguese military presence in the central highland had been more aggravating than impressive. They built their first fort beside the Bailundo capital, or *ombala,* and immediately King Numa II attacked it. In retaliation, the Portuguese burned the *ombala* but did not, or could not, subdue the king and his people. The sudden drop in rubber prices in 1899–1902 struck an economic blow at the Umbundu who, prospering from the rubber trade, had overextended their credit to outfit their large caravans. While suffering this economic reverse, the Bailundo area was being flooded with poor white settlers: *degredados,* Boers, and petty traders. As many as 500 trading posts had been set up in a few years. The Ovimbundu resented this competition, especially at the time when trade, the basis of their prosperity, was already depressed. They were also angry because of the increased Portuguese pressure for contract laborers. The Portuguese encouraged the manufacture of rum and pushed its sale among the Umbundu. In an impassioned speech before the war council, Mutu ya Kevela deplored the harmful effects of rum consumption: "Before the traders came we had our own home beer, we lived long lives and were strong."

When the trader complained again that Mutu ya Kevela had not paid his debt in the stipulated time, the captain major sent a sergeant and two soldiers to demand payment. They returned empty-handed after being subjected to insults and jeers by Mutu ya Kevela and his people. The chief not only refused to pay but would not even acknowledge the authority of the captain major. "Mutu ya Kevela had thrown down the gauntlet and it remained for the Portuguese to pick it up."[18] The captain major, with only twenty soldiers, was helpless to respond even when large crowds of Umbundu met in full view of the fort, expressing their defiance of the Portuguese. Many of the white traders were in a state of panic and took refuge in the fort.

On April 23, 1902, Mutu ya Kevela departed from Bailundo to mobilize the Umbundu, sending envoys to all parts of central Angola, from Bié to Catumbela. By the first week in May, rebellion had broken out all over the central highlands. The first phase of the war, which lasted only two months, was won by the Umbundu, but the victory was incomplete. The fort had not been taken and the question was, could the Africans, who lacked artillery, raze the forts of Bailundo and Bié before the Portuguese reinforcements arrived from the coast? Three columns of Portuguese forces were constituted to strike at the Umbundu—one coming from Luanda and two from Benguela. With the arrival of the reinforcements, the superior armaments dominated the battles and by September 15 the Umbundu resistance was broken.

Everyone agrees that the difference between the African muzzle-loaders and the European automatic rifles and artillery was sufficient to give the military victory to the Portuguese. There is a difference of opinion, however, as to the existence and importance of Umbundu disunity. One account of the Bailundo War is entitled "To Rise with One Mind," a phrase used by a friendly observer: "It scarcely seemed possible that these people could bury their differences and rise with one mind in rebellion against the Government."[19] Another account concludes: "The main objective of the insurgents was to drive the Portuguese away. The objective failed not because the Africans lacked pluck but, mainly, because they were not united."[20] Whether the Angolans were united or disunited, the fact remains that in the Bailundo War the Portuguese broke the resistance of the Umbundu people.

Mutu ya Kevela had been killed at Chipindo in the environs of

18. Soremekun, p. 458.
19. Christensen and Wheeler, p. 22.
20. Soremekun, p. 470.

Bailundo, August 4, 1902, but he was the hero who emerged from this conflict between Portuguese and Angolans. He led in battle and mobilized the people with his oratorical appeal for reform, justice, and freedom from the oppression of the slave trade, rum, and economic depression. The Portuguese authorities in Luanda did recognize the legitimate African grievances that led to the Bailundo War and attempted to redress some of them. In his book on the war the governor general acknowledged that its primary cause was the activity of the traders and petty officials, twenty-seven of whom were dismissed or suspended.[21] Among the reforms was a brief recession in the number of *serviçaes,* or contract laborers, sent to São Tomé. Henry W. Nevinson, the British enemy of slavery, wrote: "Owing to terror, the export of slaves to San Thome ceased altogether for about six months after the (Bailundo) rising. It has gone back to its old proportions now—the numbers averaging about four thousand head a year (not including babies), and gradually rising."[22]

Religious Missions

The Berlin Conference recognized "the obligation to insure the establishment of authority," which implied military police control at least "sufficient to protect existing rights." Portugal had established such authority in Angola in 1920. The conference recognized that religious missions also played a significant role in the effective occupation of African territory. In extending the invitation to the conference the German government "was guided by the conviction that all the governments... shared the wish to bring the natives of Africa within the pale of civilization by opening up the interior of that continent to commerce, by giving its inhabitants the means of instructing themselves, by encouraging missions and enterprises calculated to spread useful knowledge." The General Act of the Conference provided that:

All the powers exercising sovereign rights or influence in the aforesaid territories bind themselves to watch over the preservation of the native

21. Christensen and Wheeler, p. 81.
22. Henry M. Nevinson, *A Modern Slavery* (New York: Schocken, 1968), pp. 157–58; first published in 1906.

tribes, and to care for the improvement of the conditions of their moral and material well-being, and to help in suppressing slavery, and especially the Slave Trade. They shall, without distinction of creed or nation, protect and favour all religions, scientific or charitable institutions, and undertakings created and organized for the above ends, or which aim at instructing the natives and bringing home to them the blessings of civilization.

Freedom of conscience and religious toleration are expressly guaranteed to the natives, no less than to subjects and to foreigners. The free public exercise of all forms of Divine worship, and the right to build edifices for religious purposes, and to organize religious Missions belonging to all creeds, shall not be limited or fettered in any way whatsoever.[23]

If not prepared to equally favor all religions, each of the colonial nations was willing to recognize that missions were useful instruments of occupation. Cecil Rhodes gave land concessions to English-speaking missions in central Africa to secure British occupation from the Cape to Cairo and to frustrate Portugal's hopes of uniting Angola and Mozambique. France was staking out claims to territory north of the Congo River with the help of Roman Catholic missions. Portugal had always recognized that the Catholic Church played an essential role in its colonial expansion. In fact, Henry the Navigator undertook the explorations in Africa as Master of the Order of Christ rather than as Prince of Portugal. King Duarte and King Afonso V ceded to the Order of Christ, administered by Prince Henry, the ownership of all lands discovered or conquered. The Portuguese planted crosses on the headlands as they explored the coast of Africa, and the brother kings Manuel of Portugal and Afonso of the Kongo were united by a common faith. As early as 1491 the first church was built in Mbanza, capital of the kingdom of the Kongo, which was renamed São Salvador. The Catholic mission by its presence in São Salvador and the education offered to Kongolese in Lisbon was one of the chief instruments of establishing the Portuguese presence in that part of Angola. After King Afonso, the Church declined and by 1800 the Governor Miguel António de Melo in a report to Lisbon warned: "Now, finally, in conclusion, I would add that if Your Majesty does not

23. General Act, Art. 6, in Gavin and Betley, p. 291.

come to the rescue soon with the necessary help, the Catholic religion in this country will come to an end."[24]

Portuguese Catholic help was not forthcoming, although the government offered certain economic incentives to European priests who would work in Angola, Mozambique, São Tomé, Príncipe, and Timor. The revival of Catholic missions in Angola was accomplished by foreign missionaries, principally through the Holy Ghost Congregation, which had originated in France. In spite of considerable suspicion of these foreign Holy Ghost missionaries who arrived in Angola beginning in 1866, the most prolific Catholic missionaries in the nineteenth century were French: Father Carlos Auber Duparquet, who founded a series of missions in the Huíla district, extending all the way to the southern border, and Father Ernesto Lecomte, who during his twenty-five years of service founded mission stations in Bailundo, Bié, Caconda, Catoco, Massaca, and Cuanhama. Lecomte's dream was to establish a string of missions across Angola to the Zambezi. Among the few Portuguese missionaries of this period were two distinguished pioneers: Father José Maria Antunes, who worked closely with Lecomte in the south, and Father António Barroso, who revived the mission in the Kongo. Father Barroso with two colleagues arrived at Nóqui, the last Portuguese port up the Congo River, on the Portuguese gunboat *Bengo* in 1881 and proceeded on foot to São Salvador. Barroso recognized his dual mission to spread Catholic Christianity and Portuguese nationalism. On the first furlough from his arduous labor, he took with him to Lisbon two sons and a nephew of King Pedro Água Rosada of the Kongo "as signs of the spiritual conquest of the Congo."[25]

Portugal was apprehensive about the fact that a majority of the Catholic missionaries in Angola were foreigners. In a lecture given before the Geographic Society of Lisbon, Father Lecomte spoke to the issue of nationality, asserting the allegiance of foreign missionaries of his congregation to Portugal and its colonial aspirations:

I am speaking of patriotism; but, someone may say, are these missions Portuguese since part of the personnel is foreign? I would answer that

24. Silva Rego, p. 298.
25. Ibid., p. 310.

the nationality of this or that missionary doesn't mean that the mission itself is not Portuguese. All the Holy Ghost missions established in Portuguese territory are Portuguese; for, with government subsidies, they carry out, at great sacrifice of lives and energies, the duty of Portugal before Europe and before all humanity: the civilization of its colonies.[26]

In spite of such protestations and the fact that the foreign priests were subordinate to Portuguese bishops, the government recognized that the foreign missionaries did not prove effective occupation as securely as national personnel would have done. The apprehension turned to fear and hostility as Portugal saw Protestant missions entering from all sides.

By 1920, nine Protestant mission societies based in the United States, Canada, Great Britain, Switzerland, and Germany had established thirty-five mission stations all across Angola. Portuguese colonial officials feared the denationalizing influence of these Protestant foreign missions, which seemed more affluent than the Catholic missions. One major reason for the difference in resources is that the traditional tie between Catholic Church and Portuguese state led the Catholic missions to expect adequate subsidies from the government. This support, which was inadequate in the first place because of Portuguese poverty and indifference, decreased even more in 1910, when the revolution established a Portuguese republic with strong secular and even anticlerical influences. The Protestant missions all came from the free church tradition, with its belief in the separation of church and state, and therefore depended on the voluntary contributions of members to support missions.

Hostility to the Protestant missionaries was intensified when they seemed to be subverting Portuguese occupation of Angola by instigating the Angolans to revolt. In the Bailundo War of 1902, local officials resented the fact that no Protestant personnel or buildings were harmed by the rebels while Portuguese facilities were destroyed. In the Bakongo rebellion of 1913–14 a Baptist missionary, Rev. J. Bowskill, was arrested and imprisoned because he was identified with the Africans who were reacting against higher taxes and increased forced labor recruitment for Cabinda. Protestants also led the antislavery cam-

26. Ibid., p. 308.

paigns in England, which were aimed especially at the continuing slave trade in São Tomé and Príncipe.

The New Slavery

The international slave trade had been abolished, but the Portuguese made legal provision to supply plantation hands for their equatorial islands of São Tomé and Príncipe. In 1858 the Portuguese published a decree abolishing slavery "twenty years hence" in all lands of the Portuguese monarchy. In 1878, exactly twenty years later, Portugal issued the general regulations for contract labor, which apparently closed the door on slavery and opened a new chapter in Angolan history. In actuality the change was in name only. The slave became a servant, *serviçal;* in Umbundu, the *upika* became an *ongamba,* carrier. Technically slaves were no longer bought and sold; the laborer "has come of his own free will to contract for his services under the terms and according to the forms required by the law."[27] For those men, women, and children who were bartered for guns, kegs of rum, or bales of calico, marched to the coast, and in Benguela, Luanda, or Ambrizete and were stowed away on a ship for São Tomé or Príncipe, the change in name from slave to servant meant nothing.[28]

The Umbundu fought against this new form of slavery in the Bailundo War and lost, but others continued to oppose the "new slave trade." Angolan Portuguese condemned the shipping of laborers to São Tomé and Príncipe because it reduced the number of workers available for plantations on the mainland. They also criticized the injustices and cruelty of the system. The outcry by Portuguese was led by a Luanda weekly, properly named *A Defesa de Angola,* which published a series of articles in May 1904, the first of which ended, "The principle is self-

27. Nevinson, p. 28.
28. According to a decree of Nov. 9, 1899, "All natives of the Portuguese overseas provinces shall be subject to the moral and legal obligations of attempting to obtain through work the means of subsistence which they lack and to improve their social condition. They have full liberty to choose the method of fulfilling this obligation, but if they fail to fulfill it the public authorities may force them to do so" (Allison Butler Herrick et al., *Area Handbook for Angola,* Washington, D.C.: U.S. Government Printing Office, 1967, p. 343).

evident that . . . what favours a few at the cost of millions is un-deniably evil."[29] The merchants of Angola sent a delegation of important men to Lisbon to talk to overseas secretaries about the calamitous state of affairs of Angola due to the shortage of labor resulting from epidemics and emigration. They were honest enough to admit that the Bailundo War was "the result of crimes and violence towards the native races who had been sent like slaves to São Tomé. The delegates have to admit that all the right is on the side of those who have risen up in revolt." As a final, indeed prophetic, warning the delegation said that if Portugal would not act, foreigners would.

England, which was not only Portugal's oldest ally but its most important economic partner, became exercised about the São Tomé slave trade. The Anti-Slavery Society aroused the curiosity of a famous British journalist, Henry Nevinson, about the labor situation in Portuguese West Africa. Under the title *A Modern Slavery* (1906), he published the dramatic narrative of his visit to the island of São Tomé, his trip to Benguela, up to the Katanga frontier and back, and his journey up the coast in a steamer carrying *serviçaes*. The Plymouth Brethren missionary Charles Swan, who knew Portuguese and Angolan vernaculars, gave an even more vivid description of the slave trade:

I have never in all my African experience, extended over the past 23 years, seen in any one day so many indications that the slave trade goes on unabated! Signs of the diabolical traffic were met with all along the path—shackles, bleached bones, and the emaciated body of a young lad who had been left to die that morning, as well as slaves themselves, in the caravans we met. My men picked up 92 shackles for legs, arms, or neck, without leaving the path to look for them.[30]

William A. Cadbury of the British chocolate firm, an active member of the Anti-Slavery Society, became concerned about the charges that it was slave-grown cocoa which was being processed by English manufacturers. He had visited Lisbon in 1903 to inquire about the contract labor system in Portuguese Africa and been assured by men in the colonial ministry that new legis-

29. Duffy, *A Question of Slavery*, p. 179.
30. Charles A. Swan, *The Slavery of Today or the Present Position of the Open Sore of Africa* (Glasgow: Pickering and Inglis, n.d.), p. 38.

lation would eliminate whatever evils there had been in the system. Nevinson's reports three years later helped produce pressure on Cadbury and other manufacturers to boycott São Tomé chocolate. Cadbury then sent Joseph Burtt, whose report, more sober than those of Nevinson or Swan, turned into a more damning document. At the beginning he stated concerning the Portuguese labor system in Angola and São Tomé: "The law is a dead letter and the contract a farce. The native is taken from his home against his will, is forced into a contract he does not understand, and never returns to Angola. The legal formalities are but a cloak to hide slavery."[31]

Cadbury himself went to Angola in 1908 and the next year his company was joined by Fry and Rowntree in a boycott of São Tomé cocoa. Whereas the Bailundo War caused a cessation in the export of *serviçaes* to São Tomé and Príncipe for a few months, the international political pressure and economic boycott cut off all "emigration" to the islands for three years, 1910–1912. However, it resumed in 1913 and by 1915 it had risen to 4,874. For the period from 1916 to 1920, an average of 3,000 laborers a year were sent to São Tomé and Príncipe.[32]

Portugal and Angola had come full circle. In the fifteenth century, before the international slave trade began shipping tens of thousands of slaves annually from Africa to the Americas, Portugal was sending hundreds of slaves from the Guinea Coast and Angola to the islands of São Tomé, Príncipe, Cape Verde, and Europe. After the other European nations had abolished the slave trade, Portugal changed the name and continued sending forced labor to São Tomé and Príncipe even into the twentieth century.

31. Duffy, *A Question of Slavery*, p. 195.
32. Ibid., p. 211.

CHAPTER 5

The Violence of Colonial Peace, 1920–1960

The Berlin West African Conference had committed the signatories to substantiate any territorial claim in Africa by "the establishment of authority" (Article 35). From 1900 to 1920, Portugal was successful in establishing military authority over the whole territory of Angola, whose boundaries had just been defined by international treaty. The next task was to establish administrative authority. Although Portugal had not articulated a colonial policy from the fifteenth through the nineteenth centuries, it was in fact using the system of indirect rule by which the colonizer administers through traditional authorities, as the British administered northern Nigeria by means of the emirates. During the earlier period, Portugal always dealt with traditional rulers, whether as brothers in the Kongo, as intermediaries in the slave trade, or as vassals. Portugal now chose the system of "direct rule." The colonial office drew lines of civil authority directly from Lisbon to the most remote village in Angola with a minimum of intervention by traditional rulers. The establishment of authority by direct rule brought Lisbon into relationship with the peoples of Angola for the first time.

Portuguese Colonial Policy

Portuguese colonial theoreticians saw beyond military or even administrative authority to a goal of integration of the Angolan peoples into the Portuguese nation. Professor Silva Cunha summarized this vision of Portuguese colonial policy for his students at the Instituto Superior do Ultramar, which prepared personnel to administer this policy in Angola and the other colonies:

(a) The final objective of native policy is to accomplish the integration of native populations of the colonies into the Portuguese nation by the progressive transformation of their practices and moral social concepts.

(b) This object should, however, be pursued with the greatest prudence. The natives have their own culture, social organization and law which should be respected, although transitorily, until the transformation of their basic conceptions of life.

(c) Until such transformation is accomplished, the natives are under the protection of the State which accepts the responsibility to defend them against possible abuses and arrogance of the colonists. This protection is manifested especially in the defense of property, against exploitation in the supervision of labor contracts and in any relationship involving natives and non-whites.

(d) The means of assimilating the natives are principally, the diffusion of the Portuguese language, education, instruction and Christianization.

(e) Having adopted the Portuguese world-view and being integrated into the civilized way of life, the native has the same legal status as the Portuguese by birth, enjoying fully the rights and being subject to the obligations which the Portuguese juridical order implies.[1]

Administrative Hierarchy

To establish administrative authority and to implement this colonial policy, Lisbon formed a hierarchic structure. The government in Lisbon delegated its authority in Angola to a governor-general who was nominated by the overseas minister and confirmed by the council of ministers. The governor-general, in turn, nominated his cabinet or governing council, composed of provincial secretaries who were confirmed by the overseas minister. In consultation with the provincial secretaries, the governor-general exercised his authority through district governors whom he chose. In 1921 Angola was divided into eleven administrative districts. In the same year the parallel military structure of districts, captaincies, and posts was eliminated, a sign of the transition from military to civil administration. The civil districts were divided into 65 *conselhos* or *circunscrições,* which were directed by administrators. The smallest administrative division was the *posto,* of which there were 287 in 1921. This was headed by a *chefe do posto.* Direct representatives of the

1. Joaquim de Silva Cunha, "Apontamentos," I, unpublished mimeographed lesson notes, pp. 171–72.

Lisbon government were thus the authorities in every parcel of Angola. With very rare exceptions, all these officials were white and most of them were from the metropole. Angolans called an official *muele putu,* foreign lord.

Below this hierarchy the Africans played a minor role in the *regedorias,* the subdivisions of the *postos.* In each of these small areas a king, chief, or headman, the *regedor,* represented the foreign lord and, if courageous, might express some of the feelings and desires of the people; however, he served primarily as an errandboy for the Portuguese administrator.

An increase of the white population, and consequent growth of cities and towns, caused the government to create more municipal councils in which the "civilized" population had some representation. These organisms were elected, contrary to the appointive system in the administrative structure, but the screening process for candidates was so rigorous that only those with the approval of the hierarchy could be elected.

This hierarchic structure, which the theoreticians conceived as a means to integrate the "native populations of the colonies into the Portuguese nation," was perceived by Angolans as a means of exploitation. They felt the weight of the Portuguese administrative system in three points: taxation, forced labor, and documentation.

TAXATION

The "native" tax was instituted in 1908, but the receipts were very irregular until the administrative system was sufficiently developed to enforce the collection. This tax had two purposes: to raise revenue for governmental expenses and to force the African into the money economy. The money-tax was used by all colonial powers to bring traditional societies into their economic orbits. Tribute paid to traditional authorities was a regular part of African culture; a visitor took salt or a chicken to a king, and a subkingdom paid tribute to the kingdom in service, personnel, or kind. The peculiar feature of the colonial tax was that it was paid in Portuguese currency rather than the shells, salt, or cloth which were the traditional means of exchange. As late as 1920 the British engineer working on the Benguela railway noted that money was unknown and that calico and salt were used for barter.[2] To pay their taxes, Angolans were now forced to enter the money economy.

In 1928, each African male in central Angola paid an annual tax of 80 angolares, equal to 100 days' pay for a contract laborer.[3] The tax, which increased steadily, reaching 108 angolares in 1941 and 120 angolares in 1945, was regulated regionally according to economic opportunity and proximity to a border. Thousands of Chokwe fled to the Belgian Congo and Northern Rhodesia in the 1930s and 1940s rather than pay their tax.[4] Those who did not pay and could not flee were the most liable to be called up for contract labor.

FORCED LABOR

Forced labor was generally accepted in colonial situations, but it was defended more openly by the Portuguese than by any other colonizing nation. They contended that colonization is a twofold process of economic development and cultural evolution and that forced labor contributes to both. Colonial lands are by definition underdeveloped because they have been controlled by people who, according to the Portuguese, were not equipped to keep pace with "civilized" nations. In this analysis, economic development requires not only capital and technology, which the colonizers are expected to provide, but manpower, which is the contribution of the native peoples.

Portugal argued that there had been a shortage of manpower in all of Africa because of natural and cultural factors. According to the 1950 census, population density was 8.6 per square mile in Angola, and apologists contended that this sparse population was not used in the development of the colony because the natives were not integrated into the monetary, industrial economy. Therefore the Portuguese affirmed that some method must be employed to compel the natives to participate in the European system. The methods fell into two categories, the direct and the indirect. The direct was forced labor; the indirect might take the form of taxes, clothing requirements, or educa-

2. H. F. Varian, *Some African Milestones* (Oxford: Ronald, 1953), p. 190.
3. Childs, p. 215.
4. T. Ernest Wilson, *Angola Beloved* (Neptune, N.J.: Loizeaux Brothers, 1967), pp. 231–32.

tion. The Portuguese, therefore, accepted forced labor as an effective means of providing the manpower which was necessary for the economic development of the colony.

The second purpose of forced labor was based on complete lack of appreciation of African culture. Since the Angolans did not offer themselves voluntarily for the jobs which the Europeans wished filled, the Portuguese concluded that they needed to teach the native the value and habits of work. As noted in Chapter 2, the Angolans had well-defined work roles in their economies, and each language had a wealth of proverbs extolling the virtue of work and chiding laziness. The Ovimbundu say: *"U wa ku vetela kepia, ka ku vetele, wa ku longisa olondunge"* ("He who disciplines you with a beating in the field, does not punish you, but teaches you a lesson") and *"Ngandi wa lavisa ocisiai: elombo utima"* ("The scorn of idleness is natural: no one prizes it in his heart"). The Portuguese because of their ignorance of the vernaculars could not understand these proverbs, nor could they recognize the work ethic which was integral to the traditional economy.

The reasonable arguments of the Portuguese for using forced labor in the economic development and cultural evolution of Angola are in stark contrast to the brutal reality experienced by the men, women, and children who were caught in the system. Forced labor took three forms in Angola. The most severe type was rightly called "a modern slavery," as workers were sent from Angola and Mozambique to São Tomé and Príncipe for five years of hard labor on a coffee or cocoa plantation. So many workers never returned from São Tomé that this was considered a life, or perhaps a death, sentence. The second type of forced labor was that which furnished long-term workers for the principal business and government enterprises throughout Angola. Obligatory labor for private interest was specifically prohibited by the constitution (Article 145). The labor code (Article 38) forbade state officials to recruit laborers for private enterprises "although they should facilitate the legitimate activity of private recruiters." However, employers from both the public and the private sector requisitioned workers at the Department of Native Affairs in Luanda. Perhaps the contract used and the persons signing were different in the cases of public and private employers, but the workers were not aware of these technicalities. They felt that the Portuguese government was sending them to work, whether it was at a government agency, such as the ports of Lobito or Luanda, or at a private sugar or coffee plantation.

The total number of workers to be recruited was apportioned among the districts. Each *conselho* and *posto* then received the quota of workers it was required to furnish. The *chefe do posto* gave responsibility to the African *regedores* to bring in the men on a certain date. If any man had not paid his tax, he was on the top of the list of those to be "contracted." The *regedor* then consulted the village elders to discover those men who should be sent to work. If he did not find enough men by this process, the *regeder* was subject to beatings at the *posto* and perhaps also a fine. The *chefe do posto*'s next recourse was to send out his African policemen, the *cipaios,* to capture men. The only sure way to be exempt from contract labor was to present written proof of employment by a European. Even having fulfilled a contract in the past year was no insurance against being sent again. The word *contract* was a farce when it referred to the relation between the African worker and his white employer. However, the colonial government took very seriously its contract with the major employers of Angola to provide the number of workers they required. The recruiting fee which employers paid to the administrative services in many cases was equal to or exceeded the cash payment to the worker for eighteen months' labor.

Observers have differed as to the number of men under contract at any one time. Basil Davidson, the British Africanist, saw official figures in Luanda indicating that 379,000 workers were contracted in 1954 and published his eloquent criticism of the contract labor system in *An African Awakening.*[5] Portugal commissioned a sympathetic Englishman, a Colonel Egerton, to answer Davidson, and in his reply, *Angola without Prejudice,* Egerton cited another official figure to prove that Angola had 99,771 contract laborers in that year.[6] The exact number of contract

5. Basil Davidson, *An African Awakening* (New York: Macmillan, 1955), p. 202.

6. F. C. C. Egerton, *Angola without Prejudice* (Lisbon, Agency-General for the Oversea Territories, 1955), p. 20.

laborers was impossible to determine, but the impact of the system was clear. Angolans saw the *chefe do posto* and other administrative officials as the enemy who was able to force any "native" to work anyplace, under any conditions, for any employer.

The third type of forced labor was that demanded by the *chefe* locally for a variety of public works. Highway construction and maintenance required large numbers of workers since even the main highways were built and maintained by hand until 1962. Men, women, and children were forced to spend a few days to several weeks at a time repairing the dirt roads, which always suffered severe damage in the rainy season. Professor E. A. Ross of the University of Wisconsin presented a Report on Employment of Native Labor in Portuguese Africa to the Temporary Slavery Commission of the League of Nations in 1925. The first entry in his report described this local forced labor in Angola:

Sixty-five natives working on the public highway, two-thirds of them women, twelve with babies on their backs. I inquired how much time they had worked for the Government in the last year.

Case 1.—In the last 5 months has worked on the highways 3 months—a month at a time.

Case 2.—Paid his 1923 head tax (40 escudos—$1.00) and then worked 3 months on end getting out timber for a house. Got nothing but 1.20 escudos ration money per day, which was not more than enough to buy two fifths of the normal ration. Also worked some weeks on the road for which he got no pay.

Case 3.—Named three places at each of which he worked two weeks either roadmaking, or helping build a house for the road boss. No food was supplied to him, no wage was given him—he paid his taxes besides, for which he got the money by selling his produce.

Case 4.—Worked on the nearby road a week at a time until its completion. No ration or wage or tax receipt.

Case 5.—Worked three months—a month at a time—about 20 miles from here, one month on one road, two months on the other. Got nothing whatever. Neither his wife, nor the wives of the other men worked on the highway.[7]

Local forced labor was also used to cultivate the gardens and fields of the *posto* and to provide skilled laborers such as carpen-

7. Edward Alsworth Ross, *Report on Employment of Native Labor in Portuguese Africa* (New York, 1925), p. 6.

ters, masons, or blacksmiths to work on projects which the *chefe* or administrator considered of public utility.

The three types of forced labor were justified by Portugal not only as necessary but as benevolent. The paternalistic colonial policy considered the natives to be "under the protection of the State which accepts the responsibility to defend them against possible abuses and arrogance of the colonists; this protection is manifested especially in the defence ... against exploitation in the supervision of labor contracts."[8] The Portuguese government might regard itself as the protector of workers, but the Angolans saw the state as the chief exploiter.

DOCUMENTATION

Documentation was the third point at which the administrative system touched every Angolan's life. The system required one or more documents for any step outside the village and its traditional culture. Each adult male was required to carry an identification booklet, or *caderneta,* which included his tax receipt and labor status. Any travel from one administrative area to another required a special pass, or *guia.* To register for school, a pupil was required to present a birth certificate as well as a diploma from the previous class. A birth certificate had to be requested for each occasion since it was only valid for six months. The cost of each document in time and money was exorbitant in relation to the people's standard of living.

The only way an African could escape the burden of native tax and forced labor was to master the maze of documentation and become an *assimilado.* Portuguese colonial policy was based on the division between native (*indígena*) and nonnative, or between native and civilized person (*civilizado*). An *assimilado* was an African who moved legally from the status of *indígena* to *civilizado.* *Indígenas* or natives were "individuals of the black race and their descendants who were born or habitually live in (Angola) and who do not yet possess the enlightenment and the personal and social habits presupposed for the integral application of the public and private law of Portuguese citizens."[9] According to this

8. Silva Cunha, pp. 171–72.
9. Statute for Portuguese Natives in the Provinces of Guinea, Angola and Mozambique, Decree-Law No. 39666, May 20, 1954, Article 2.

definition, race, parentage, birthplace, and residence were involved, but the fundamental distinction between native and nonnative was cultural. The native was not considered culturally prepared to be integrated into civilized society. The civilized person, *civilizado,* was also classified as a citizen, *cidadão;* however, this designation did not refer to civil citizenship in the sense of nationality. Both native and nonnative were of Portuguese nationality and in that sense were citizens or subjects. However, the native was not a political citizen. Marcelo Caetano, former overseas minister and prime minister of Portugal, made the distinction in these words: "Natives are Portuguese subjects, under the protection of the Portuguese state, but without forming part of the Nation—which is considered as a cultural community or as a political association of citizens."[10] The distinction between different meanings of "citizen" was sufficient reason for continuing to use the popular term *assimilado,* although legally it was by losing the status of native and acquiring citizenship that an Angolan could be exempt from the native tax and forced labor. The Statute for Portuguese Natives stipulated that an African who proved that he had fulfilled the following requirements could lose the status of native and acquire citizenship:

Be eighteen years old;
Speak the Portuguese language correctly;
Exercise a profession, art or trade which offers earnings necessary for the support of the individual and the dependent members of his family, or possess goods sufficient for the same purpose;
Be of good conduct and have acquired the enlightenment and habits presupposed for the integral application of the public and private law of Portuguese citizens; and
Not have failed to fulfill military obligations or be a deserter.

The candidate proved his readiness for citizenship by successfully gathering a sheaf of sealed papers, documents, and official forms as required by law. Since the bureaucracy was built out of official papers, the best proof of being ready for citizenship was to be able to work one's way through a maze of *requerimentos,*

10. Marcelo Caetano, *A Constituição de 1933—estudo de direito político,* 1956, p. 23, quoted by José Carlos Ney Ferreira e Vasco Soares de Veiga, Estatuto dos Indígenas Portugueses das Províncias da Guiné, Angola e Moçambique, 2d ed. (Lisbon: Tipografia, Escola da Cadeia Penitenciária de Lisboa, 1957), p. 13.

certidões, and *atestados.* Frequently the administrative officials who approved the application for citizenship had no personal contact with the candidate. With sufficient funds, an agent could be hired to pilot the papers through the channels of the various government departments and deliver the official declarations that his client was a Portuguese citizen.

The number of Angolans who qualified for citizenship and could pay the necessary fees was infinitesimal, as shown by the fact that by 1950 only fewer than one percent of the African population were *assimilados.* These few Angolans had escaped the native tax and forced labor, but they had acquired a new burden. Portuguese colonial policy, as summarized above, affirmed that "the final objective of native policy is to accomplish the integration of native populations of the colonies into the Portuguese nation." In fact the *assimilados* had been required to declare that they had abandoned their African culture, but they were not integrated into the Portuguese nation. They were caught in the conflict between two cultures and were citizens of neither. As the gifted Angolan author António de Assis Júnior wrote in 1917, the *assimilado* was caught "between two fires."[11]

Transportation

Leopold II of Belgium is credited with the saying that *"coloniser c'est transporter."*[12] A transportation network was essential both to establish civil authority and to open the continent to commerce. Portuguese administrators with no engineering training or equipment used local forced labor to construct and maintain 20,000 miles (35,000 kilometers) of roads by which they could reach the remote corners of their areas.[13] By 1960, 435 miles (696 kilometers) were paved but the quality of the rest of the roads was so poor that even many of the 3,029 miles (4,847 kilometers) of first-class highway were impassable in the rainy season. Second- and third-class roads were even worse, and

11. Wheeler and Pélissier, *Angola,* p. 98.
12. Lord Hailey, *An African Survey, Revised 1956: A Study of Problems Arising in Africa South of the Sahara* (London: Oxford University Press, 1957), p. 1535.
13. Afonso Costa Valdez Thomaz dos Santos, *Angola, coração do império* (Lisbon: Agência Geral das Colónias, 1945), p. 208.

11,875 miles (17,000 kilometers) of the total was simply classified as "other." Whatever the quality, these roads were designed to serve European administrators. Africans had no cars to drive on roads which they built with such suffering. Of the 43,055 vehicles (including cars, trucks, and motorcycles) registered in all of Angola in January 1960 virtually none belonged to Africans. To add insult to injury, African men walking or working along the road had to snatch their hats from their heads as a car approached. The safe assumption was that a car would be carrying white people and in the colonial situation the worst crime was lack of respect, *falta de respeito.*

In addition to furnishing the means for the administrative system to embrace the total population of Angola, the network of roads also brought produce to the railroads. Roads could be built by men, women, and children using their own hoes and baskets under the supervision of an untrained *chefe do posto.* Railroads demanded more engineering skill and much more capital, yet they were necessary if Africa was to be opened up to European commerce. The financing of the railroads was always Portugal's main difficulty.

RAILROADS

In 1848 a railroad between Luanda and Calumbo was proposed, but the route was only studied in 1862. In 1884, when the delegates were gathered in Berlin, Portugal finally issued a decree calling for bids to build a railway from Luanda to Pamba in the area of Ambaca. The preface to the decree showed that Portugal was conscious of the rivalry among the European nations for commercial advantage:

Considering that at this moment when the interests of Africa are being debated in Europe and when the most powerful nations are engaged in opening the marvelous world, it is indispensable that without loss of time we complete this project of the Railway to the interior which for years has been studied and planned, and that we may conquer definitely for Luanda the privilege, which is its due, to be the true door by which civilization and commerce can penetrate central Africa; considering that it would be lamentable, after so much study, sacrifice and labor, if it could be alleged that we had done nothing for the development of our African possessions, and if we thought to begin at other points the enterprise of the Railway to the interior on which we have labored for so long and which only lacks the final impulse.[14]

The Caminho de Ferro de Luanda was put into operation in 1901, when it reached as far as Ambaca, 173 miles from Luanda. When completed, the line covered a total of 378 miles (613 kilometers), its main line running from Luanda to Malange, with two spurs to Dondo on the Cuanza River and to the Golunga Alto coffee area.

In 1884–85 the naval officers-explorers Hermenegildo Carlos de Brito Capelo and Roberto Ivens, as part of Portugal's attempt to establish claim to the territory between Angola and Mozambique, crossed Africa from Moçâmedes to Quelimane. A concession was then requested for a railway from Moçâmedes to Sá da Bandeira, which was to be the first step in a cross-Africa line. This was authorized in 1890, but no capital was forthcoming, so in 1905, the state began construction and reached Sá da Bandeira, 155 miles (248 kilometers) across the Namib Desert and up the escarpment, in 1923. During World War II the gauge was changed from the narrow, .6 meter (23.6 inches) to the standard African gauge of 1.067 meters (42 inches), and then in the 1950s this line was pushed 496 miles (792 kilometers) into the interior to Serpa Pinto. South from Sá da Bandeira the Caminho de Ferro de Moçâmedes had a branch line reaching 81 miles (128 kilometers) south to Chiange.

Two small private railways were built to serve single industries: the Amboim Railway, with 77 miles (123 kilometers), carried coffee from the Gabela plateau to Pôrto Amboim, and the Cuio Railway transported sugar from the Dombe Grande and Luacho plantations.

The list of stations on the Caminho de Ferro de Benguela (CFB) mixed euphonic African names—Caimbambo, Longonjo, Lépi—with a sprinkling of Portuguese heroes—Marco de Canavezes, Mariano Machado, Teixeira de Sousa. The single British name was that of Robert Williams. That ambitious Scot was judged worthy to have the Caala station named Vila Robert Williams since he produced the capital to build Angola's one

14. Ibid., pp. 190–91.

international railway. As in the construction of the Luanda and Moçâmedes railways, the Benguela Railway had been stalled for lack of capital. The Portuguese established a special fund from taxes on alcohol and rubber in 1899 to finance the railway, but this money was used by the government in Luanda for general expenses. Portugal was also having financial problems so in 1902 it let out a modest bid for some fifty miles of line to Mount Saôa. Williams responded by requesting a concession to build a railroad all the way from Katanga to the coast, without any financial aid from the government.

Robert Williams had arrived in Africa in 1891 and associated himself with Cecil Rhodes at Kimberley and on the Rand in South Africa. In 1898, Rhodes sent Williams to Northern Rhodesia to prospect for mineral deposits. Africans had been smelting copper ingots on the watershed between the Congo and the Zambezi for many years before Europeans cast covetous eyes on that rich area. Williams had to negotiate a concession from King Leopold of Belgium, who had secured control over Katanga in 1891–92. After prospecting rights for five years were granted in 1900, Williams confirmed the wealth of the mineral deposits and conceived the idea of building a railroad west from the copper belt through Angola, which would follow the old slave trail and shorten the distance to Europe by 3,000 miles.

The Portuguese government granted a ninety-nine-year concession to Williams, and the CFB was founded with a capital of £3 million, 90 percent of which was owned by Tanganyika Concessions Company and 10 percent by the Portuguese government. Although Portugal could not finance the railway with its own capital, some Portuguese still protested the Williams concession, calling it the "Loss of Angola."[15] A pamphlet with this name, concerned about the establishment of Portuguese sovereignty across Angola, affirmed, "Where there is one Englishman, there is England."[16] Williams and the Tanganyika Concessions Company were not interested in Angola politically; they wanted a corridor through Angola and a port for the exploitation of the Katanga mineral wealth. Tanganyika Conces-

15. *Perda de Angola—a concessão Williams* (Lisbon: Diário Illustrado, 1903).
16. Ibid., p. 30.

sions' share of the profits from the mines was assured by its partnership in Union Minière du Haut-Katanga, which was formed in 1906 and went unchallenged in its domination of Katanga from that time until the independence of Congo in 1960.

Since Williams's goal was the transportation of minerals requiring large freighters, he realized that Benguela Bay was too shallow to be the terminal port of the railway. Therefore he requested the concession from a port 21 miles (33 kilometers) north of Benguela, Lobito, where a three-mile sandspit formed a deep bay. The name Lobito comes from the Umbundu word *upito,* the passage through the hills that was used by caravans carrying goods and slaves to and from the interior. Captains who wished to avoid the taxes imposed on slaves in the legal port of Benguela anchored their ships in the dense mangroves of Lobito.

At the beginning of the twentieth century practically no Angolans lived on the coastal strip in the area of Lobito, Catumbela, and Benguela. The CFB brought in Kroos and Senegalese from West Africa and 2,000 Indians from Natal to lay the tracks along the coast and across the desert and mountain strip about 150 miles from Lobito. They even imported camels from North Africa for transportation across the desert. The West Africans adapted themselves to the strenuous work and rigorous, arid conditions, but the Indians, accustomed to more water and amenities in Natal, had to be repatriated. Only after reaching the highlands was local labor available.

World War I halted construction of the railroad because of difficulties in obtaining materials and financing; for six years the CFB terminated in Chinguar, 322 miles (515 kilometers) from Lobito. In 1920 the construction resumed and finally reached the border with the Belgian Congo on August 26, 1928. Including the six-year interruption, it took twenty-five years at a cost of $40 million (over 80 percent from British sources) to construct 838 miles (1,343 kilometers) of railway. In 1931, when the connecting lines in Katanga were completed, the CFB became a link in the only African transcontinental railway.

Of the Angolan railways, only the Benguela Railway fulfilled the Portuguese hopes of penetrating the interior to open the

Table 1.   Traffic and revenues of Angolan railways, 1960

	Amboim	Benguela	Luanda	Moçâmedes
Passengers	10,246	725,504	221,941	73,706
Tonnage	34,022	3,608,551	445,836	226,707
Receipts (U.S. $)	219,160	23,169,880	1,955,400	639,720

Source: Calculated from data in *Anuário estatístico 1960* (Luanda: Imprensa Nacional, 1961).

continent to commerce. The relative importance of the four major lines is shown in Table 1.

At least 70 percent of the passengers were Africans, judging by the fact that 716,000 of the 1,031,397 total traveled in third and fourth class.

The Luanda Railway provided transportation and communication within the Kimbundu area, while the Benguela line, running through the Umbundu area, furnished the means by which the latter extended their influence from Lobito to the Zaïre border. Since they adapted more quickly to European civilization than other ethnolinguistic groups in central Angola, the Umbundu became the clerks, telegraph operators, and in a few cases even the stationmasters along the whole line. The CFB employees and their families attracted other Umbundu and in 1960 there were 7,725 Umbundu in and around Luso and 4,341 near the border station of Teixeira de Sousa. Many Umbundu also found work on the Moçâmedes line since the coastal zone was sparsely populated and the conservative Nhaneca-Humbe peoples through which that railway ran did not seek employment with Europeans.

PORTS

The promotion of trade and commerce which dominated the Berlin Conference and motivated the building of the railways had as its goal the integration of Africa into the world market economy. Domestic commerce was chiefly valued as it stimulated and fed into the world economy. Angola had twenty-six ports for coastal shipping, but only three of those ports, the

Table 2.   Tonnage handled through major Angolan ports, 1960

	Imported	Exported
Luanda	325,943	443,311
Lobito	329,412	1,374,755
Moçâmedes	43,520	38,816
Total for Angola	760,399	2,029,179

Source: Calculated from data in *Anuário estatístico 1960.*

terminals of the railways—Luanda, Lobito, and Moçâmedes—
were essential to the world commercial network. A fourth world
port was added in 1967 when Gulf Oil began exporting oil from
Cabinda.

Lobito, combining the advantages of the best natural harbor
and the terminus of the only transcontinental railway, had the
best equipped and busiest port. The port of Luanda did not
have a wharf for berthing oceangoing vessels until 1945. The
growth in traffic in the port of Luanda from the end of World
War II until 1961 accompanied the increase in population and
the centralization of government offices, commerce, and industry in the capital. During this period, 1920–1961, Moçâmedes
was a distant third in facilities and traffic although in 1957 a
quay able to receive oceangoing ships was inaugurated. As Table
2 shows, imports through Luanda and Lobito were about the
same in 1960, but the tonnage exported through Lobito was
much greater because of the minerals brought by the CFB from
the copper belt of Katanga and Northern Rhodesia.

AIR TRANSPORTATION

A public corporation, Divisão dos Transportes Aéreos (DTA),
was created in 1938 to furnish domestic air transportation for
Angola. By 1960, DTA had regular flights to twenty-six airports,
serving the capitals of all fifteen districts and even such small
communities as Camabatela, Forte Roçadas, Portugália, and
Toto. Luanda was the center of the network, with 43 percent of
the passengers arriving at or departing from the capital. All 436
international air flights in 1960 were through Luanda.

Communications

Communications are as essential as transportation for administrative control or commercial development of a country. Postal, telegraph, and telephone services in Angola were provided by a government agency, Direcção dos Serviços de Correios, Telégrafos e Telefones (CTT). The increase of mail during this period reflected both commercial expansion and the growth in the number of persons who had effectively entered into a literary culture from the traditional African oral culture. The pieces of mail handled by the CTT increased from 5,438,216 in 1944 to 64,601,129 in 1961. Within this total increase in mail, the expanded distribution of newspapers and periodicals from 617,651 in 1944 to 3,196,999 in 1961 is an even clearer sign of the spread of literature in Angola.

In 1961, sixteen newspapers and fifteen magazines were being published in Angola. Ten cities had their own newspapers, but all the other periodicals were produced in Luanda. Three of the newspapers had a circulation of more than 10,000, but most of them were between 1,000 and 5,000, and all were in Portuguese.[17]

Reaching more Angolans than the press were the seventeen radio stations broadcasting from fourteen cities across Angola. In 1960, 53,183 radio receivers were registered in Angola and there were undoubtedly others functioning which had never been registered. Only the government station in Luanda, operating with ten kilowatts, was powerful enough theoretically to reach the whole colony, but in fact the reception was poor in most of Angola. Its location at the coast and climatic conditions made even the official radio station difficult to hear in the interior unless it hooked up with other transmitters, as it did for special programs. Until the war started in 1961, all the stations broadcast only in Portuguese.

The concentration of publishing and broadcasting in the urban centers, the exclusive use of Portuguese, and the limited number of radio receivers restricted the communications network to about 10 percent of the population of Angola before the outbreak of the war in 1961.

17. *Angola: Curso de extensão universitária, ano lectivo de 1963-64* (Lisbon: Instituto Superior de Ciências Sociais e Política Ultramarina), pp. 313-20.

Economy

The first purpose of the Berlin West African Conference, as expressed by Otto von Bismarck, was "to bring the native of Africa within the pale of civilization by opening up the interior of that continent to commerce."[18] History confirms that Bismarck and his European colleagues had transposed means and ends in their articulation of the purpose of the conference. Their goal was really to open up the interior of Africa to commerce and the means was bringing the Africans not "within the pale of civilization," but within the world market economy.

The administrative authority established according to the system of direct rule and the infrastructure of highways, railroads, ports, and communications contributed directly to the goal of opening up the interior of the continent to commerce. How successful was Portugal in reaching this goal in Angola from 1920 to 1960? The answer to this question may be found in an examination of Angola's economy in this period. At the conclusion of Chapter 2 we noted that in 1920 most Angolans were in process of transition from a subsistence to a market economy. Whether subsistence or market, the Angolan economy was essentially rural and agricultural. For our brief analysis the agricultural economy of Angola from 1920 to 1960 can be divided geographically into north, central, and south.

ECONOMY OF THE NORTH

The agriculture of the north of Angola revolved around three principal crops—cassava, coffee, and cotton. Cassava was Angola's biggest crop in volume[19] and except for some export of *crueira,* the cut and dried form of the root, this was a subsistence crop. Coffee and cotton were cash crops.

The development of coffee as a cash crop was the most important economic fact of the 1920–1960 period in the north. As early as 1830, Africans had harvested coffee from semispontaneous bushes and sold it to Portuguese traders. The first commercial estate was established in 1937. Coffee exports

18. Protocol No. 1 Meeting of November 15, 1884, in Gavin and Betley, p. 129.
19. David M. Abshire and Michael A. Samuels, eds., *Portuguese Africa: A Handbook* (New York, Praeger, 1969), p. 261.

gradually increased until they reached a high of 11,000 tons in 1895, but soon fell off to 3,000 to 4,000 tons annually in the first two decades of the twentieth century. Only after World War II, with the acute commodity shortages of the Korean War period, did the price rise so dramatically that production and export were greatly stimulated.[20] From 1948 to 1954 the price climbed from 8.61 escudos to 29.39 escudos per kilo. Since the coffee plant takes several years to bear fruit, the production did not increase immediately with the rise in price, but by 1961 coffee exports reached 118,000 tons, more than double the 1948 total of 53,400 tons. The area devoted to coffee also increased during this same period from 120,000 hectares in 1948 to 500,000 in 1961.

The coffee boom produced prosperity for the Portuguese and frustration and resentment for the Angolans. Portuguese were attracted to Angola by the high coffee prices and so the Portuguese population in the northern coffee-producing area increased dramatically from 1950 to 1956. A cautious estimate of the number of Africans displaced by Europeans in the coffee area in just one year, 1955, is staggering: 5,000 in the township of Uíge and 10,000 in the township of the Dembos. Portuguese settler production increased much more rapidly than African production and the proportion of total production contributed by Africans declined from 39 percent in 1941 to 26 percent in 1958.

The African resentment against Europeans, and more specifically against the government, also grew because of the exploitative methods used to produce cotton. Portugal had very little industry of its own in the metropole, and what little it had produced poor-quality goods. The textile industry was the largest in Portugal, but it had difficulty competing internationally. To help solve Portugal's economic problems, a Cotton Export Board (Junta de Exportação de Algodão) was created with headquarters in Mozambique and representation in Angola so that the two colonies could provide cheap raw materials for the Portuguese textile industry. In addition, the production of cotton was forced on Africans. Many were sent to work on plantations.

20. Wheeler and Pélissier, p. 137.

Elsewhere, principally in the Cassange area, an even more oppressive system was put into effect. Each African family was forced to grow cotton on a prescribed patch of land. No wages were paid and the harvest was sold at a low, fixed price to Cotonang, a Luso Belgian firm with a government-granted monopoly of cotton. When one patch was worn out the Africans were forced to move to a new one that was always farther away from home.

Coffee and cotton provided the basis for the economic growth of the north of Angola from 1920 to 1960 and the profits from these two cash crops balanced Portugal's foreign trade accounts, strengthened the metropolitan textile industry, increased profits of foreign investors, and provided lucrative employment for the growing number of white settlers. All this was done at the expense of the Africans, who lost their land and were forced to work on plantations or plots or were brought in from other regions of Angola on contract. This system brought the north of Angola into the world market economy and decreased even further the dependence on subsistence agriculture.

ECONOMY OF CENTRAL ANGOLA

In central Angola the Umbundu continued their movement from a subsistence to a market economy, which had begun before the turn of the century. Four stages in Umbundu economic development have been identified.[21] The Umbundu traditionally had a diversified economy in which hunting and beekeeping occupied a major portion of the labor energy and the rest was divided between trade and war, crafts, wild plant and small animal collection, fishing, and subsistence agriculture. From 1875 to about 1910 the diversity of economic activity continued, but trade and war became the dominant occupations at the expense of hunting and beekeeping, while the other activities continued in about the same proportions. As the Portuguese established military, administrative, and economic domination, trade and war were eliminated and hunting, beekeeping, crafts,

21. Jorge Vieira da Silva and Júlio Artur de Morais, "Ecological Conditions of Social Change in the Central Highlands of Angola," in Franz-Wilhelm Heimer, ed., *Social Change in Angola* (Munich: Weltforum Verlag, 1973), pp. 93–110.

and plant and small animal collection were reduced to a bare minimum. In the third period, from 1910 to 1930, agriculture expanded to take up the slack so that subsistence and cash crop agriculture occupied most of the labor energy, supplemented by small stock and poultry plus wage labor. The fourth stage of Umbundu agriculture, beginning about 1930, saw the elimination of all activities except subsistence and cash crop agriculture, small stock and poultry raising, and wage labor. The main expansion was in cash crop agriculture and wage labor.

The growth in corn exports from zero in 1910 to 100,000 metric tons in 1950 is the surest sign of the dramatic increase in cash crop agriculture among the Umbundu. The amount of corn exported is accurately known since the government controlled all export through the Grémio de Milho and the Junta de Exportação de Cereais. The amount of corn produced in subsistence agriculture is impossible to determine. In the 1960s the corn production that did not enter the channels of trade was estimated to vary from 150,000 to 200,000 tons per year. If this is a reasonable estimate, the decline of subsistence agriculture in relation to cash crop has been exaggerated. Whatever the proportion between the two types of agriculture, there is no doubt that the peoples of central Angola moved toward monoculture and that their intensified production of corn, for both subsistence and market, had two negative effects: because corn is a soil-depleting crop, the already poor soils were impoverished more rapidly; and, under pressure to produce for the market, the farmers reduced the length of fallow periods so the soil was not able to renew itself. Whereas coffee and cotton in the north were primarily grown in European plantations, all the corn was still produced by Africans on small family plots.

Essential to the development of cash crop agriculture were the white traders (*comerciantes*), who more completely occupied Angola for Portugal than did the administrative officials. The *comerciante* had a monopoly on the exchange of African produce for the necessities that came from outside the village: salt, sugar, fish, oil, cloth, and tools. Barely literate and without capital, the white trader exploited the status awarded by a white skin and metropolitan connections to set himself up in an adobe building with a tin or tile roof which was both store and residence. The government at times regulated the location of traders so they could come under some surveillance and control by the authorities. Even so, the traders in Angola had a great advantage over Asian, Syrian, Lebanese, and Greek traders in other parts of Africa because they were Portuguese and thus compatriots of the local officials. Not infrequently the trader came from the same region in the north of Portugal as the *chefe do posto*. Personally the *chefe* and *comerciante* might bicker or even fight, but they stood together against the Africans.

In central Angola during this period sisal plantations became a significant part of the Angolan economy. Sisal (*Agave sisalana*) became a profitable crop during World War II, and production increased from 3,137 tons valued at $330,960 in 1951 to 23,197 tons with the value of $13,151,960 in 1961. Such prosperity attracted many more growers to the Benguela subplateau, where the *conselhos* of Cubal, Ganda, and Bocoio accounted for 60 percent of the total sisal production. All the plantations were owned by Europeans since sisal demands large amounts of capital to purchase the machinery that processes the fleshy leaf. Just as more capital was being invested, the world price of sisal dropped so that in 1954 a greater tonnage (31,378) was exported, but only brought $4,171,525.

Sugar, one of the oldest industries in Angola, was controlled by three Lisbon-based companies, Companhia de Açucar de Angola, Sociedade Agrícola do Cassequel, and Companhia Agrícola de Angola. Their plantations were located on the coastal plains—two in the Luanda area, one between Lobito and Benguela, and the fourth at Dombe Grande, south of Benguela. Sixteen thousand persons were employed in the sugar industry, practically all of them as contract laborers.

In the south the cereals millet and sorghum are subsistence crops. Cattle has brought this area also into the market economy. Contrary to the view once commonly held by Europeans, Africans treat cattle as a productive and marketable item as well as a status symbol. Information gathered by the Missão de Inquéritos Agrícolas de Angola shows clearly that the peoples of southern Angola market their cattle systematically.

WHITE COLONIZATION

In addition to spontaneous white settlement attracted by coffee and sisal, the Portuguese government was under pressure from advocates of planned settlement to intervene directly by selecting the prospective white settlers and providing them with free transportation, land, housing, animals, seed, subsidies, and technical advice. The arguments of those in favor of planned settlement helped shape colonial policy from 1920 to 1960 so that Lisbon or Luanda concentrated their efforts and expenditures on stimulating government colonization rather than spontaneous settlement.

Before launching its own major schemes the government requested the Benguela Railway Company to establish agricultural settlements along the rail line. Despite expenditure of $2.8 million in the first two years and good marketing facilities, the rural settlements attracted only nineteen colonists between 1935 and 1949 and of that number only nine remained until 1949.

Beginning in the 1950s, Portugal concentrated its supreme effort in rural colonization on two projects: Cela and Matala. The planners designed Cela, 90 miles (144 kilometers) inland from Novo Redondo on the central highlands, to receive 8,400 families (totaling 58,900 individuals) by 1980. The projection for Matala was to settle 1,000 families in the Cunene River valley. The government was profligate in its support of the two projects, but by 1960 it was clear that they would not achieve their goals. Each project had only 300 families and the colonists stayed in the settlements only as long as it took them to make arrangements for other employment in cities or towns. The estimated cost of settling each family in Cela was $100,000 and in Matala, $25,000. Rural settlement must be assessed a failure in Angola, whether measured from the perspective of the government which invested such large amounts for these meager results, from the viewpoint of the colonists who fled to urban areas as soon as possible, or judged by Africans who were deprived of some of their best land which was then cultivated by whites with huge government subsidies.

The white population was scattered in rural trading and administrative posts and in the planned rural settlements, but most

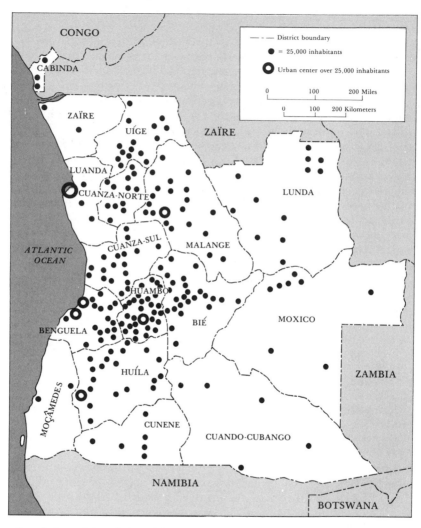

Population of Angola in 1970. United Nations Map No. 2643, January 1974. The boundaries and names shown on this map do not imply official endorsement or acceptance by the United Nations.

of the Portuguese who left Europe for Angola settled in urban centers. According to the census, any population center with 2,000 inhabitants was considered urban. From 1940 to 1960 the urban population increased from 5.4 percent to 11 percent. Only four of the twenty-nine urban centers had more than 20,000: Luanda, Nova Lisboa, Lobito, and Benguela. The coffee development produced a significant town in the north in the 1950s. Uíge, which had only eleven commercial establishments and a few mud buildings in 1945, had expanded by 1956 to a sizable town with 179 commercial establishments, modern buildings, and electricity.

ECONOMIC DEVELOPMENT

Thus the Portuguese succeeded in the period 1920–1960 in bringing many more Angolans within the "pale of civilization"—if that is what the world market economy is. Certainly it expanded commercial opportunities in the interior of Angola. The market sector of the agricultural economy grew significantly as shown in Table 3. In the north, coffee and cotton drew thousands of Africans directly or indirectly into the market economy and removed many acres from subsistence agriculture. In central Angola, the effect of corn as an export crop and sisal was to change peasant farmers to proletarian workers, and in the south the Humbe and Ambo peoples were more directly and regularly involved in the market economy through their sale of cattle. In the early 1920s long-term-contract laborers were requisitioned for the ports and railways, diamond mines, and sugar plantations. Later in the period the new coffee, sisal, and cotton

Table 3. Angolan agricultural market production, 1938 and 1960

	1938		1960	
	Tons	U.S. dollars	Tons	U.S. dollars
Coffee	16,637	$1,432,744	87,217	$50,558,560
Cotton	2,773	581,000	8,894	5,855,040
Corn	517	11,557	117,111	6,598,080
Sisal	992	50,360	57,941	15,019,160

Source: Calculated from data in *Anuário estatístico 1960.*

plantations competed for the limited labor supply. The absence of the most vigorous men from their villages further weakened the subsistence sector of the economy.

In the period from 1920 to 1960, the Angolan economy enriched the oligarchy, composed of the increasing white population and a tiny black elite, at the same time that the vast majority, 90 to 95 percent of the population, was impoverished. The standard of living of the overwhelming majority of Angolans declined during this period for reasons connected with the rise of a cash economy. The concentration of production of coffee, cotton, sisal, and corn for export reduced the land and labor available for raising the variety of foods in the traditional diet. Furthermore, the wages earned from contract labor plus the receipts from the sale of cash crops did not compensate for the loss of production in the subsistence economy. The ecosystem theory helps to explain the economic impoverishment of Angolans:

It is well understood in ecological theory that a more mature and diversified ecosystem in contact with one less mature drains the net productivity from the latter and helps to maintain and even increase its immaturity. In most developing countries, the surplus of net productivity in an incipient cash crop economy of a rural ecosystem is usually drained by the evolved urban trading system, maintaining its development and precluding, therefore, any notable development in the rural sector. It can even be said that the tendency in this case is to decrease the diversity of the rural system and increase its immaturity in order to bring out new possibilities for export.[22]

In addition to the economic loss to the Africans in their transition from the subsistence to the market economy, they also suffered a social loss. The increase in migrant or contract labor, which drew the most vigorous males to plantations or urban areas, contributed to the disintegration of the kinship group and the deterioration of village life.

MINERALS

The silver and copper eldorados sought by the Portuguese in Angola in the sixteenth and seventeenth centuries never mate-

22. Ramon Margalef, *Perspectives in Ecological Theory* (Chicago: University of Chicago Press, 1968), p. 95.

rialized, but in 1912 diamonds were discovered in Lunda. Five years later the Companhia de Diamantes de Angola (Diamang) was formed and given a monopoly to exploit diamonds in the whole of Angola. British, Belgian, and American firms provided the capital for Diamang, with the Portuguese government holding 5 percent of the shares. One condition of the fifty-year concession was that the government would receive 40 percent of Diamang's earnings; in 1954 the percentage was increased to 50.[23] Diamang was under contract to DeBeers Consolidated Mines Ltd., a subsidiary of Anglo-American Corporation of South Africa. The DeBeers cartel allotted quotas to producers, regulated prices, and controlled the diamond flow of all major producers in the capitalist world. A state within a state in the Lunda district, Diamang was Angola's largest employer and provided its own security, health, education, and welfare services in return for the monopoly it enjoyed on the exploitation of minerals and manpower. By 1936 the value of diamonds exported reached $4 million or 32 percent of Angola's total exports. The quantity and value of diamonds continued to increase and at the end of this period the value of diamonds exported had risen to $19,849,720. Although the value had increased almost fivefold in the twenty-four years, the percentage of the value of diamonds in Angola's total exports had decreased from 32 percent to 14 percent, mainly because of the dramatic increase in coffee exports.

As we have seen, the major economic growth in Angola depended on foreign capital. The Benguela Railway was built with British capital. British also joined with Belgian, American, and South African interests to form Diamang. Portuguese capital played a greater role in coffee production, but here too German and American investors had a stake. The exploration for petroleum was also undertaken with foreign capital, beginning in 1927 when Belgians formed the Companhia de Combustíveis do Lobito (CCL) as a joint stock company to act as a distributer of oil products, household gas, and coal in Angola. In 1952 the company was granted exclusive rights to explore for oil in the Congo and Cuanza river basins. This operation was also fi-

23. Abshire and Samuels, p. 297.

nanced by foreign capital through Petrofina, the largest industrial enterprise in Belgium. Petrofina struck oil in Benfica, near Luanda, in 1955 and the following year the first tanker left Luanda with crude petroleum for processing in Portugal. In 1957, with government approval, the CCL formed the Companhia Concessionária de Petróleos de Angola (Petrangola), to which all its rights were transferred. Petrofina invested an initial $31 million and the Angolan government has a one-third interest in the company. Petrangola constructed a $65 million refinery near Luanda with a capacity of 650,000 tons per year.

António de Oliveira Salazar, who became minister of finance in 1928 and prime minister in 1932, changed Portuguese colonial policy from indifference with dashes of mercantilism to a mobilization of the colonial resources for the benefit of the metropolitan economy. In practical terms this meant that Angola kept Portugal solvent by providing hard currency. From 1953 to 1962, Angola's imports from Portugal averaged $60 million while its exports to the Metropole averaged $26,900,000. Outside the escudo area the proportions were reversed: Angola imported an average of $69,040,000 and exported $108,920,000 annually. Portugal was able to use Angola's credit in hard currency to balance its escudo deficit. A triangular flow of foreign exchange went from outside the escudo area to Angola, from Angola to Portugal, and from Portugal the exchange flowed back out of the escudo zone.

Salazar attempted to change Portuguese colonial policy by limiting the foreign investments that had been the basis of all major economic development in Angola. A decree in 1937 required that at least 50 percent of the capital of corporations exploiting land under concessions be owned by native-born Portuguese (Decree Law 28,228, November 23, 1937); in 1943 the requirement was broadened, ruling that half the capital of any enterprise be Portuguese and that nationals be appointed to the board of directors (Naturalization of Capital Law No. 1994, April 13, 1943). The economic growth of Angola after World War II could have been considerably greater, but it was strictly limited by Salazar's policy until 1965, when the pressure from the war of independence forced Portugal to return to reliance on foreign investments.

Missions

Portugal succeeded in imposing a colonial administrative system on Angola, building an infrastructure of roads, railroads, and communications and drawing Angolan labor and natural resources into the world market economy so they could contribute to, and in fact, sustain, the Portuguese economy. For the Angolans to participate in the economic and political systems, however, they needed to be assimilated into the civilization of which these systems were a part. To recall the words of Professor Silva Cunha at the beginning of this chapter, "The means of assimilating the natives are principally, the diffusion of the Portuguese language, education, instruction and Christianization" Portugal, like all colonial powers, assigned these tasks to Christian missions, which until the 1950s administered practically all educational institutions as well as most health and welfare programs in Africa.

The Portuguese recognized the Christian missions as essential instruments of enculturation, but lacked the resources to assure that the culture being transmitted was truly Portuguese. Although Portugal considered itself a Catholic nation, the Catholic missions were staffed almost entirely by foreign missionaries. The Protestant missions were completely foreign in source of funds and personnel. Portugal feared the denationalizing influence of the missions at the same time that it depended on them to serve its goal of assimilating the Angolans into Portuguese culture.

CATHOLIC MISSIONS

The traditional interdependence between Church and state was challenged during the brief period of the Republic—1910 to 1926—and the government even created nonreligious missions "to spread Portuguese civilization, give prestige to the Fatherland, and nationalize the indigenous population."[24]

To the relief of the Church, this curious experiment—a kind of Portuguese Peace Corps—ended in 1926 when the Minister of Colonies, João Belo, published the Statute of Missions of Af-

24. Silva Rego, p. 314.

rica and Timor.[25] The missions referred to by the statue were the Catholic missions, which had been deprived of certain privileges by the Republic. The statute marked the first step toward the recognition of the Church as the full partner with the state in the "civilizing mission." In this same year, Salazar entered the government and led it to take further steps in this direction. Article 45 of the 1933 Constitution calls "The Catholic religion . . . the religion of the Portuguese nation." Elaborating on this theme, Pope Pius XII in 1940 said: "The Catholic faith, as it was in a certain way the life-blood, which sustained the Portuguese nation from the cradle, was certainly the principal, if not the only source of energy, which carried your land to the apogee of glory as a civil and missionary Nation, 'spreading the Faith and the Empire.'"[26] The occasion for this letter was the signing of the Concordat and the Missionary Accord by the Vatican and the Portuguese government. The following year, the Missionary Statute, which applied the Concordat and the Missionary Accord to the colonies, affirmed: "The Portuguese Catholic missions are considered institutions which are useful to the Empire and have an eminently civilizing purpose."[27]

After 1940, Portuguese government subsidies for Catholic missions in Angola increased regularly, from $199,273 in 1940 to 283,032 in 1945, 359,000 in 1950, 718,356 in 1955, and $1,129,027 in 1960.[28]

Angolans were not necessarily aware of this financial support of Catholic missions, but they recognized clearly the close tie between the Catholic Church and the state. Catholic certificates of baptism and marriage were legal, which greatly facilitated life in the extremely bureaucratic society created by Portuguese colonialism, whereas Angolans married in the Protestant churches were still registered officially as "single" and their children as "illegitimate." Local Catholic catechists were paid by the government and enjoyed other perquisites such as exemption from taxes and contract labor. The discrimination between Catholic and Protestant was crucial for a majority of Angolans because

25. Ibid., p. 316.
26. Ibid., p. 594.
27. Ibid., p. 607.
28. Eduardo dos Santos, *L'état portugais et le problème missionaire* (Lisbon: Junta de Investigações do Ultramar, 1964), pp. 112–19.

they lived in religiously defined communities. In a culture that was communal rather than individual, the Angolans' personal identity and life-style as well as their social organization depended on the community to which they belonged. Conversions in Angola, and indeed in most of Africa, have been communal. When a family wished to identify with the Protestant or Catholic community, it moved across the stream or over the hill from the traditional settlement. The new converts constructed a wattle-and-daub building for a school-chapel and the new community was formed. This Protestant or Catholic community usually kept the name of the traditional village ruled by the elders, although it might choose a new name for its section. In areas served by both Catholic and Protestant missions, the one not represented in the original split would probably soon succeed in winning some converts; the village would then be composed of three communities: Protestant, Catholic, and traditional.

Having divided the villages on the basis of Church affiliation, each population developed its own self-identity and formed an image of its neighbors. The Protestants resented the privileges that the Catholics enjoyed by virtue of being members of the official religion. Catholics admired the Protestants' zeal for education and the orderly life imposed by the Puritan ethic, but at the same time considered them a little "too smart" (*espertos*). A seemingly contradictory term used by Catholics to characterize the Protestants was *vakuafulu*. According to Padre Alves's dictionary, *afulu* means "pacific, meek, suave in manner, American, Protestant (ostentatiously kind)." The dictionary claims that the word derives from *oku vulwa,* meaning "to be stupid, simple, indolent or slow." Popularly, *afulu* is supposed to be the Umbundu adaptation of the English word "fool." Some Portuguese who knew English thought the early Protestant missionaries fools because of what was considered an exaggerated kindness to the Africans. According to this interpretation, these Portuguese introduced the English word into Umbundu. Whether "too smart" or "ostentatiously kind," the image of Protestant missionaries and their adherents in the eyes of the Catholic community evoked a combination of admiration and hostility.[29]

29. Albino Alves, *Dicionário etimológico Bundo-Português,* I (Lisbon, 1951), p. 93.

Christian churches, by producing divisions within villages, introduced the potential for conflict, but at the same time they provided both incentive and structure for the creation of new communities. The authority that had once been exercised by traditional rulers passed to such church leaders as catechists, elders, and pastors. The churches created new systems of authority and law within local villages, but the most striking feature of Protestant missions in Angola was the identification of each of the major mission agencies with one of the principal ethnolinguistic groups: the Baptists with the Kongo, the Methodists with the Kimbundu, and the Congregational with the Umbundu. The Protestant missions provided vehicles by which the ethnolinguistic groups could move from their traditional African to modern Western means of communication and social structure.

KONGO/BAPTIST

In each region the mission's first task was to establish effective means of communication. This involved learning the respective language and in most cases reducing it to writing. In the Kongo/Baptist area, the Baptist Missionary Society (BMS) linguist, Holman Bentley, published a directory and grammar of the Kongo language, and in 1893, only fifteen years after the arrival of the first Protestant missionaries, completed the translation of the whole New Testament. The Protestant belief in the authority of the Scriptures coincided with the Angolans' faith in the almost magical power of the written word. In fact that the BMS was the instrument by which the Kongo received the Bible in their own language was important not only for Christian indoctrination, but also for their communal identity and self-esteem.

Similarly, the Protestant mission was the vehicle by which the traditional social structure was given some recognition by Western culture. Thomas Lewis, who baptized five Kongolese in São Salvador on December 2, 1887 and conducted Communion the following Sunday in his home, indicates the respect with which the missionaries regarded the local culture:

We did not impose any formal constitution upon this company of Christians. We were content to tell them that there was a New Testament which we had not yet translated (only a few portions were completed in 1887), and that it was to be the rule and guide of the Christian Church; and we left it at that, so that the native church might develop it its own way according to the African genius.[30]

In polity the Baptists are congregational; i.e., each local congregation has final authority over its own life. However, the fact that the Baptist missions did not produce a series of isolated congregations scattered over the tropical hills of the Portuguese Congo is proof of the sincerity of the affirmation, "We did not impose any formal constitution upon this company of Christians." Rather, the many small congregations were bound together in three regional churches in a hierarchy of ecclesiastical responsibility. This hierarchical structure was a reflection of the Kongo social structure in which local villages paid allegiance to area rulers and finally to a central king.

The Protestant community in the Kongo area of Angola was proportionately larger than that of any other area. The 1960 census divided Angola religiously as follows: 51 percent Catholic, 17 percent Protestant, and 32 percent non-Christian. However, among the Kongo the division was 52 percent Catholic, 46 percent Protestant, and 2 percent non-Christian.

KIMBUNDU/METHODIST

As in the identification of the Baptists with the Kongo, the Methodist mission in the Kimbundu area recognized the importance of communications. Among the first group of missionaries to arrive in Luanda in 1885 was the gifted Swiss-American linguist Heli Chatelain. In three short years he learned Kimbundu, reduced it to writing, prepared a grammar and dictionary, and translated the Gospel of John, which was published in 1888. Chatelain wrote:

The future of native Angolan literature in kimbundu . . . is now practically assured. J. Cordeiro da Matta, the negro poet of the Quanza River, has abandoned the Portuguese muse in order to consecrate his talents to the nascent national literature. The autodidactic and practical Am-

30. Thomas Lewis, *These Seventy Years* (London: Carey, 1930), p. 22.

baquistas of the interior have begun to perceive the superiority for purpose of private correspondence, of their own tongue.[31]

Chatelaine was too sanguine. The Portuguese influence was so strong among the Kimbundu people that of the major Angolan languages, Kimbundu is the least used today.

The freedom of policy and polity found among the Baptists in the North ("We did not impose any formal constitution upon this company of Christians") was strange to Methodism. The historian of Methodist missions, Wade Crawford Barclay, writes: "There is no record of the Missionary Society having given instructions to its missionaries to transfer to their respective fields the exact pattern of Church organization existing at home. It was assumed by all, without question, that this would be done."[32]

The Kimbundu were the most alienated from their traditional culture of all Angolan peoples, and so were the most susceptible to accepting the ready-made ecclesiastical structure defined by the Methodist Disciple. It is especially surprising, therefore, given this fact, to discover that the functioning of this imposed structure was strongly influenced by African customs and kinship patterns. We see the influence of kinship ties on the choice of leaders, so that certain families maintain ecclesiastical power as they might once have held power in traditional society. The Methodist Church throughout its history has also had to deal with the split within the Kimbundu people between the Catetenses, who live at the coast near Luanda, and the upcountry Ambaquistas, near Malange.

UMBUNDU/CONGREGATIONAL

In the Umbundu area the development of the Congregational missions (American Board of Commissioners for Foreign Missions—ABCFM) followed more or less the same pattern as the Baptist and Methodist had in the Kongo and Kimbundu areas. The American Board linguists, William Henry Sanders and Wesley M. Stover, published a vocabulary and grammar of

31. Chatalain, p. viii.
32. Wade Crawford Barclay, *History of Methodist Missions: Widening Horizons 1845–1895,* vol. 3 (New York: Board of Missions of the Methodist Church, 1957), p. 148.

Umbundu in 1884, followed by a school primer in 1886 and the New Testament in 1897. In this linguistic period, the work was concentrated on the mission station, but soon schools began to spring up across central Angola. They taught reading not only as a useful skill but as an essential qualification for church membership, thereby increasing the demand for literature in Umbundu.

To give more emphasis to literature production, the ABCFM in 1921 moved its press to Dondi, the mission where the other central institutions (hospitals, secondary schools, and theological seminary) had been established to serve the whole Umbundu-speaking area. That was also the year that the High Commissioner of Angola, José Mendes Ribeiro Norton de Matos, published Decree 77 regulating the establishment and functioning of all missions. Articles 2 and 3 dealt with the use of native languages, prohibiting the publication of vernaculars except as parallel texts to the Portuguese. [33]

The necessity of publishing everything in diglot not only raised technical problems in the preparation of literature, but greatly increased the cost. However, the Protestant churches in the area served by the ABCFM grew rapidly in the 1920s so even the cost of diglot did not unduly restrict the publication and distribution of Umbundu literature. This literature program served as an essential vehicle to carry the Umbundu language from the traditional oral culture to the modern literary culture without a traumatic discontinuity. "Indeed, the main common possession of the Umbundu, the Umbundu language, is, as a literary vehicle and object of study, almost a missionary monopoly." [34]

The Protestant missions in central Angola also enabled the Umbundu to transfer to new Christian communities some of their social structure. In 1900 the names Bailundo, Chiyaka, and Galangue would have been instantly recognized as Umbundu kingdoms. By 1930, the same names would be identified as Protestant mission-churches. The best evidence that the Protestant

33. John T. Tucker, *Angola: The Land of the Blacksmith Prince* (London: World Dominion, 1933), p. 175.
34. Adrian C. Edwards, *The Ovimbundu under Two Sovereignties* (London: Oxford University Press, 1962), p. 25.

church in central Angola inherited the social structure of the Umbundu communities in which it had been planted was produced by a survey in the 1950s, which indicated that all the ordained ministers were members of royal lineages. Whether consciously or not, the people chose as the leaders of the new Christian communities persons who were qualified for leadership by traditional standards.

The Protestant missions played an ambivalent role in Portugal's colonial policy of integrating the Africans into the "civilized way of life." The missions contributed to literacy in Portuguese and the organization of peoples into Christian communities, but they did so with non-Portuguese funds and personnel. The Portuguese classified the Protestant missions by their national origins as British, Swiss, or American. The Angolan Protestants by language and political necessity were subject to the Portuguese colonial administration, but they also felt a loyalty to their foreign benefactors and at times even identified themselves as "British," "Swiss," or "American." The Protestants' dependence upon foreign resources prompted the Portuguese to charge Protestantism with being a denationalizing influence. The charge was self-substantiating because the Portuguese government's harassment led Angolans to associate oppression, deprivation, and poverty with Portugal, whereas opportunity, facilities, and affluence were associated with England, Holland, Switzerland, Canada, and the United States.

Education

Education in Angola was divided, as early as 1913, between those schools designed for Europeans and assimilated Africans and others for the mass of Angolans. The first type of school was located along the coastal strip or in the hinterland where Portugal exercised administrative control. By 1880 in the north, schools for Europeans, mestizos, and assimilated Africans were scattered along the main communication lines between Luanda and Malange at Barra do Dande, Barra do Bengo, Icolo e Bengo, Zenza do Golungo, Ambaca, Pungo Andongo, Cazengo, Dondo, and Muxima. In the south, schools were functioning by 1880 in Novo Redondo, Benguela, Dombe Grande, Quilengues, Caconda, Huíla, and Moçâmedes. Educational statistics are not exact for the period, but the growth of the school population can be discerned from the reports of 587 students in 1880 and 2,408 in 1901. Since the white population of that period was so small, it is not surprising that 88 percent of these students were mestizos or assimilated Africans.[35]

The principal impediment to the expansion of this part of the educational system was the lack of trained teachers. Even when available they were poorly and irregularly paid. Therefore, a few especially effective and dedicated teachers of that period deserve special mention: Nicolau Rogeiro, an African educated totally in Angola who taught around Icolo e Bengo; Alfredo Netto, an African educated in Europe who taught in Luanda and in the interior; Francisco Pinto da Rocha, son of early settlers in Moçâmedes and educated at the national *liceu* in Lisbon, who returned to teach in his hometown; and António Boavida, a parish priest in Ambriz who worked patiently as a primary school teacher.[36]

MISSION EDUCATION

Education for the mass of Africans was entrusted—more by default than by decision—to the Christian missions, Catholic and Protestant. For the Catholic missions, which had two practical reasons for promoting education, the ends in view shaped the type of education provided. First, the common church members who had been baptized by the thousands had to be taught to *rezar*, i.e., repeat prayers and bits of Catholic doctrine. Whether the prayers or chants were in Latin, Portuguese, or the local native language, it was a matter of memorization. Reading was not an essential discipline. Second, the church needed to encourage and prepare those who might be called to a religious vocation. Since the seminary course was in Portuguese, the national language was stressed. These two contrasting purposes produced many catechetical classes hardly worthy of the name "school," and relatively rigid preseminary courses for an elite who became fluent in Portuguese and were expected to continue studying in the seminary.

35. Samuels, *Education in Angola*, p. 43.
36. Ibid., p. 44.

The Protestant missions had a different goal. They wanted each person to be able to read the Word of God in his own language. This required schools above the catechetical level academically but below the seminary standards. Catechist-teachers were needed to go to new villages with their New Testaments and hymnbooks to teach the people how to read, write, count, and sing hymns. In 1914 the American Board and Canadian Congregationalists founded Currie Institute in answer to the desire for a better-trained leadership. However, this was still for the purpose of training local village leaders rather than the more assimilated elite of the Catholic seminaries. The Institute course included carpentry, masonry, agriculture, and tailoring in addition to Bible and the three R's so that the village leader would be able to live on a higher standard and serve as an example to his people. The Methodist Mission established a comparable leadership training institution in Quessua.

The first period in the history of mission education in Angola, before 1920, was characterized by a lack of government action and freedom for missions to shape educational institutions to serve their ends. The second period began December 9, 1921, when Norton de Matos, the high commissioner, published Decree No. 77. This law altered the course of missionary education by prohibiting the use of native languages in schools. The provision was reinforced by requiring that the local village teachers be licensed by administrative officials and the licenses "cannot be given unless the native teacher is able to speak the Portuguese language."

More of a threat to the established programs than the language requirement was the assumption by the government of authority over all education. The decree did offer, together with a "free concession up to 500 hectares of land" and "the free cutting of timber . . . for buildings," annual subsidies for qualified European professors in mission schools and native professors in permanent rural schools. However, the subsidies were never accepted by the Protestant missions. It is impossible to say whether they would have been available if claimed. With or without subsidies, all schools were placed under the direct control of the government.

The school has been the most widely used and most effective

means of evangelization in all of Africa south of the Sahara. In Angola the word *escola* did not refer simply to an academic institution; it meant the church as an ecclesiastical organization and in fact referred to the Christian community. The Umbundu word *Ndukuasikola,* literally, "I am of the school," meant "I am a Christian."

The panic with which most Protestant missionaries received Decree 77 was due to the fact that its publication coincided with the extremely rapid expansion of the Christian work. The means of expansion was the village school and according to the new law it was to be brought under government supervision, with all workers being required to use Portuguese.

The Annual Reports of the West Central Africa Mission of the American Board of Commissioners for Foreign Missions indicate a growth in Protestant school population in one area of central Angola from 4,176 in 1910 to 12,596 in 1920. Reading was a requirement for church membership. The rapid rise in the number of pupils was followed by a phenomenal harvest of church members, increasing from 625 in 1910 to 983 in 1920 and then jumping to 8,475 in 1930.

The required use of Portuguese instead of the pupils' maternal Bantu languages as a means of instruction was accompanied by a change of goal. The missions had established their own systems of education, published their own books, trained and placed their own teachers. The goal was to receive the mission diploma. During the period from 1921 to 1950 that goal changed to acquiring an official certificate, which depended primarily on the pupil's mastery of the Portuguese language. To promote better teaching of the official language the government required that each mission have at least one European teacher with minimum academic credentials, offering an annual subsidy of 3,000 angolares ($120) "to each mission which may have in its permanent employ a European professor, whether missionary or not, who may possess the conditions and ability to teach the Portuguese language well." This encouragement was changed into a requirement by decree 755 of March 26, 1928, that "private establishments for free education or such directed by foreign individuals or entities, must have for the carrying out of the Portuguese course a teaching staff of Portuguese nationality which must have as a minimum the third year of *liceu*, or the course of the higher grade primary schools."

During the thirty-year period of 1921–1950 the government proposed educational schemes for *indígenas* emphasizing manual arts and agriculture, but they were never implemented on any significant scale.

PRIMARY EDUCATION 1950–1960

The third period in the history of education in Angola began at the inauguration of a new system of education for Africans, O Ensino Rudimentar, the Rudimentary Education Act of 1950. Whereas Decree 77 had asserted the government's authority over all education and established Portuguese as the medium of instruction, it did not define the curriculum or provide the bureaucratic machinery for its supervision. Twenty-six years later the Rudimentary Education Act gave detailed instructions as to what should be taught, when, by whom, and under what conditions. The Education Law of 1950 implemented the Missionary Accord of 1940 between Portugal and the Vatican. If it had been enforced rigidly, it would have outlawed all Protestant schools and forced all African children to attend Catholic schools. However, no one expected the law to be enforced, least of all the Catholic Church, which was charged with the administration of the rudimentary schools. Father Silva Rego, the missiologist at the Overseas Colonial Institute in Lisbon, complained of the impossible task given to the Church: "The rudimentary education is entrusted . . . to the Catholic missions. The State freed itself of this education and requires that the Catholic missions undertake it, but and this is important, the State does not give the necessary resources to make it possible."[37]

Although the government support for Catholic schools was admittedly inadequate, the new law did reinforce the Catholic educational system by establishing normal schools to prepare teachers to administer the rudimentary curriculum. The first normal school under this law was located at Cuima near Nova Lisboa and entrusted to the Holy Ghost Fathers with full finan-

37. *Alguns problemas sociológico-missionários da Africa negra* (Lisbon: Estudos de Ciências Políticas e Sociais, No. 32, 1960), pp. 104–5.

cial support of the state. Only Catholic students were admitted and upon graduation they were placed in Catholic mission schools and supported by the state. By 1954 the Cuima school had 153 students and at the end of this period new normal schools for young women had just been built or were projected for each diocese.

The main feature of this period in the history of education in Angola was not the increase in students but the establishment of the machinery by which more pupils could be officially registered with the education department. Whereas until 1950 only the small group of elite that had mastered enough of the national language to attempt an examination, along with the Portuguese children of towns and cities, achieved some official recognition. Under the Ensino Rudimentar the youngsters beginning their ABC's in a rural school could be registered and examined at the end of the year by a jury of government examiners.

The main goal of rudimentary education, as conceptualized by the educational authorities, was: "to contribute to the elevation of the native masses by means of the first level of instruction regarding the realities of the life of the people who are underdeveloped [*pouco evoluidos*] without alienating them from their class, their traditional hierarchy or from physical labor." To this end, agricultural work and manual arts were included in the program to avoid the creation of *calcinhas* ("short-pants")—a colonial pejorative referring to young men who felt estranged from their traditional culture but who were not accepted by the ruling class. Ironically, the effect of the Rudimentary Education Act was the opposite of what its creators intended. The demand to register all pupils required parents and teachers to spend extravagant amounts of time acquiring the necessary documentation. The official juries gave almost exclusive attention to the pupil's knowledge of Portuguese. The successful students were those who mastered the official language and the maze of bureaucratic requirements. Only the failures were not alienated from "their class, their traditional hierarchy or from physical labor." In 1956 the terminology was changed from Rudimentary Education to Ensino de Adaptação, Education for Adaptation. The course was shortened by one year, but no fundamental changes were instituted.

The general effect of governmental action in the field of education from 1921 to 1951 was to impede the development of mass education. Above it was noted that one mission agency (ABCFM) reported 12,596 pupils in one area of Angola in 1920. This was 369 more than were registered officially in 1954 in the Protestant schools of all Angola. By ever-increasing requirements and inspections concerned with documents and statistics, the government crippled the movement for mass education that had a good start thirty-four years earlier.

SECONDARY EDUCATION

Secondary education had been available in Angola only in Catholic seminaries or a few private schools or *colégios* until 1933, when the government built the first official high schools or *liceus* in Luanda and Sá da Bandeira. The Jesuits had administered a school in the seventeenth century which educated many Africans, mulattoes, and Portuguese. From this college emerged both a native clergy and a half-caste administrative class. The educated mulattoes formed most of Luanda's lesser bureaucracy. In the eighteenth and nineteenth centuries there was no formal provision for secondary education in Angola. The Catholic seminary in Huíla was transferred to Luanda in 1906 and began *liceu* classes in the bishop's residence in 1907. The twenty-four students who entered when the course began consisted of eight Africans, fourteen mestizos, and two whites born in Portugal. The Angolan students came from Luanda, Ambriz, Libolo, Golungo Alto, Benguela, Cambambe, and São Tomé. Few graduates of that seminary were ever ordained, but an Angolan elite was formed who found employment either in commerce or government service. Among the graduates were Alberto de Lemos, who wrote a history of Angola and organized the provincial census of 1940 and 1950; Narciso do Espirito Santo, who was for many years a senior functionary in the Lobito municipal government and founded an important weekly newspaper; and Jaime Ramos Monteiro, who became head of the provincial treasury and served as a voting member of the legislative council. The inauguration of the Republic in Portugal in 1910 limited the secondary course in the Luanda Seminary and the first government high school was not built until twenty-three years later.

The *liceu* course was so theoretical and classical that many educators recognized the need for another kind of secondary school. Vocational education had been advocated for Angola for several decades; in fact, a vocational school was constructed in Luanda between 1876 and 1880, but it never functioned. The first government vocational (*industrial e comercial*) schools were inaugurated in the early 1950s. They offered courses in commerce, electricity, mechanics, and home economics.

Although education in Angola expanded in the 1950s (see Table 4), the proportion of young people in school was still very low. According to the 1960 census, 1,183,292 Angolans of the 4,830,449 total were between the ages of five and fourteen. Of them, 105,981 pupils were registered in primary schools. If the age group from fifteen to nineteen is added, it makes a total of 1,561,877 potential students; of them, 117,768 were registered in primary and secondary schools of all types. This means that 7.5 percent of school-age Angolan young people were in school in 1960/61, a percentage considerably below the proportion of the population in schools in the British colonies before independence, though above the percentage in the French-controlled areas.

The few dozen students who finished secondary school in Angola each year had to seek higher education elsewhere if, indeed, their academic accomplishments, will, and resources com-

Table 4. Growth of secondary education in Angola, 1954–1961

	Students in academic high schools			Students in vocational high schools		
	Govt.	Private	Total	Govt.	Private	Total
1954–55	1,510	1,610	3,120	1,252	530	1,792
1960–61	3,959	3,527	7,489	4,365	136	4,501

Source: From Herrick et al., *Area Handbook for Angola* (Washington, D.C., 1967), pp. 126–27.

bined to give them such an opportunity. António Agostinho Neto, who was to be the first president of Angola, set out for Portugal to study medicine in 1947. With some private funds and a scholarship from the American Methodists, he succeeded in finishing his course and qualifying as a doctor in 1958, in spite of frequent interruption by arrests, interrogations, and imprisonments. The government provided housing in the Casas dos Estudantes do Império, in Lisbon and Coimbra, which became centers of intellectual radicalism and anti-Salazar politics. In the 1950s the first students from central Angola went to the metropole for higher education, but they all fled from Portugal shortly after the outbreak of the war in 1961 and finished their various courses in other countries.

In spite of being the poorest nation in Europe, Portugal fulfilled the role of a colonial power from 1920 to 1960 by establishing administrative authority and building transportation and communication networks in Angola, which is fourteen times the size of the metropole. Salazar's New State (Estado Novo) provided political stability in Portugal and consistency in its colonial policy. Staying out of World War II was economically beneficial to Portugal as Portuguese and foreign investors profited from the sale of colonial raw materials sold at high wartime prices. Angola's resources, human and material, were brought into the world market economy and provided Portugal with the foreign exchange to keep its own underdeveloped country in balance.

The obverse of each Portuguese profit was an Angolan loss. The administrative system was built on taxes and restrictions which impoverished Angolans. The colonial economy that supported Portugal's trade was based on forced labor. The profits from export crops were made at the expense of the Africans, who lost their traditional fields and had their social structure undermined. Missions and schools opened a few doors to Angolans for employment and social position, but they chiefly stimulated expectations that were frustrated by Portuguese colonialism.

One of the principal characteristics of colonialism is the communications barrier between the colonized and the colonizers. The colonizers were convinced that Angola was becoming more prosperous economically and more stable politically while the colonized, on the other side of the communications barrier, were translating their frustrations into political movements and preparing to fight Portuguese colonialism. An illustration of the ignorance that such lack of communication produces is this optimistic prediction made by a military and administrative official as he concluded his history of the Portuguese Congo: "The District, as for that matter all Angola, does not have racial problems. Blacks and whites work side by side without conflict or hate.... Whether economically, politically or socially the Portuguese Congo will give to this restless world an example of the effectiveness of the Portuguese civilizing force in the lands of Africa."[38] The author, Hélio Esteves Felgas, one of the more knowledgeable Portuguese officials, was so blinded by colonialism he did not recognize the political ferment that was agitating the north of Angola. In 1958, as Felgas was publishing his book describing the peaceful prospects in northern Angola, Holden Roberto, the Kongo nationalist leader, was in Accra at the All Africa Peoples' Conference circulating a manifesto in the name of the União das Populações de Angola (UPA) which called for the national liberation of Angola.

"The final objective of native policy [was] to accomplish the integration of native populations of the colonies into the Portuguese nation." Yet the instruments that Portugal used—administration, transportation, communications, religion, and education—did not serve this objective; instead, they contributed to the creation of a new Angolan nationalism.

38. Hélio Esteves Felgas, *História do Congo Português* (Carmona, 1958), p. 198.

CHAPTER 6

The Clash of Nationalisms: Angolan vs. Portuguese, 1961–1965

In Angola the colonial period, strictly speaking, was very brief—from 1920 to 1961. Having already achieved military control by 1920, Portugal then proceeded to establish administrative control, promote white colonization, and build the infrastructure to enable Angola to contribute politically and economically to the metropole. Portugal did not recognize that during this same period anticolonialism was not only keeping pace with colonialism, but was developing into Angolan nationalism.

African Associations

The republican period in Portugal (1910–1926), which produced a multiplicity of Portuguese political parties, also spawned a variety of African associations. In Lisbon *assimilados* and mestizos from the various Portuguese African colonies organized a number of organizations, each claiming to represent and promote the progress, rights, and interests of the masses in all five Portuguese African colonies and to be strictly constitutional and legal in all their activities. Among them the Liga Africana supported the Pan-Africanism of W. E. B. Du Bois, while the Partido Nacional Africano leaned toward the negro nationalism of Marcus Garvey and defended the African personality and character: "We are not simply Portuguese. Before being Portuguese we are Africans. We are Portuguese of the negro [sic] race. We are proud of our double quality. But we possess, above all, the racial pride . . . of being negroes [sic] . . . We must cooperate with the whites."[1]

At the same time in Luanda, *assimilados* and mestizos formed

---

1. Wheeler and Pélissier, p. 119.

the Liga Angolana, which was not a true political party but an elite lobby of Angolans with a program of improving conditions for the mass of Africans as well as advancing the *assimilados* within the European system. Since the inspiration of these associations was more Pan-African than Angolan, whites did not feel that they really belonged in the Liga Angolana even though a few did join. Hostile whites called it the Associação de Mata-brancos (The Association of White-killers), even though the Liga was moderate and very loyal to the Republic.

Africans in Luanda had less political freedom than in Lisbon between the two world wars. The Liga Africana in Lisbon had a statutory provision "to revoke all discriminatory legislation in Portuguese Africa," whereas the Liga Angolana in Luanda could not include such a purpose in its statutes. Salazar's New State reorganized these associations both in Lisbon and Luanda to bring them under the direct control of the Portuguese government. In Luanda, the older generation of Liga leaders, who were culturally assimilated Africans, accepted working in strictly legal collaboration with the colonial administration. A younger generation, advocating anticolonialism rather than simply reform of colonialism, urged extension of Liga membership as well as its cultural, social, and political activities to the uneducated masses of Africans.

In 1950 a group of Luanda Africans sent to the United Nations a document which stopped short of condemning colonialism but criticized Portugal's administration of the colony of Angola:

because in the course of 469 years of its permanence in Angola it [Portugal] not only has not fulfilled the agreements assumed in International Conferences, but has violated the treaties and demonstrated incontestably incompetence in administration of the Colony of Angola, practicing acts of slavery, robbery and homicide which are described in this message . . . because to colonize is not only to exploit, but to civilize, instruct, educate. . . .

The Angolans closed their exposition by imploring the United Nations to action:

to order as urgently as possible the end of the Portuguese administration of Angola and Congo, the Government being handed over to the natives who would administer the country under the Protectorate of a nation which would be named by the natives.[2]

This petition to the United Nations was soon passé as Angolans joined Africans across the continent in condemning colonialism itself—not just criticizing the particular abuses of each colonial situation. The step from reformism to anticolonialism took, at the most, a decade—1945 to 1955. The step from anticolonialism to nationalism, however, was more difficult, as it has been in all Africa. It required self-examination and redefinition by peoples whose territory had been defined by European colonial powers until that time. It involved a search in the past for cultural roots, an assessment of the present state of tradition, and a projection into the future to discover the direction of African history. In Angola, two movements appeared in the mid-fifties which attempted to mobilize the people into an effective anticolonial force and then to develop Angolan nationalism. The Movimento Popular de Libertação de Angola (MPLA) and the União das Populações de Angola (UPA) differed both in the cultural roots with which they sought to identify and in their analysis of the historical significance of the Angolan struggle.

The MPLA

The MPLA found its roots in the *assimilado*-mestizo community which had formed the various associations in Luanda and Lisbon during the republican period. For its historical analysis of the struggle in which it was involved it drew upon Marxist ideology. By 1948 the Portuguese Communist Party had established a secret cell in Luanda. Two other clandestine groups were also spreading Marxist influence among the city's young intellectuals. The Partido Comunista de Angola (PCA) was formed in 1955, according to Mário de Andrade, the principal historian of the MPLA. Elements from the PCA and other nationalist leaders participated in the formation of the Partido da Luta Unida dos Africanos de Angola (PLUA) in early 1956.

2. "*Mensagem do povo negro de Angola dirigida às Nações Unidas para: Sua Excelência o Presidente da República dos Estados Unidos da América do Norte, Washington.*"

PLUA then issued a manifesto which invited Angolans to organize themselves clandestinely for a united, armed struggle against Portuguese colonialism. As the urban nationalist movement gathered adherents in Luanda, the Movimento Popular de Libertação de Angola was formed in December 1956, claiming to be "truly the first party of the masses."

This claim represents more the ideology of the movement than the social reality. Only individuals who had emerged from the masses through their educational and economic opportunities were attracted by the MPLA's intellectual appeal. Such an appeal depended upon the strong, capable leadership that has characterized the MPLA from its beginning. Among the influential leaders were Mário Coelho Pinto de Andrade, Viriato Francisco Clemente da Cruz, and Lúcio Lara, but the man who survived all the internal struggles, who conducted international diplomacy to gain foreign support at the crucial times, and who became the first president of the People's Republic of Angola (PRA) is Dr. António Agostinho Neto.

ANTÓNIO AGOSTINHO NETO

Dr. Agostinho Neto was elected president of the MPLA at the First National Conference held in Leopoldville in December 1962.[3] He personified in his birth, nurture, education, profession, and political experience the kind of nationalism that MPLA would offer to Angola. Born on September 17, 1922, near Luanda, Neto had roots in the Catete people of the Kimbundu group. The Catetense were closer to the capital than the upcountry Ambaquistas but still participated more fully in traditional Kimbundu culture than the urban population of Luanda. His father, a Methodist pastor, the Reverend Agostinho Pedro Neto, shared the common Catetense enthusiasm for education, which was reinforced by the Angolan Protestant conviction that school and church were equally important institutions in the Christian community. A Methodist church report used the colorful simile, "A church without a school is like a couple with-

3. John A. Marcum, *The Angolan Revolution,* Vol. I: *The Anatomy of an Explosion* (Cambridge, Mass.: The MIT Press, 1969), p. 300.

out children." Maria da Silva Neto, his mother, was also a teacher and had a kindergarten in the *musseques*[4] of Luanda.

Neto began his primary education in a village school, then his father was transferred to the church in Luanda, which facilitated his son's high school education. Angola's only two public high schools were located in Luanda and Sá da Bandeira. The few privileged Africans who completed primary school elsewhere in Angola could continue their education only if they could move to one of these cities or pay the high fees of a private *colégio*. Neto went through high school on a government grant for excellence in scholarship and bought books and supplies from the small wage he received as secretary to the Methodist bishop, Ralph E. Dodge. Dodge reports that

even as a boy, Neto was quiet, reserved, a bit shy but always correct and businesslike. . . . António always got good marks in school and progressed from one grade to the next with yearly regularity. . . . The pattern of the Portuguese was to admit the African students in the same school with the Europeans but thin them out especially in the upper grades. António was one of the few who was able to complete his education in Angola up to the university level.[5]

Neto had set medicine as his goal, but when he completed *liceu* in 1944, Angola had no university or postsecondary courses. So he worked for three years in the government health services and quietly participated in the formation of a cultural association in Luanda. Since overtly political organizations were forbidden, a cultural association provided the only forum in which social and political issues could be discussed. Poetry was a medium that Neto and his colleagues found useful for rallying the indignation of literate urban Africans against the injustices of Portuguese colonialism and for expressing empathy with the Angolan masses. It is doubtful that his literary attempt to identify with the people was recognized by the rural populations, who lived in an oral culture. Even when the urban, *assimilado*-mestizo writers

4. *Musseque* means sandy, arable land. The plural is used for the extensive areas surrounding the European city of Luanda where the Africans lived and cultivated small plots of manioc and other food crops. Oscar Ribas, *Tudo isto aconteceu: Romance autobiográfico* (Luanda: Edição do Autor), p. 630.

5. Marcum, I, 330–31.

were producing revolutionary poetry, the peasants identified this elite with the Portuguese colonists.

In 1947 the Methodist Board of Missions in New York granted a scholarship to António Agostinho Neto. Before he left Angola to continue his studies in the medical faculty of the University of Coimbra in Portugal, he wrote "Farewell at the Hour of Parting":

> My Mother
>   (all black mothers
>   whose sons are gone)
> you taught me to wait and hope
> as you hoped in difficult hours
>
> But life
> killed in me that mystic hope
>
> I do not wait now
> I am he who is awaited
>
> It is I my Mother
> hope is us
> your children
> gone for a faith that sustains life . . . [6]

Neto's passage through the medical course was tortuous, not because of academic problems but because of politics. He had his first taste of prison life in 1951 when he was arrested for collecting signatures for the Stockholm Peace Appeal.[7] After his release from three months in the infamous Caxias Prison near Lisbon, Neto did not avoid political involvement. He became a member of the central committee of an anti-Salazar youth group, the Movimento de Unidade Democrática—Juvenil (MUDJ), and was arrested in 1952 for taking part in a demonstration. His academic education was interrupted, but his political education and reputation were enhanced as he was arrested again in February 1955 and only released in June 1957. Such international figures as Jean-Paul Sartre, André Mauriac, Ara-

6. Agostinho Neto, *Sacred Hope*, trans. Marga Holness (Dar es Salaam: Tanzania Publishing House, 1974), p. 1.

7. Ibid., p. xxv.

gon and Simone de Beauvoir, Nicolás Guillén, and Diego Rivera joined in protesting his imprisonment.[8]

Neto had his textbooks with him in prison, but barely passed his final examination in 1958. In order to practice in Angola, Dr. Neto still had to complete the tropical medicine course, which he did in 1959. Later that year, he and his Portuguese wife, Maria Eugénia, and their baby son returned to Angola. A few months before Neto's arrival the first president of the MPLA, Ilídio Machado, was arrested along with fifty-four other Europeans, mestizos and Africans suspected of subversion. Neto had barely begun his medical practice in Luanda when he was again arrested on June 8, 1960, for "subversive activities against the external security of the State."[9] He was one of fifty-two persons seized in this second wave of arrests in a year. Dr. Neto's friends, patients, and supporters planned a demonstration in Catete, the administrative center of his native area, to demand his release. Portuguese officials learned of the plans and when the demonstrators arrived, they were met by soldiers who fired on the peaceful crowd, killing thirty and wounding over 200.

The authorities were particularly apprehensive in June 1960, not only because of the increase in subversive activities within Angola but also because of the imminent independence of the Belgian Congo, set for June 30. In prison, Neto expressed his confidence in the victory of Angolan nationalism:

> Here in prison
> rage contained in my breast
> I patiently wait
> for the clouds to gather—
>
> Here in prison
> rage contained in my breast
> I patiently wait
> for the clouds to gather
> blown by the wind of history.
> No one can stop the rain.[10]

The Portuguese thought they could "stop the rain" by trans-

8. Ibid., p. xxvi.
9. Ibid., p. xv.
10. Ibid., p. 68.

ferring Dr. Neto to Lisbon and then to the Cape Verde Islands, where he continued to practice medicine but under constant police surveillance. By this time, Neto was recognized as one of the principal leaders of the MPLA, having functioned as president of the steering committee for the brief time he was in Angola, and then being named honorary president.[11]

After a year in Cape Verde, Dr. Neto was rearrested and transferred on October 17, 1961, to the Aljube Prison in Lisbon, and another international campaign was launched to free him. This one attracted even more public attention than the first campaign in 1956, as the *Santa Maria* incident and the launching of the war of independence in early 1961 had brought Angola to prominence. A number of leading writers in Britain voiced their protest by writing to the London *Times:*

> We wish to draw urgent attention and that of your readers to the plight of one of Angola's outstanding men, the writer Agostinho Neto, whose life, there is reason to fear, may now be in serious danger. It is not too much to say that the importance of Agostinho Neto in Portuguese-speaking Africa is comparable with that of Leopold Senghor in French-speaking Africa. We believe that every effort must now be made to save this distinguished poet of Portuguese Africa's nationalist awakening.[12]

The Portuguese government was moved, perhaps by international pressure or by internal reasons, to release Neto in March 1962 and place him under restricted residence. However, the underground railway that had taken scores of African students and other nationalists out of Portugal in 1961–62 now succeeded in carrying Neto, his wife, and two small children across the straits to Morocco.[13]

When Neto and his family arrived in Leopoldville in July 1962, he was the most internationally known Angolan nationalist. Within Angola, Neto was identified with the Kimbundu-assimilated-mestizo-intellectual social class. His ancestry bound him to the Catetense and the wider Kimbundu

11. Ibid., p. xxx; and Marcum, I, 39–40.
12. Neto, p. xxxv.
13. Marcum, I, 263.

community. Nine years in secondary school in Luanda (1934–1943) and three more as a government employee in the health department made him at home in the European-mestizo-*assimilado* intellectual circles of the capital. Dr. Neto had received not only a medical education during his ten years in Portugal but also a political education through his anti-Salazar and anticolonial activities and his two and a half years in prison.

MÁRIO COELHO PINTO DE ANDRADE

Six years younger than Agostinho Neto, Mário Pinto de Andrade finished secondary school in Luanda and went to the University of Lisbon to study philology in 1948. A mestizo, born in Golungo Alto on August 21, 1928,[14] he was the younger brother of Father Joaquim Pinto de Andrade, who was the chancellor of the Luanda archdiocese when the war broke out in 1961. Mário de Andrade was in Lisbon until 1954, when he moved to Paris to study social sciences at the Sorbonne. There he joined the team of international intellectuals associated with the cultural review *Présence Africaine*. Andrade wrote several articles under the pseudonym Buanga Fele and edited an anthology of African poetry in Portuguese. More than any other leader, Mário de Andrade contributed to the positive intellectual image of the MPLA in Europe by his writings and international political activities. In 1956 he organized the meeting of nationalist leaders from the Portuguese colonies into an interterritorial Movimento Anti-Colonialista (MAC). Andrade helped guide MAC through various forms until it became the Conferência das Organizações Nacionalistas das Colónias Portuguesas (CONCP), which coordinated the activities of MPLA, PAIGC (Partido Africano de Independência da Guiné e Cabo Verde), and FRELIMO (Frente de Libertação de Moçambique) through the independence struggle. Andrade was the first president of CONCP as well as acting president of MPLA. At the First National Conference in Leopoldville, where Agostinho Neto was elected president, Mário de Andrade became secretary for external affairs of the MPLA executive committee.

14. Ibid., p. 40.

VIRIATO FRANCISCO CLEMENTE DA CRUZ

The third of the MPLA founder-leaders, Viriato da Cruz, like his two colleagues Neto and Andrade, was a graduate of the government *liceu* in Luanda. Born March 25, 1928, at Kikuvu, near Pôrto Amboim, the young mestizo was only twenty-one years old when he became editor of the influential and short-lived literary review *Mensagem*. He was also a leader in the cultural group which took as its slogan, "Let us discover Angola." Cruz, who made important contributions to Angolan nationalism, analyzed this social and literary movement:

[It] should reassume . . . the combative spirit of the African writers of the end of the nineteenth century and the beginning of the present century. This movement would combat the exaggerated respect for the cultural values of the West (many of which are already past); inspire the youth to rediscover Angola in all its aspects through collective and organized effort; exhort them to produce results for the people; solicit the study of modern foreign cultural currents, but with the aim of rethinking and nationalizing their positive and valid creations; require the expression of the popular interests and authentic African nature, but without making any concessions to the thirst for colonial exoticism. Everything should be based on an esthetic sense, intelligence and on African reason and will.[15]

The urge to "rediscover" Angola was appropriate to Viriato da Cruz and other Angolans who had abandoned or been torn from their mother culture. In his poem "Makezu," da Cruz pictures an African granny-vendor in the *musseques* of Luanda shouting "*makezu*" ("mush") to attract the attention of the servants, washerwomen, and artisans so they would buy her manioc mush as they leave their homes to walk to work in the city. But this new generation

> . . . took to a new custom called civilization.
> They only eat bread and sausage
> or take coffee and bread . . .
>
> Our roots take their strength from mush.[16]

---

15. Mário de Andrade, *Antologia temática de poesia africana* (Lisbon: Livraria Sá da Costa Editora, 1975), p. 6, translated by L.W.H.

16. Ibid., pp. 122–23; translated by permission of the publisher.

As poet, politician, and organizer, Viriato da Cruz held the important position of secretary-general of the MPLA from its founding in 1956 until 1962.[17] Da Cruz was on the long list of those to be arrested in 1957 when the political police (Polícia Internacional e de Defesa do Estado, PIDE) established head-quarters in Angola. However, he managed to flee to Portugal and then to France, where he joined Mário de Andrade and other mestizo intellectuals such as Lúcio Lara, forming the active nucleus of the MPLA leadership in exile.[18]

Through such leaders as Neto, Mário Pinto de Andrade, Viriato da Cruz, and Lúcio Lara, MPLA developed a movement with roots in the urban, *assimilado*-mestizo community and an ideology shaped by Marxism.

The UPA

The second nationalist movement, the União das Populações de Angola, was led by members of families that belonged to the traditional power structure of the Kongo kingdom and took as its motto, "Land and Liberty." On the death in 1955 of Dom Pedro VII, a king of the Kongo who had remained submissive to the Portuguese authorities during his thirty-two-year reign, Kongo royalists resident in the Belgian Congo urged the choice of a successor who would better represent African inter-ests. Eduardo Pinock, who led the self-exiled group, had been born on March 28, 1905 at São Salvador, where he attended the local Baptist mission school. Like so many Bakongo, Pinock had found more economic opportunities across the border and for many years held what was then an unusually responsible post for an African, that of railroad stationmaster at the Congolese port of Matadi.[19] In the choice of a new king, Pinock and his as-sociates supported the candidacy of a respected community leader and Protestant, Manuel Kiditu, named for his maternal uncle, Dom Manuel Kiditu, a former king (1912–1915). The Portuguese officials vetoed this choice and crowned António José de Gama, described by his critics as "an old handyman and

17. Marcum, I, 41.
18. Ibid., pp. 41–42.
19. Ibid., p. 56.

printer at the Catholic mission of São Salvador, who suffered from sleeping sickness and had only an elementary education."[20]

Having failed in their attempt to choose their own king, the Protestant reformers then urged that Eduardo Pinock be named first councillor of Dom António III. The Portuguese officials, threatened by this suggestion, not only refused to accept the nomination of Pinock as councillor, but forced the king to prohibit any São Salvadorean from returning home from the Belgian Congo after June 30, 1956. Having suffered two political defeats in efforts to use the kingship to achieve political reform, and faced with involuntary exile, the emigrés decided that they must organize an underground political movement.

Manuel Barros Nekaka in Leopoldville had been trying to organize Angolans to rally support for the Kingdom of the Kongo since 1942. When the efforts of the Protestant reformers to capture the throne in 1955 failed and the border was closed to the return of the emigrés, the Angolans in the Belgian Congo took new initiatives. On May 20, 1956, Nekaka, Pinock, and others, including Holden Roberto, sent a letter to an American State Department official in Leopoldville, asserting that historically and legally the Portuguese Kongo constituted a territory separate from Angola, to which it had been unjustly joined in 1884.[21] In 1956 an anonymous petition was sent from São Salvador do Congo to the United Nations by "natives of the territory of the formerly independent kingdom of the Congo," listing their grievances: forced labor, lack of health and education services, economic exploitation, arbitrary arrests, land seizure and expropriation.[22]

In July 1957, Angolans from Leopoldville and Matadi met in Leopoldville to organize the União das Populações do Norte de Angola (UPNA).[23] They named Barros Nekaka president and Francisco Borralho Lulendo, of the Matadi group, secretary. Although the Belgian Congo gave the Angolans more economic opportunity than their own country, the political restrictions

20. Idem.
21. Ibid., p. 62.
22. Ronald H. Chilcote, *Emerging Nationalism in Portuguese Africa: Documents* (Stanford, Calif.: Hoover Institution Press, 1972), pp. 44–48.
23. Ibid., pp. 43, 54, 63, 65; and Marcum, I, 63.

were almost as severe. Therefore, UPNA sought to send a representative abroad to lobby for their rights in Africa, in the United States, and at the United Nations. The first opportunity to speak in a larger forum came through an invitation to participate in the All-Africa People's Conference in Accra in 1958. Nekaka was unable to go to Ghana so the assignment was given to his nephew and protégé, Holden Roberto.

HOLDEN ROBERTO

Born on January 12, 1923, at São Salvador, Angola, Roberto was named after a British Baptist missionary, Robert Holden Carson Graham.[24] Two years later, Roberto was taken to the Belgian Congo by an aunt, and his parents soon followed. He was educated at Leopoldville, where he was graduated from a Baptist mission school in 1940 and then sent back to São Salvador to "rediscover his roots and perfect his Portuguese." After a year in the Mbanza Kongo, he returned to the Congo where he worked as an accountant in the Belgian administration and then at Nogueira, a Portuguese trading company in Leopoldville. Roberto said that it was during a three-week visit to Angola that he was shocked into political activism by witnessing the brutalization of a helpless old man by a callous Portuguese *chefe do posto*.[25]

Although Holden Roberto had no formal postsecondary education, he profited from an intense, practical political education with teachers who were not academicians but African nationalist leaders from the countries which achieved political independence during that period. Roberto had become acquainted with two future ministers of the Congo, meeting Patrice Lumumba at the Cercle des Evolués when they were both Belgian civil servants in Stanleyville, and Cyrille Adoula while playing on the same soccer team in Leopoldville. Accepting the invitation to attend the First All-Africa People's Conference in Accra, Roberto established relations with George Padmore, Kwame Nkrumah, Sékou Touré, Kenneth Kaunda, Taieb Slim, Tom Mboya, and Frantz Fanon. At the second such conference in Tunis the next year, he was elected to the conference steering

24. Marcum, I, 64–65.
25. Ibid., p. 65; and Pierre A. Moser, *La révolution angolaise* (Tunis: Société l'Action d'edition et de Presse, 1966), p. 66.

committee and formed an enduring friendship with Tunisian President Habib Bourguiba. Attached to the Guinean delegation, Roberto also attended the Fourteenth General Assembly of the United Nations.

As soon as Roberto began to meet African leaders with a broader vision, he discovered that the idea of resurrecting the old Kongo kingdom was considered a tribal anachronism. Communicating this criticism to his home organization, he persuaded them to drop the regional term so that the Union of the Peoples of the North of Angola (UPNA) became the Union of the Peoples of Angola (UPA).[26]

The Revolt Begins

Before 1961, the two main nationalist movements—MPLA and UPA— existed underground or in exile and only surfaced in foreign capitals, at Pan-African meetings, or at the United Nations. At the beginning of 1961, however, two events occurred which forced the Portuguese and the nationalist movements themselves to recognize the seriousness of the Angolan anticolonial sentiment. Before dawn on February 4, 1961, Africans attacked prisons in Luanda. And on March 15, 1961, bands of men began a series of attacks which spread in the next few days to most of the Portuguese trading centers, administrative posts, and coffee plantations in the north of Angola.

In the capital, on February 4, 100 to 200 Africans armed with knives and clubs attacked two prisons and a police station, hoping to free political prisoners who, it was rumored, were to be transferred to Portugal. Reportedly, seven Portuguese police were killed, about forty Africans machine-gunned, and none of the prisoners freed. Agostinho Neto explained the significance of the attacks: "The operation was not, in fact, a success, because the prisoners were not freed, but from that moment the People became conscious of the imperative to fight, and the Portuguese had to face an unexpected situation, a prelude to the difficulties in which they would find themselves in order to maintain their domination."[27]

26. Marcum, I, 169.
27. *Libertação nacional: Textos e documentos do MPLA sobre a revolução angolana* (Edições Maria da Fonte, 1974), p. 33.

The violence continued for a week in Luanda. On February 5, armed European civilians leaving funeral services for the seven policemen turned on African bystanders. Five days later a raid on another Luanda prison resulted in seven deaths and seventeen wounded. Portuguese vengeance was awesome. The police helped white civilian vigilantes organize nightly slaughters in the African townships or *musseques.*

The outburst of violence in Luanda received world press coverage because many foreign journalists had arrived in Luanda at the end of January to report the hijacking of the Portuguese luxury liner *Santa Maria,* supposedly en route to Angola. Captain Henrique Galvão, who had become a critic of Portuguese colonialism through his experience as an administrative official in Angola, organized the seizure of the *Santa Maria* in cooperation with General Humberto Delgado, the opposition candidate for the presidency of Portugal in 1958. The plan had two parts: first, to commandeer the ship after it left Venezuela and take it to Africa; and second, to overpower the Spanish West African territories of Fernando Po and Río Muni, which would then be the base for an air attack on Luanda. On January 20, 1961, Galvão, recognizing the quixotic nature of the venture, called it Operation Dulcineia. "We were romantics fighting for our lady, Liberty," he said.[28]

The plan was aborted when Captain Galvão decided to stop at Saint Lucia in the Windward Islands to leave a wounded crewman and a sick passenger who needed medical attention. Even so, Galvão considered Operation Dulcineia a success since it called the attention of the world to the plight of the Spanish and Portuguese, and aroused the hopes of the Iberian peoples that the dictatorships of Franco and Salazar could be overthrown. The governor-general of Angola had given credibility to the rumor that Angola was the ship's destination by declaring that he had taken "all possible measure for the defense and security of this Portuguese possession in Africa in view of the approach of the *Santa Maria* commandeered by Henrique Galvão."[29] So

28. Henrique Galvão, *O assalto ao "Santa Maria,"* trans. Manuel Pires de F. Matos (Lisbon: Edições Delfos, 1973), p. 147.
    29. Ibid., p. 217.

the *Santa Maria*, sailing into the harbor of Recife, Brazil, on February 2 after a thirteen-day adventure, focused the attention of the world on Portugal's largest colony, Angola.

This world attention increased the impact of the predawn attacks on the Luanda prisons, but no one knew exactly whom to credit or blame for the incidents. At that time there were two MPLAs—one outside Angola, a head without a body, and one inside, a body without a head.[30] MPLA representatives in exile who were able to make public statements claimed only "the participation" of MPLA elements in the February 4 events. As time passed the MPLA assumed full credit for the predawn attacks, and the Angolan national anthem begins: "O Fatherland, never will we forget the heroes of the fourth of February."

Holden Roberto had returned to the Congo after its independence on June 30, 1960 and begun a program of political activity aimed at Angola. UPA couriers were dispatched to Luanda and Nova Lisboa to distribute party tracts among African soldiers in the Portuguese army.[31] UPA also beamed political broadcasts to Angola to exhort Angolans to prepare for action against Portuguese colonialism. The political activity which could now be carried on openly in the Congo by UPA was being done clandestinely in Angola. In fact, when UPA decided to organize the attacks on March 15, it called three organizers from northern Angola to coordinate plans. About February 28, 1961 they were sent back into Angola[32] and, according to the account of one of these emissaries, he instructed the people in the area to burn bridges, crops, houses—to destroy property but not persons.

On March 10, after having sent orders into Angola, Roberto left Leopoldville for the United Nations Security Council meeting in New York. On the day set for the revolt, Roberto gave a press conference without referring to the happenings in Angola but condemning Portuguese colonialism. He maintained that UPA had 40,000 regular members and over a half a million sympathizers.[33]

30. René Pélissier, "Résistance et révoltes en Angola (1845–1961)," vol. 3 (unpublished manuscript), p. 1225.
31. Marcum, I, 135.
32. Ibid., p. 141.
33. Ibid., p. 142.

On March 15 and 16, Angolan mobs, instigated if not actually led by UPA, attacked about thirty small settlements, administrative posts, and coffee plantations in two separate areas of northwest Angola. The first was along the Congo-Angola border near São Salvador, the second the Dembos area reaching to within 75 miles (120 kilometers) of Luanda. For four months the area under attack by Angolans increased until it covered all of northwest Angola from the Atlantic to the Kwango. Only in August did the Portuguese military superiority make itself felt so that the nationalists were pushed back into the two pockets in which the original attacks had occurred in March.

When reports reached New York about the undisciplined nature of the outbreak, Roberto deplored the "extreme violence" of African attacks whose ferocity he described as an "expression of desperation against Portuguese terrorism over the past five hundred years," and added, "We are deeply sorry that women and children have been killed." The Portuguese widely circulated photographs of the corpses—black and white, young and old, men and women—murdered by the mobs who lashed out with their *catanas* (knives).[34]

It is difficult to understand why the poorly organized Angolan nationalists, using only knives and a few muzzle-loading guns, could have been so effective. The lack of preparedness and slow reaction by the Portuguese is even more difficult to explain when we realize they had received warnings of imminent attacks for several months before March 15.

Reasons for the Rebellion

The official Portuguese explanation of the rebellion in the north was simple—"armed bands coming from the exterior"[35]—but this was refuted in fact by the very traders, officials, and plantation foremen who had escaped. They were taken by surprise precisely because the attackers were their regular customers, clients, or workers. However, it is true that the independence of the Congo on June 30, 1960, gave freedom to

34. Idem.
35. Pereira da Costa, *Um mês de terrorismo (Angola: Março-Abril de 1961)* (Editorial Polis, 1969), p. 13.

Angolan emigrés to organize politically and to extend their influence and activities back into Angola.

The Portuguese also suggested Kongo tribalism and religious rivalry as causes of the rebellion. They attributed the brutal nature of some of the attacks to "atavistic tribal practices" and cited the death of "loyal Bailundos" as proof of the tribal character of the revolt.[36] However, the ethnic hypothesis does not stand up when it is recognized that a majority of the attacks during the first week were in the Dembos, a predominantly Kimbundu rather than Kongo area. The Portuguese official interpretation of the events laid blame also on the Protestants and noted that the Kongo district was the area of Angola with the highest percentage of Protestants. This charge was a corollary of the Catholic criticism that the Protestants were religiously heretical and politically subversive. There is no doubt that the UPA grew out of the Kongo Protestant community to challenge the dominant political power based on the identification of Catholic Church and Portuguese state.[37]

A more plausible explanation for the 1961 rebellion in the north of Angola is related to coffee, land, and labor.[38] The price of coffee had dropped in 1960 and the African producers suffered more acutely since they could not call on the government or commercial banks to compensate them for their loss of income. The slump of 1960 accentuated the general threat to African farmers presented by the expansion of estate coffee production on European land concessions. The expansion of the plantations also required additional contract labor, which added more inflammatory elements. The correlation between the number and location of violent attacks and the expansion of European-owned coffee plantations seems to substantiate the assertion that this was the inflammable material in which the explosion took place. Was it ignited by spontaneous combustion or set alight by some spark?

36. Jeffery M. Paige, *Agrarian Revolution: Social Movements and Export Agriculture in the Underdeveloped World* (New York: Free Press, 1975), p. 274; and Eduardo dos Santos, *Maza: Elementos de etno-história para a interpretação do terrorismo no noroeste de Angola* (Lisbon: Edição do Autor, 1965) pp. 45-50.
37. Paige, p. 275.
38. Ibid., p. 277.

Holden Roberto, the president of UPA, at different times affirmed both. In a memorandum to the United Nations he explained how the revolt began on a coffee plantation called Primavera near Madimba, some sixty-five miles from the Congo-Angola border:

On the evening of March 14 the conscript laborers at Primavera gathered before the house of the coffee plantation manager, a Sr. Reis, and demanded six months' overdue back pay. He allegedly refused to listen and without further ado, took out his gun and fired at the workers, killing several of them. Armed with their catanas (machetes), the farm workers promptly fell upon Reis and killed him and his family. Hearing of the Primavera incident, other Portuguese settlers began shooting Africans on sight. The latter responded by burning crops, pillaging houses and demolishing bridges. The news spread, incidents multiplied—the revolution had begun as a kind of spontaneous combustion.[39]

Roberto contradicted his own description of the revolt as "spontaneous combustion" when he spoke at the Second Anniversary of the Revolution in Leopoldville on March 15, 1963: "We gave this password [to engage in the fight for independence] on March 15, 1961 and the responsibility is wholly ours."[40] As a matter of fact, the grievances of the Angolans against the Portuguese were so numerous and serious that any one or a combination of incidents could have triggered the revolt: the drop in coffee prices, the loss of land, a violent clash on one plantation, the independence of the Congo, or the encouragement of the United Nations.

The Portuguese Reaction

The question of why the Portuguese were so ill prepared for the rebellion is more difficult to answer, however, especially when it is recognized that personal warnings were given to traders, Portuguese officials, and missionaries by friendly Africans and that a rebellion had started in the Cassange basin east of Malange at the end of 1960.

The peasant revolt in the Cassange basin was never integrated

39. Marcum, I, 134.
40. Chilcote, p. 83.

into the nationalist mythologies. As noted before, the Portuguese government forced the population of that area to cultivate cotton and sell it at a fixed price to Cotonang, which held a complete monopoly in its marketing. In a generally deteriorating situation, three factors combined to produce the rebellion, which is sometimes known as Maria's War.[41] First, the independence of the Congo on June 30, 1960 aroused the political hopes of Angolan nationalism, especially in the areas such as the Cassange basin that bordered on the newly independent nation to the north. Second, a sharp drop in the price of cotton reduced the average receipts of producers from forty-eight dollars (U.S.) in 1959 to thirty-four dollars in 1960. Third, a messianic-nationalist movement inflamed the discontent of the peasants against the forced cotton production and the sharp decline in income.

One of the principles of the movement ordered the peasants to kill their animals, which they did in November and December of 1960. Then they abandoned their fields and refused to pay taxes. The people considered this passive resistance, but Cotonang and the Portuguese government did not think it less dangerous for being called "passive." The authorities arrested the ringleaders of the movement, but this did not stop the people's revolt. In January 1961, at planting time, the farmers burned their seed, abandoned their tools, and tore up their identification booklets. To show their enthusiasm, they sang the praises of Lumumba, Pinock, and Maria.

Passive resistance gave way to a more active second phase in which rebels with *catanas* and *canhangulos* (muzzle-loading rifles) attacked rural stores, two administrative posts (Tambo Aluma and Marimba), and a Catholic mission. However the traders, officials, and missionaries were not harmed; they were simply disarmed and allowed to flee. The Portuguese underestimated the strength behind these assaults.

While public attention was focused on the Luanda prison attacks on February 4 and the ensuing funerals and reprisals, the Portuguese sent two companies of infantry (*caçadores especiais*)

41. Marcum, I, 124–26. The name Maria's War came from the mispronunciation of the name of the leader, António Mariano.

from Malange to Cassange. Direct combat in the basin began on February 6 near Quela. For the first time the Portuguese air force dropped napalm and fire bombs on Angolan villages. Estimates of the number of victims in Maria's War ranged from a few hundred to 20,000,[42] but the best authority on the period accepts the more modest estimates of "hundreds, perhaps thousands, of African lives."[43]

Both the peasants' war in the Cassange basin in January and the February attacks on Luanda prisons worried the Portuguese, but they still hesitated to use major military power. Perhaps they did not recognize that the uprising in the northwest was more serious than the rebellion in the Cassange basin. Certainly the Portuguese did not understand the intensity of the resentment of the Africans, nor were they aware of the deep penetration of the UPA. In Luanda and Lisbon, officials could also see the possible negative reactions to massive Portuguese military response. In spite of their rhetoric that the Portuguese would never abandon Angola as the Belgians did the Congo, the experience of their northern neighbor was clearly in mind and the Portuguese did not wish to frighten the Angolan whites into fleeing. The withdrawal of their limited troops from the center, south, and east to crush resistance in the northwest might have touched off rebellions all over Angola. Finally, Portuguese mobilization would have supported the argument of the anticolonial nations in the United Nations that Lisbon really was a threat to peace.[44]

The Portuguese in Angola, accepting their own government's propaganda, believed that the whites were in Africa on a civilizing mission. Therefore, the assumedly inferior blacks owed respect and gratitude to them as representatives of a superior civilization even though the individual Portuguese settler might be illiterate. The blacks, too, had been shaped by the colonial pattern so they knew when to say, "*Sim, Senhor!*" and how to keep their hatred hidden, even from themselves. It is not surprising, therefore, that a general disorientation and panic set in

42. Pélissier, III, 1282.
43. Marcum, I, 125.
44. Pélissier, III, 1366–68.

when Africans, who had seemingly accepted the assumption that lack of respect for whites was the greatest crime, drew out *catanas* and slaughtered white bosses, foremen, and traders, not even sparing women and children. In spite of the stifling atmosphere which forced all political comments to be made in hushed tones, Angolans shouted "*Mata!* [kill] *UPA!*" as they assaulted stores, government posts, and coffee plantations. The two words that came to Portuguese stunned minds to express these events which did not fit into the colonial mentality were *acontecimentos* (happenings) and *confusões* (confusions). The events seemed to admit of no rational explanation.

MILITARY ACTION

However, the seriousness of the *acontecimentos* of March 15 finally convinced the Portuguese that they were faced with a challenge which could not be easily crushed with a few bombs, as in the peasants' war in the Cassange basin, nor would civilian reprisals be possible or effective as in Luanda after the February 4 attacks. On March 30, two weeks after the major revolt in northern Angola, Salazar began to act. First he centralized military and political power in each colony in the hands of the governor-general. Within a few days, paratroopers and other special forces arrived in small numbers by air. On April 13, Salazar reshuffled his government and he himself occupied the post of national defense minister, explaining his actions by saying: "The reason is Angola. To act rapidly and with force is the objective which will put to the test our capacity to make decisions."[45]

The steamship *Niassa* arrived at Luanda on May 1 with the first large contingent of troops from Portugal. They paraded down the Avenida Marginal from the port with Dr. Adriano Moreira, the new overseas minister, and Col. Kaúlza de Arriaga, the subsecretary of the air force, in the reviewing stand. On May 13 the newly arrived troops left Luanda for the north to begin the military reoccupation of Angola. The long military column was accompanied by scores of civilian vehicles with goods and fuel for localities that were still holding out against the Ango-

45. Hélio A. Esteves Felgas, *Guerra em Angola* (Lisbon, 1961), p. 79.

lans. They took four days to cover the 350 miles (550 kilometers) to Negage via Lucala, Vila Salazar, and Camabatela, leaving supplies and reinforcements along the way. By July 1, 1961, it was estimated that Portuguese troop strength in Angola had reached 17,000.

Hélio Felgas, the Portuguese historian of this period, affirms that their forces reoccupied the whole northwest area in less than four months. This period began with the taking of the post of Lucunga on June 13 and ended October 7, during which time fifty posts and commercial settlements, spread over three districts and occupying an area more than twice the size of Portugal, were reconquered. Many others were reinforced and the frontier area was garrisoned. On October 7 the governor-general, referring to the reconquest, said: "If we can divide the war into distinct phases, we would say that we have terminated the military operations and are beginning the next phase of police operations, although this will still be in a military manner."[46]

In the period 1961–1965 the size of Portugal's armed forces in Angola increased from 9,000, including 2,000 to 3,000 Europeans, to 50,000 officers and men. These regular military forces were reinforced by Forças Militarizadas (militarized forces), which included the OPVDC, PSP, and PIDE. The Provincial Organization of Volunteers and Civil Defense (OPVDC) was a militia which served as an auxiliary to the regular armed forces with special responsibility for protection of life and property against guerrilla attacks. The OPVDC had a permanent staff of military commanders. The Public Security Police (PSP), which had performed normal police duties in towns and cities before the war, took on special paramilitary duties, protecting plantations in the war zone and patrolling highways and rural areas. The International Police for the Defense of the State (PIDE) had sent its first agents from Lisbon to Luanda in 1957 and by 1965 had about 500 agents in Angola. This, of course, did not include the paid informants who were many times more numerous than the actual agents. In addition, the militarized forces included the judicial police and railroad brigades.

46. Felgas, p. 204.

The military response to the nationalist attacks can be measured by the fact that in 1969 slightly more than half of the total European male population between the ages of twenty and sixty-five were engaged in either military or paramilitary activities.[47]

The military set itself to fulfill a threefold mission: to secure the borders, maintain internal security, and conduct a social action program to gain or maintain the loyalty of Africans through psychological warfare. To fulfill this third objective, military personnel assisted the expanding educational system by building schools and teaching in classrooms, particularly in war zones. Some health services and first aid were also provided by military personnel.

STRATEGIC HAMLETS

To facilitate both military and psychological warfare, the Portuguese forced the Angolans to settle in strategic hamlets. Portugal had earlier employed "rural concentrations" in the north of Angola in the fight against sleeping sickness (trypanosomiasis). Bakongo were forced to abandon their inaccessible villages and build houses along the main roads so nurses could innoculate the population against the disease. This system was adapted in 1961 to the pattern of strategic hamlets used against guerrilla fighters in Malaya, Philippines, and Vietnam. Military officials argued that concentrating the Angolans into larger villages alongside the roads patrolled by the military would deny the insurgents the aid and comfort they formerly received from the local populace. Civilian officials supported the plan, maintaining that strategic hamlets provided the opportunity to extend medical, educational, agricultural, and sanitary services to the people.

After the Portuguese had regained control of the towns, administrative posts, and plantations, the strategic hamlets became the central focus of the military program in the north. The government constructed 130 to 150 hamlets with the capacity for about 2,000 persons each.[48] The estimates of the population

---

47. Gerald J. Bender, "The Dilemmas of Counterinsurgency: The Portuguese Strategic Hamlet Program in Angola" (unpublished research paper), p. 19.

48. Ibid., p. 30.

of the northern area in general and the strategic hamlets in particular is disputed. According to the 1960 census, the Zaïre and Uíge districts had a total African population of 503,318. Most of the people fled to the Republic of the Congo or hid in the forests between 1961 and 1965. The Portuguese claimed that as many as 200,000 had returned and were living in the hamlets, but the exact number in the hamlets is impossible to ascertain.

REFORMS

Recognizing that the conflict in Angola could not be won by military means alone, the Portuguese mobilized politically almost as rapidly as they did militarily. Reforms were instituted to respond to the three main charges against Portuguese colonialism. To counter the charge that Africans were second-class citizens in Angola, the Portuguese government revoked the Statute of Natives (Estatuto dos Indígenas, Decree Law No. 39,666) of May 20, 1954. By a decree (No. 43,893) of September 6, 1961, the distinction between "civilized" and "noncivilized" was legally abolished. To replace the native tax book, the identity card that had been the sign of citizenship, and therefore restricted to whites and assimilated blacks, became available to all. However, most rural Angolans found this reform more bother than benefit. The government sent teams of functionaries into remote areas to take pictures, collect fingerprints, and register the vital statistics necessary for the new identity cards. People were expected to pay for services in time and money, and when they finally received the card, it guaranteed no new privilege. The special head tax levied on Africans was also abolished, and a new "general minimum tax" (Imposto Geral Mínimo) was instituted, which, however, doubled the tax for the former *indígenas.*

The Portuguese next reformed the educational system, recognizing it as a weapon in the struggle between Portuguese and Angolan nationalism. Believing that this weapon should be in the hands of the government, the Portuguese moved in 1961 to assume direct responsibility for the education of the total Angolan population instead of leaving African education to the missions. The first task was to train more teachers and the most urgent need was among the rural Africans. Therefore, in 1962, vacation courses of two and a half months were established to train *monitores* to teach the first year of the rural education course. The next year the government repeated the first-year course and added a second-year course in seven centers with 791 students. By 1965 each of the fourteen districts had a *monitores* course with a total of 2,413 students.[49] Since these students became *monitores* or teachers on government salary after completing the first two-and-a-half-month course, this new program almost doubled the number of teachers in Angola in the first five years of the war.

To prepare primary teachers with more adequate training, the government established two more levels of normal schools: *escolas de habilitação* and *escolas de magistério*. The former received students who had completed primary school and gave them a four-year program which included community development courses as well as the rudiments of an academic education. The six *escolas de habilitação* established by 1965 were administered by the Catholic Church and had 649 students. At a higher level, the education services established a two-year program at three *escolas de Magistério* for students who had already completed their fifth year of secondary school. These three schools had 205 students. The new teacher training programs allowed an increase of 81 percent from 1961 to 1965 in the number of primary pupils, from a total of 105, 781 to 191,693.[50]

To cap this educational development, which was accelerated in response to the war, the government established the University of General Studies in 1963 with three campuses: Luanda (faculties of arts and medicine); Sá da Bandeira (faculty of education); and Nova Lisboa (agronomy and veterinary science). In 1963 the three campuses had 314 students and by 1966 they almost doubled the number to 600, practically all whites.[51]

The educational reform was qualitative as well as quantitative. Until 1961 all primary textbooks came from Portugal and described exclusively European geography and customs. Parrot pedagogy prevailed. Some educators had been preparing new

49. Herrick et al., *Area Handbook for Angola*, p. 135.
50. Ibid., p. 126.
51. Ibid., p. 133.

curriculums and texts, but they did not receive official support until March 1961, when the government recognized that new materials with illustrations and vocabulary from the daily life of the students were essential if mass education were to succeed. The new books still looked at Angola through Portuguese eyes, but some effort was made at least to look at Angola. Prewar books were exclusively Portuguese; postwar books were colonial-Angolan.

The Portuguese expanded the educational system in Angola on the assumption that this reform would be a significant part of a counterinsurgency program. Since Africans complained of not having access to education, the provision of schools, teachers, and new books should, according to Portuguese analysis, produce loyalty to Portugal. However, the experience in Angola would seem to support those who contend that social and economic improvements may be more subversive than supportive of the established regime. Rather than satisfying the population's expectations and desires, the government's efforts, which the people never judged to be sufficient, exacerbated the frustrations and further alienated the people.[52]

The third reform that Portugal instituted in response to the outbreak of war was the elimination of forced labor. African laborers were no longer recruited forcibly through government administrative officers. Instead, the government licensed private labor recruiters to go into the villages and enlist men to work in coffee or sugar plantations, fisheries, mines, and the like. Even without the direct coercion of the administrative officials, the private recruiters succeeded in supplying the number of workers required. The recruiters could count on the Africans' constant need of cash income to pay taxes and buy the necessities of life. It was difficult for the Africans who had been forced all their lives to obey the administrative officials to distinguish the new recruiters with official licenses from Portuguese administrators.

NATIONALIST REACTION TO REFORMS

Portugal instituted reforms in 1961 to correct three of the evils against which the Angolans rebelled: the legally inferior status of

52. Bender, *Dilemmas*, pp. 8–9.

the *indígena,* lack of educational opportunities, and forced labor. Angolans were pleased to take advantage of new educational opportunities, more employment openings, and some slight administrative benefits. However, they did not consider that these reforms had fundamentally changed the unjust relationships between the Portuguese and the Angolans. One thing that was not changed by the reforms was the throttle on free speech. No one in Angola could publicly criticize the government programs or propose reforms.

Only the Angolan nationalist leaders in exile could criticize the reforms and express the more radical view that the time had passed to reform colonialism: it must now be discarded in favor of self-determination and political independence. In fact, the nationalist criticism considered the Portuguese reforms not only ineffective and hypocritical, but positively evil. Angolan nationalists held that by signing these decrees and making speeches, the government convinced the Portuguese that justice was being done. The exiles feared that even some Angolans would be lulled to sleep by these palliative measures, and the reforms would salve the consciences of the Western powers which were supporting Portugal. According to the nationalist leaders, the worst feature of the reforms was that they concealed the real issue—a conflict of nationalisms. Portuguese nationalism had reluctantly opened itself to receive Angolans as citizens within the Lusitanian nation, but they were still second-class citizens with restricted educational and economic opportunities. Angolan nationalism protested not simply against forced labor, but against an economy that was geared to the enrichment of Portugal and other European or American investors. They demanded not only more schools, but an educational system that would teach Angolans the values of their traditions and the facts about their land and society.

In their rejection of reform, the Angolan nationalists were supported by the United Nations. Through a historically significant coincidence, the Angolan nationalist movements were being formed just at the time that Portugal became a member of the United Nations. Between 1955 and 1960, Angolan nationalism benefited as the United Nations took an increasingly active role in defining the relationship between members and their non-self-governing territories.

The Role of the United Nations

Angola became the test case when the General Assembly approved a list of twelve principles which declared that *prima facie* there is an obligation to transmit information in respect to a territory that is geographically separate and is distinct ethnically and/or culturally from the country administering it (Resolution 1541 XIV, December 15, 1960).

With the outbreak of the war in 1961, Angolan colonialism was transformed from a legal case to an issue of international urgency. Just after the attempt to free Luanda prisoners on February 4, 1961, Liberia and twenty-six other African and Asian countries requested an urgent meeting of the United Nations Security Council. Portugal protested that the rebellion was a domestic affair, while African and Asian delegations argued that the "juridical fiction" of Angola being an integral part of Portugal should not impede the Security Council from consideration of the question.

The Security Council agreed to discuss Angola at a special meeting (March 10–15), where Ceylon, Liberia, and the United Arab Republic introduced a resolution calling on Portugal to implement Resolution 1514 (XV) on the Granting of Independence to Colonial Countries and Peoples. On March 15, 1961, the very day the rebellions broke out all across northern Angola, the resolution was rejected because it failed to secure the required majority. (The vote was five in favor—Ceylon, Liberia, USSR, United Arab Republic, and United States—and none against, with six countries—Chile, China, Ecuador, France, Turkey, and the United Kingdom—abstaining.)

Following the events of March 15, forty African, Arab, and Asian nations brought the question of Angola before the United Nations General Assembly. On April 20 the General Assembly, with only Portugal and South Africa voting against, adopted a resolution (1603 XV) similar in its operative provisions to the one rejected in the Security Council. It stated that the failure to. "act effectively and in time for ameliorating the disabilities of the African peoples of Angola is likely to endanger international peace and security." It called upon Portugal to "consider urgently the introduction of measures and reforms" in order to implement the provisions of the declaration on ending colonialism, and it established a five-member subcommittee on Angola to report on the situation.

The United Nations played a more important role for Angolan, Guinean, and Mozambican nationalism than for other African nations. Portugal had not provided opportunities as Britain, France, and even Belgium had done for the discussion of political issues by the leadership of their colonial people. After the Republic (1926), any expression of African nationalist aspiration was prohibited in Portugal or in any of its colonies. Although nationalist leaders from other colonies were arrested and restricted in their political activities, they were allowed to form parties, publish literature, and, up to a point, criticize the colonial regimes. The United Nations, therefore, provided the essential forum for the articulation of Angolan nationalism when Portugal banned it.

The Development of National Movements

The initial Angolan military successes and the international recognition of Angolan aspirations put pressure on the two main Angolan political parties to become more truly national movements. To this end, the parties sought to be more inclusive in their leadership and to form united fronts.

The UPA, which was firmly rooted in the Bakongo and depended on the leadership of Roberto, Pinock, and Nekaka, reached out to include important non-Kongo elements. Rosário Neto (no relation to Agostinho Neto), a Kimbundu exile, opened the UPA office in Leopoldville at the time of Congolese independence in 1960 and became vice-president. João Batista, a Cuanhama corporal in the Portuguese army, fled from his post in northern Angola in 1960 and became a UPA commander. Alexandre Taty, a Cabinda Catholic seminarian, became second vice-president of UPA, and a prominent Luanda mestizo, Aníbal de Melo, was chosen to be the party's political director. In late 1961, Jonas Malheiro Savimbi, an Umbundu student who had fled in 1960 from Lisbon to Switzerland because of harassment by the PIDE, took the post of secretary-general of UPA. Savimbi's entry moved the UPA toward its goal of becoming a national party by providing prominent representation of the largest ethnolinguistic group and counteracting UPA's anti-intellectual image. Therefore, by the end of 1961, UPA could claim to be a national party, at least on the basis of its representative leadership.

UPA next moved to extend its constituency support from the BaxiKongo in the area of São Salvador to include other peoples of the same ethnolinguistic group. The Bazombo to the east had formed a legally recognized mutual aid society, the Association Mutuelle des Ressortissants de Zombo (ASSOMIZO), in Leopoldville in 1956. After Congolese independence, AS-SIMIZO transformed itself into a political party, the Alliance des Ressortissants de Zombo (ALIAZO), which was a nonviolent and conciliatory alliance reflecting its leaders' Christian training and middle-class values. Under nationalist pressure, ALIAZO dropped its ethnic label and became the Partido Democrático de Angola (PDA) in January 1962. It aspired to play the role of mediator between UPA and MPLA but, when it failed in this, PDA joined UPA on March 27, 1962 to form the Frente Nacional de Libertação de Angola (FNLA), which issued the following statement of objectives:

To direct the struggle for Angolan national independence on the basis of fraternal collaboration among all Angolan ethnic groups ... To install ... a democratic regime that will respect the provisions of the Universal Declaration of Human Rights, that will institute agrarian reform ... a planned economy, and industrialization of the country ... to adopt a policy of nonalignment ... [53]

The FNLA could hardly be considered a "national" front, however, since at the base the UPA and PDA represented only two of the peoples belonging to the Kongo ethnolinguistic group.

The MPLA followed the same process of including leadership from outside its urban-Kimbundu-mestizo base in naming António Jabes Josias, one of Holden Roberto's former associates from São Salvador, to be president of its Congo committee. The committee also included Jorge M. Freitas, earlier connected with Barros Nekaka's group in Leopoldville. However, the MPLA placed more emphasis on uniting various Angolan groups to give it a national character than on seeking individual leaders

53. Statement of the objectives of FNLA, in Chilcote, pp. 102–5.

from various regions or communities. This approach was to its advantage since it had confidence that its better-trained leadership would assure a dominant position for MPLA in any united front. The MPLA achieved a short-lived front at the end of 1960 when representatives of MPLA, UPA, ALIAZO, and a small Cabindan movement, AREC (Association des Ressortissants de l'Enclave de Cabinda), met in Leopoldville and formed the Front Commun des Partis Politiques de l'Angola (FCPPA). A power struggle took place within UPA between those who favored the united front and those who opposed it. Holden Roberto led the latter group, contending that meaningful unity depended upon a real consensus of political views and that Angolan unity was "total as far as elements of the population on the field of battle [are] concerned. . . . There is no other kind of unity."[54]

Internationally, the MPLA pressed for a common front in 1961 at the Third All-Africa People's Conference in Cairo, which warned against "imperialist or neocolonialist" maneuvers tending to provoke "divisions amongst the people," and at the Council of the Organization of the Afro-Asia Peoples' Solidarity Conference held in April 1961 in Bandung. The MPLA used the meeting of the nationalist movements for Portuguese colonies in Casablanca to put pressure on the UPA to join a coalition. At this meeting the Conferência das Organizações Nacionalistas das Colônias Portuguesas (CONCP) was formed. Discussions between the MPLA and the UPA, ALIAZO, and the Mouvement de Libération de l'Enclave de Cabinda (MLEC) did not result in coalitions or united fronts.

The two major parties also attempted to extend their influence and support through auxiliary labor, student, and health organizations.

Government-in-Exile

The most daring initiative taken by Angolans to create a national instrument to oppose Portugal was FNLA's formation of a government-in-exile a week after UPA and PDA had created the Frente Nacional de Libertação de Angola (FNLA) in April 1962. The Govêrno Revolucionário de Angola no Exílio (GRAE),

54. Marcum, I, 309.

which originally was to be located inside Angola, was established instead in Kinshasa (then Leopoldville), since no area in Angola was securely held by Angolan nationalists. Holden Roberto assumed the presidency and Manuel Kunzika, president of PDA, became the first vice-president of GRAE. Jonas Savimbi occupied the position of foreign minister, which was the most strategic position after the presidency, since one of the main purposes of GRAE was to gain international recognition for the FNLA and the Angolan war of liberation. When the Organization of African Unity (OAU) was formed a year later, in May 1963, GRAE received its official recognition and that of some twenty African states.

The OAU recognition of GRAE was not only the high point of FNLA's political fortunes, but also raised new and exaggerated expectations among its militants and sympathizers. GRAE expected greater financial support through the OAU's Liberation Committee, but actually received less than it had been receiving previously through bilateral assistance. Holden Roberto's prediction of military victory within two or three years also led Angolans to expect GRAE's forces to carry the attack on Portuguese colonialism to all regions of Angola. Umbundu who had joined the GRAE army with the hope of penetrating their region in central and southern Angola became disillusioned and mutinied when Roberto seemed to be waging a "border war." Tension mounted within GRAE when Roberto had some sixty of the mutineers arrested and put into Congolese jails.

The dissent and rebellion within GRAE sssumed more serious proportions with the resignation of three top non-Kongo leaders. At the OAU conference in Cairo in July 1964, Jonas Malheiro Savimbi resigned his post as minister of foreign affairs. Then Dr. José João Liahuca, the director of the GRAE health and welfare agency, SARA, and José Kalundungo, chief of the general staff of the GRAE army, submitted their resignations. All three were Umbundu and attributed their frustrations to what they considered Holden Roberto's tribal orientation. Savimbi recalled that the Executive Committee of the UPA, the propelling force behind the GRAE, was composed of nineteen members, of whom eighteen were Kongo and of these, twelve were from the traditional Kongo capital, São Salvador, the home

Table 5.   Casualties in Angolan fighting, 1963–1965

Year	Killed	Wounded	Imprisoned	Total
1963	840	350	2737	3927
1964	749	469	1130	2348
1965	548	465	780	1793

Source: "*BAC 5 * 6 boletim anti-colonial Feb. –Mar. 1973*" (Lisbon, mimeographed), p. 13.

of Holden Roberto. Kalundungo argued similarly: "To show you Mr. Holden's attachment to tribalistic principles, we need only tell you that of the twenty-two officers trained in Algeria, only six belonged to ethnic groups different from his own."[55]

The dissidents argued that Holden Roberto and his organizations UPA/FNLA/GRAE were not only crippled by tribalism but also by inefficiency and undue dependence on American assistance. They made these arguments not so much on the basis of ideology but because of the practical effects of these policies. The war was stalled and nothing was being done to liberate the majority of Angolans who lived in central or southern Angola. Savimbi was undoubtedly articulating the convictions of his colleagues from central Angola when he said, "The guerilla army should live and progress into the interior with the total support of the population."[56] In a matter of months, Savimbi would begin mobilizing another movement with the goal of pushing into the interior.

GRAE suffered another reverse in mid-1964 when Holden's long-time friend Cyrille Adoula was replaced as prime minister of the Congolese Republic by Moïse Tshombe, who had close ties with Portugal. The internal weakness of the two principal movements, MPLA and FNLA, during 1964 and 1965 is reflected in the lower level of military activity. According to the Portuguese military command in Angola, the number of Angolan casualties declined, as shown in Table 5.

55. Chilcote, p. 162.
56. Ibid., p. 160.

In 1964 the MPLA began to recoup its fortunes, while GRAE was under heavy attack from Savimbi and other influential dissenters. The overthrow of Fulbert Youlou, president of Congo Brazzaville, by the revolutionary government of Alphonse Massamba-Debat provided the MPLA with a base from which it could operate much more freely. Russia and Eastern Europe provided materiel, while Cuban advisors established a training base at Brazzaville. The most active and best educated of the young militants were sent for military training and other study to Eastern Europe.[57]

Economic Response to the War: 1961–1965

Salazar, who was basically an economist, realized that a prompt military and political reaction was not sufficient to defend Angola. Comprehensive and rapid development of Angola was needed for Portugal to maintain political control. In June 1961, Decree Law No. 44016 established the outline of a new program for economic development in the overseas provinces and the integration of the financial and production structures of each province into an Escudo Area Common Market.[58] The outline was filled in gradually from 1961 to 1965 and, as we will see below, in the latter year the Portuguese made a more dramatic response to the economic pressures brought by the colonial wars.

Both military and economic responses to the nationalist threat demanded a more rapid expansion of the infrastructure. The total mileage of roads, 20,000 (35,000 kilometers) in 1961, which made it theoretically possible for Portuguese officials to reach all corners of Angola, was impressive. However, only 435 miles were paved. By May 1966, 2,190 miles (3,504 kilometers) were paved, 504 were graded and ready for paving, and 1,287 miles (2,059 kilometers) were improved roads with some engineering. More contracts had also been let to achieve the goal of uniting the capitals of all the districts by paved roads, which was seen as both a military and an economic necessity by the government.[59]

57. Wheeler and Pélissier, p. 216.
58. Herrick et al., p. 357.
59. Ibid., pp. 332–33.

The war stimulated the development of the air network within Angola but isolated the colony even more from the outside world. For internal flights the domestic airline, DTA, purchased two Fokker Friendships (F-27), which speeded up the longer domestic flights. However, Air France and Sabena discontinued their regular flights to Angola. Only Portuguese Air Transport (TAP) and South African Airways (SAA) connected Angola to a limited outside world: Rhodesia, Mozambique, and South Africa on the continent and Portugal in Europe.

Agriculture was the basis of Angola's economy, so any economic reform had to deal first with agriculture. Within that sector the most urgent demand for change came from the Cassange region, where the compulsory production of cotton had caused the peasant rebellion in 1960–61. Immediately following the outbreak of the war in March 1961, compulsory cotton cultivation and cotton concessions were abolished. Then, as part of the overall economic reform, the Portuguese government established a Cotton Institute in Angola to replace the board in Lisbon which had regulated the trade before 1961. Similarly, the Lisbon government substituted coffee and cereal institutes for trade boards that had operated out of the Portuguese capital in the prewar period. The institutes dealt with virtually all commercial aspects of these three crops, including marketing, price fixing, crop storage, and quality control, and also gave technical assistance to growers. New research facilities were provided to promote agricultural development. The Institutes and research centers served commercial agriculturalists, who were almost exclusively European. Some of the government agriculturalists wished to promote the development of the traditional sector of agriculture, but their lack of appropriate structures for extension work and their ignorance of the Angolan languages and cultures, together with limited resources, restricted severely their moving beyond good intentions.

In April 1961 the government gave emergency aid to the coffee farmers in the northwest, who were most seriously affected by the uprising, by establishing an agricultural and livestock credit fund. In 1964 its function was extended by law to include the promotion of agricultural development in general.

Portugal instituted these economic reforms to strengthen it-

Table 6.   Angolan foreign trade, 1961–1965

Year	Exports	Imports
1961	$135,593,850	$114,369,150
1962	149,250,150	136,428,810
1963	163,935,450	147,402,300
1964	205,363,200	165,000,150
1965	201,155,850	196,040,600

Source: Allison Butler Herrick et al., *Area Handbook for Angola* (Washington, D.C., 1967), p. 320.

self to bear the burdens imposed upon it by the wars in Angola, Mozambique, and Guinea. However, the impact of the reforms was not nearly as beneficial to Portugal as the increased income from mineral production. Iron and petroleum had been explored before 1961, but only came into significant production after the outbreak of the war in Angola.

Iron had been mined since 1957 and by 1965 it constituted a major export item. In 1959, iron ore production totaled 349,000 metric tons and by 1964 it reached 905,000 metric tons. In a more dramatic fashion, the production of petroleum increased from 9,000 metric tons in 1956 to 904,737 metric tons in 1964. Over half was processed in the Luanda refinery.[60]

The attacks on the coffee plantations in the north, the flight of whites to Europe, and the general atmosphere of uncertainty following the uprisings in 1961 disrupted local economies. However, government statistics indicate that Angola's foreign trade increased steadily from 1961 to 1965, with only a slight decline in exports in 1965. Even in that year Angola had a favorable balance of trade, as Table 6 shows.

Communications

Each side in the colonial war felt the need to tell its story to the widest audience possible. The vast majority of Angolans were entirely dependent on direct and informal oral communication for information. Radio was the most important channel of public

60. Ibid., pp. 308–9.

communication. The Portuguese had eighteen stations which they controlled through government subsidies and censorship to assure that only the official view of the news was transmitted. The number of licensed receiving sets increased 25 percent from 1961 to reach a total of 73,000 in 1964.[61] An estimated 25 percent of the Angolan population understood some Portuguese. One or two stations broadcast several hours weekly in African languages, but they were listened to more as a curiosity than as a source of information by Angolans. The government station in Luanda also beamed programs in French to the Congo and in English to South-West Africa.

The African nationalists broadcast to Angola over the respective host government-owned stations: MPLA from Brazzaville and FNLA from Kinshasa. Programs from Russia, South Africa, Great Britain, West Germany, and the Netherlands and the Voice of America were some of the foreign broadcasts that reached Angola with regular news and entertainment, sometimes in Portuguese.

Angolans differ over which is their national day—February 4 or March 15—but all agree that 1961 was the year in which the decisive war began between Angolan and Portuguese nationalisms. The years 1961–1965 constituted the first phase of that war of independence. If the history of Angola is one of five centuries of conflict, how did this conflict differ from those of the previous centuries?

First, for the first time Africans revolted against colonial rule in the name of Angola. The Kingdom of the Kongo had fought to assert its own authority repeatedly since the first Portuguese arrived in 1482. The Kimbundu, organized into a variety of political units, had resisted Portuguese conquest and allied themselves with or opposed the Bakongo to the north according to their political or commercial interests. The Bailundo revolted against the abuses of the Portuguese in 1902 and although they sought alliances and support from Huambo, Bié, and Chiyaka, they had no colonywide plan or vision.

The Portuguese tried to deny the existence of Angolan

61. Ibid., p. 242.

nationalism, claiming that the war was simply a series of tribal skirmishes. Official news stories stressed the conflict between the Bakongo and "loyal Bailundos." The Cuanhamas, who were drafted in the south, were sent to the northern front and praised for their heroic feats against the Bakongo. The Portuguese refused to admit that Angola might be a nation and not simply a colony or an overseas province of the Portuguese nation.

The Portuguese introduced a new patriotic song which ended: "*Angola é nossa. Angola é Portugal*" ("Angola is ours. Angola is Portugal"). However, when the Angolans sang lustily the line "Angola is ours" and whispered "Angola is Portugal," the song was banned. Even the Portuguese began to admit to themselves, if not publically, that the real enemy was not simply rebellious tribes but Angolan nationalism.

The second distinctive characteristic of the 1961 war was the combatants' sense of its being a life-and-death struggle. The Portuguese feared that the loss of their African colonies, especially the richest, Angola, would mean the economic end of Portugal, already the poorest nation in Western Europe. On the other side of the battle line, the Angolan nationalists knew that their only alternatives were independence or permanent exile. Compromise or reconciliation were no longer acceptable options.

Third, the 1961 war was internationalized in a unique way. Other countries had intervened militarily in the territory now known as Angola on previous occasions, but they were only using it as a battleground to grab some local advantage. Even when the nations met in Berlin (1884–85), they were concerned about keeping trade open in the Congo basin and did not recognize the existence of Angola as a political entity. After 1961, various countries intervened to try to shape Angola according to their interests. The United States and Western Europe spoke in favor of self-determination for Angola, but preferred it to continue as a Portuguese colony to any of the alternatives that they could see. South Africa and Rhodesia had no great respect for the Portuguese, but feared Angola as an independent, black-ruled nation. Newly independent African nations sympathized strongly with Angolan nationalism, but their practical assistance was limited to the provision of diplomatic channels, bases in neighboring countries, and token military financial contributions. The socialist countries encouraged Angolan nationalism by furnishing arms, training, and finances as a means of attacking the West.

The life-and-death struggle of two nationalisms, supported by different international interests, had reached a stalemate in 1965. By that time, Portugal had succeeded in recapturing control of all the towns, administrative posts, and plantations in the north, and the Angolan economy was growing steadily. Angolan nationalists, with the added pressure from African nationalist movements in Guinea and Mozambique, were forcing Portugal to spend almost half its national budget on defense. Fifty thousand Portuguese troops were tied down in Angola alone, and Portugal was under increasing pressure from the international community to grant independence to its colonies.

Both the Portuguese and Angolans conceded that the struggle would be long and expensive. Yet each claimed that victory was certain. To prepare for this prolonged struggle to achieve ultimate victory, each side in 1965 was planning new offensives.

CHAPTER 7

The Internal Conflicts of Angolan and Portuguese Nationalisms, 1966–1976

Angolan and Portuguese nationalism fought each other to a standoff as they clashed militarily and politically from 1961 to 1965. Portugal succeeded in confining the Angolan nationalists to a few refuges in the "rotten triangle" in the hills of northern Angola. Yet to do this Portugal had to maintain an expeditionary force in Angola proportionately much larger than that of the United States in Vietnam at the height of the Indochina war. In addition, Lisbon had to support the military, economic, and psychological pressure of more violent and disciplined attacks by PAIGC in Guinea and FRELIMO in Mozambique. This required the Portuguese government to spend nearly half of its national budget on the three colonial wars.

The two Angolan nationalist movements leading the attack on Portuguese colonialism had suffered various political and military defeats in the first four years of the war. Yet they were far from conquered. The Angolans' strength lay more in the support they enjoyed both inside Angola and in the international community than it did in military power.

The stalemate of 1965 prompted both sides to prepare new initiatives to carry on the war to victory. In the last chapter of the history of Portuguese Angola, however, the more crucial struggle was the internal conflict within each nationalism rather than the external clash between Portugal and the Angolan movements.

Within Angolan nationalism a new movement, UNITA, appeared which fragmented even more the forces facing Portuguese colonialism. The Angolans spent more time and energy

fighting among themselves, or seeking a solution to their internecine warfare, than they did opposing their main enemy, Portugal.

Similarly, Portuguese nationalism was racked by dissension
and internal conflict. Politically, the opposition maintained pressure on the regime in Lisbon by presenting candidates at all
elections, although in most cases they withdrew on the eve of the
elections in frustration at the restrictions placed on them. Economically, the regime's insistence on the vital importance of the
colonies was challenged by commercial and industrial leaders
who advocated concentrating economic interests in Europe
rather than in Africa. Religiously, opposition to the Salazar-
Caetano regime appeared in the Catholic Church both in the
metropole and in the colonies. Finally, the opposition became so
strong within the Portuguese armed forces that the "movement
of the captains" executed the coup on April 25, 1974, which not
only ended the fifty years of authoritarian rule in Portugal but
gave victory to Angolan nationalism in its struggle against Portuguese colonialism.

MPLA's New Front

The FNLA/Zaïre alliance had effectively excluded MPLA
from a major military role in the northwest region of Angola so
it looked to Zambia in the east as a base for a new front. In 1964,
the MPLA opened an office in Dar es Salaam, where it could
work more closely with FRELIMO, its CONCP ally, and also
have access to a friendly port for the importation of materiel.
When Zambia became independent in October 1964, the eastern
border of Angola became accessible so a new MPLA office was
established in Lusaka. MPLA ordered its personnel into the
Moxico and Cuando Cubango districts of eastern Angola in
1965 to begin building a "minimum network of political cooperation."[1] Some military supplies began to flow from Dar es
Salaam to Lusaka, and in May 1966, MPLA reported firing its
first shots on the eastern front. The Portuguese Defense Minister, General Gomes de Araújo, returned to Lisbon from an in-

---

1. Basil Davidson, *In the Eye of the Storm: Angola's People* (Garden City, N.Y.:
Doubleday, 1972), p. 242.

Areas of military activity in Angola, 1966–1974. Adapted from Allison Butler Herrick et al., *Area Handbook for Angola* (Washington, D.C.: U.S. Government Printing Office, 1967), p. 379.

spection tour in Angola in September 1966 confirming that a new front had indeed been opened in the east by MPLA units infiltrating from Zambia.[2]

UNITA: A Third Liberation Movement

Another initiative undertaken by Angolan nationalism in 1966 was the creation of a third liberation movement, the União Nacional de Independência Total de Angola (UNITA), which was organized in March 1966 in the village of Muangai in eastern' Angola, 300 miles (480 kilometers) from the Zambia border. Jonas Savimbi had been seeking a new role for himself in the struggle against Portuguese colonialism in the twenty months between his resignation as a foreign minister of GRAE in July 1964 and the founding of the third major Angolan liberation movement in March 1966. His search entailed a long trip to North Vietnam, North Korea, and China which was arranged in part through the diplomatic assistance of Ahmed Ben Bella of Algeria. Savimbi had to explain to Chairman Mao Tse-tung and Premier Chou En-lai why he had opposed Viriato da Cruz, who had the backing of China when he left the MPLA and sought to work in the FNLA in 1962–63. If Savimbi's position at that time was displeasing to the Chinese, he could at least assure them that he now intended to carry on a people's war inside Angola. On his return to Africa, Savimbi talked with Agostinho Neto and Daniel Chipenda about possible collaboration with the MPLA, but evidently decided instead to form a new movement.

In the midst of this travel, Savimbi was still fulfilling his final requirements for his degree in political and legal sciences, which he received from the University of Lausanne in July 1965. He had started his educational career in a mission school, as did most rural Angolans. His father, Lot Malheiro Savimbi, who was a lay leader of the Protestant community in central Angola, had been graduated in 1921 from Currie Institute, a male training school in the Dondi Mission. The mission expected that all graduates would receive work assignments with their diplomas, but Lot Savimbi disappointed the missionaries and church lead-

2. John A. Marcum, *The Angolan Revolution*, Vol. II: *Exile Politics and Guerrilla Warfare 1962–1976* (Cambridge, Mass.: The MIT Press, 1978), p. 178.

ers when he took his diploma and went off to work on the
Benguela Railway. However, he soon proved to himself and to
the church that he could be just as useful a Christian working as
a telegraph operator or stationmaster on the railway as he could
by serving the church as pastor, teacher, or nurse. When Lot
Savimbi retired after twenty-five years of service on the railway,
he became mission school inspector and, finally, director of the
Chilesso Mission at the same time that his son, Jonas Savimbi,
founded UNITA.

Jonas Savimbi's travels had convinced him that he could find
allies in Asia and Africa for a new initiative against Portuguese
colonialism, but it was more important to find the Angolan constituency that would support him. First he identified colleagues
from central Angola who had left GRAE with him and who were
helped across the Congo River to Brazzaville by MPLA.
Twenty-four of these defectors, predominantly Umbundu, writing as the Amigos do Manifesto Angolano (Amangola), issued a
statement in December 1964 calling upon exiled Angolans to
move back inside their country and mobilize the masses for
guerrilla warfare.[3] MPLA supported Amangola until it became
clear that the dissidents from the FNLA were not disposed to
apply for membership in the MPLA.

A second constituency open to Savimbi's blandishments was
the group of exiled Angolan students in Western Europe and
North America. Many of the students active in the União Nacional dos Estudantes Angolanos (UNEA), which supported
GRAE, had become disillusioned with the lack of military activity
by both major movements and even more disappointed with the
constant conflict between the FNLA and MPLA. Consequently,
Savimbi found a student constituency ready to listen to his criticisms of the two movements and anxious for some new initiatives. UNEA took a position of nonalignment in relation to the
two movements and called for unity of all Angolans.

Savimbi found a third constituency in Zambia among the Angolan refugees who had been active in the UPA/GRAE office in
Lusaka. They were mainly Lunda-Chokwe and Ganguela

3. Ibid., p. 161; and Jorge Alicerces Valentim, *Qui libere l'Angola?* (Brussels:
Michele Coppens, 1969), pp. 40–42.

(Luenas and Luchazes) from eastern Angola who were disappointed with the inactivity of the two movements in their home territories.

After contacting potential allies and assessing the strength of a new Angolan constituency, Savimbi began to formulate the rationale for a new party. In a letter to former missionaries of the United Church of Christ, he set forth the gist of his political thinking:

> Only the Angolan people within the country is capable of freeing itself from foreign domination. . . . The unity of Angolan forces really dedicated to the liberation of our country is the most important condition for victory. . . . This unity has to result from an equilibrium of all Angolan nationalist forces. . . . this equilibrium will mobilize our People against the enemy in a popular and proportional representation of all the social groups . . . . Angolan society is divided into tribes, into clans, and classes. There cannot be any durable solution for Angolan divisions if the social structure is not considered. . . . The MPLA only includes representatives of the "Kimbundus". GRAE only contains "Kikongos." These two parties together still leave outside the political struggle more than half of the population. . . . It is necessary that a new political formation representing other Angola forces should be constituted. . . . Today it is internationally known that the MPLA is affiliated with pro-Communist ideas and methods. . . . Sr. Roberto Holden was supported by western forces. . . . It is vital to avoid a direct or indirect confrontation of the great powers on our soil.[4]

When Savimbi reached Zambia in October 1965, he persuaded Kenneth Kaunda to invite Holden Roberto and Agostinho Neto to Lusaka for discussions regarding a united front of all Angolan forces. When they declined the invitation, Savimbi proceeded with his plans to form a third movement. In March 1966, Savimbi hiked into Angola and held a conference in Muangai at which UNITA was formed. Not much was heard about UNITA, however, until Christmas Day, 1966, when several hundred UNITA partisans attacked the border railroad town of Teixeira de Sousa.[5] By casualty count, UNITA would have to consider the attack a defeat since it lost perhaps 300 of its ill-armed and ill-trained soldiers, while only six or seven Por-

4. Letter of Jonas Savimbi, dated Sept. 21, 1965.
5. Marcum, II, 191–92.

tuguese were killed. However, by interrupting the Benguela
Railway and stopping Zambian and Zaïrean copper shipments
for a week, UNITA had forced the world to take notice of its
entry into the Angolan war.

Savimbi returned to Lusaka in February 1967 and then flew
on to a meeting of African leaders in Cairo. In March, during
Savimbi's absence, UNITA forces twice derailed trains, closing
the Benguela Railway to Zambian copper traffic for several
weeks. To avoid Zaïre's and Zambia's anger, the MPLA and
FNLA were quick to dissociate themselves from the rail disrup-
tions. When Savimbi returned to Lusaka in June 1967, he was
arrested and expelled from Zambia. He then found himself back
in Cairo, where he had resigned from GRAE three years before
and had begun the pilgrimage that led him to found an
Angola-based movement. Some observers predicted that without Savimbi, UNITA could not survive,[6] but it did, and Savimbi
slipped back into Angola a year later. From June 1968 until
April 1974, Savimbi made a virtue of necessity and led UNITA in
its struggle against Portugal from the bush of eastern Angola.

Savimbi has always been the uncontested leader of UNITA.
One sign of his leadership has been his ability to attract strong
nationalists from other regions and other ethnolinguistic
groups. The secretary-general of the movement and political
commissar of its guerrilla forces was a Cabindan, Miguel N'Zau
Puna. Born about 1939,[7] Puna attended a seminary in Malange,
then worked for the port administration at Nóqui before going
to Tunisia, where he studied agronomy for five years. He returned to Angola with Savimbi in 1968 and played key roles in
UNITA as political strategist and military commander. José
Samuel Chiwale, born about 1944 in Huambo, taught school and
in 1965 went to China for military training. In the early 1970s,
Chiwale emerged as UNITA's top military leader.[8] Samuel
Chitunda was the *nom de guerre* of Samuel Piedoso Chingunji,

6. Ibid., p. 193.
7. Ibid., pp. 194, 398n.
8. Ibid., pp. 194, 398n.

born about 1938 in Bié. He received his military training in the Portuguese army, in which he became an officer.[9] Jorge Isaac Sangumba, UNITA's principal external spokesman, earned a university degree in New York and then established a modest office in his apartment in London. Smart G. Chata, a Chokwe, was elected one of three vice-presidents.

The recruitment of these leaders reflects the development of the mid-sixties as Angolan nationalism reached out to enlist more peoples of Angola in the political struggle against Portuguese colonialism.

Portugal's Economic Initiative

Portugal's new initiative against Angolan nationalism was economic rather than military. In 1935, Salazar had laid the foundation of his economic system, which was designed to exclude or severely limit foreign investments and to exploit the colonies for the benefit of the metropole. The colonial wars forced Salazar to change this policy and by Decree Law 46,312 in April 1965 the door was opened to foreign capital.[10] This new policy plus the stimulation of the increasing military expenditures gave Angola its most rapid economic growth, which benefited principally the Europeans although some of the prosperity trickled down to a few of the more privileged urban Africans.

Angola's gross internal product increased more than threefold from $850 million in 1963 to $2,800 million in 1973[11] as a result of both private investment and government action. The government's Third Development Plan (1968–73) invested 41.8 percent of its $962 million budget in extraction and mining, 12.5 percent in transportation and communications, 8.9 percent in social services, and 8.3 percent in agriculture, forestry, and stock raising.

The private sector produced the dramatic economic growth

9. Ibid., pp. 194, 398n.
10. Carlos G. Nensala, "The Role of Fiscal Policy in the Economic Development of Angola" (M.A. dissertation, Catholic University of America, Washington, D.C., 1973), p. 24.
11. United Nations A/9623 (V): Report of Special Committee on the Implementation of the Declaration on the Granting of Independence to Colonial Countries and Peoples (1974), October 8, 1974, p. 6.

that reinforced Portugal's will and ability to sustain its defense against African nationalists. In 1966, as MPLA and UNITA were opening the new military fronts in the west, the Gulf Oil Company found oil in the waters off the Cabinda enclave and in December signed a contract giving Cabinda Gulf Oil, a subsidiary of Gulf Oil, exclusive rights to prospect and exploit in the area. The company was required to invest at least $2.8 million during 1967 and 1968.[12] By the end of 1972 the Cabinda Gulf Oil Company had invested $209 million in Angola, and in the same year Gulf paid $61 million in income taxes and royalties to the Portuguese authorities,[13] representing 13 percent of the total Angolan provincial budget for the year and 60 percent of the province's 1972 military expenses.[14] Rebocho Vaz, governor-general of Angola, indicated how keenly aware the Portuguese were of the importance of a protected supply of oil for their war effort:

As you know, oil and its derivatives are strategic materials indispensable to the development of any territory; they are the nerve-center of progress, and to possess them on an industrial scale is to ensure essential supplies and to dispose of an important source of foreign exchange.

Apart from this, in the mechanized wars of our times, its principal derivative—petrol—plays such a preponderant part that without reserves of this fuel it is not possible to give the Army sufficient means and elasticity of movement. The machine is the infrastructure of modern war, and machines cannot move without fuel. Hence the valuable support of Angolan oils for our armed forces.[15]

The economic support of the Portuguese war effort increased as the production of petroleum multiplied more than tenfold in five years, from 537,152 tons in 1967 to 7,055,144 tons in 1972. By 1973 petroleum had surpassed coffee as Angola's most valuable export. Not only Gulf, but two other companies with European capital, Petrangol and Angol, also signed contracts with Portugal for exploitation of oil in Angola, contributing to an

12. African Development, November 1973, p. 11.
13. United Nations A/9023 (III): Report of Special Committee on the Implementation of the Declaration on the Granting of Independence to Colonial Countries and Peoples (1973), October 11, 1973, p. 13.
14. United Nations A/AC 109/L. 842, February 28, 1973.
15. *African World Annual,* 1967–68, p. 29.

increase in production. Churches and other voluntary organizations in North America and Europe protested against Gulf's investment in Portugal's war effort, but the adverse public opinion that these campaigns generated was not sufficient to discourage other corporations from seeking opportunities to invest in Angolan oil. Exxon, Texaco, Sun Oil, the Amerada Hess Corporation, and the Cities Service Company were all negotiating contracts which had reached various stages of agreement by the time Portuguese rule of Angola came to an end in 1974.

The production of iron, like that of petroleum, became significant in Portugal's economy in the mid-sixties and increased steadily as the nationalist military and political pressure escalated. The value of iron production rose from $1.4 million in 1967 to $45.8 million in 1970.

In value, the production of diamonds rated above iron. It had maintained a steadily growing production rate for many years but did not multiply as dramatically as oil and iron during the escalation of the war. Yet, during this critical period in Portugal's effort to provide economic support for its war, the value of diamond production increased from $40.8 million in 1967 to $59 million in 1971.[16]

Almost as dramatic as the increase in exploitation of minerals and agricultural produce was the growth of the manufacturing sector of the Angolan economy. During the period from 1962 to 1972, the respective gross production value increased more than fivefold, rising from $7,475,000 to $39,748,000. In the period from 1968 to 1972, the annual rate of industrial growth reached about 20 percent.

The only part of the economy that did not grow to meet the challenge of Angolan nationalism was the subsistence sector. This, of course, reinforced the arguments of the liberation movements. According to their analysis, the Portuguese were exploiting Angola's raw materials to profit the metropole and the foreign nations that had increased their financial investments in the colony. The Angolan economy, following the typical colonial pattern, was directed toward exports; by 1970 the export value was about $74 per head, representing about double

16. United Nations A/9023 (III), p. 20.

the African developing countries' average, surpassed only by Zambia with its copper exports. Three years later, Angola's exports had jumped to $124 per capita. However, the subsistence sector, upon which most Angolans depended, remained stagnant at about $70 per capita[17] for the twenty years from 1953 to 1973.

Economic Opposition

Angola's economic growth in the late sixties and early seventies seemed to justify Portugal's determination to keep control of its largest and richest colony. Yet, as the cost of the colonial wars escalated, the debate sharpened within Portuguese nationalist circles over whether Portugal should orient its economy toward Europe or Africa. The Salazar-Caetano view of Portuguese nationalism conserved the anachronistic principle that the sending of inferior products to the protected colonial markets and receiving of raw materials at depressed prices was sound economics. Portugal should have learned from its experience in prolonging the slave trade through the nineteenth century that such colonial dependence actually stunts the growth of both the metropolitan and the colonial economies. Opposition to this colonialist economic position did appear among some young technocrats, who became known as Europeanists since they saw the economic future of Portugal in Europe rather than in Africa. When Caetano succeeded Salazar as prime minister in 1968, he appointed some of these technocrats to important government posts, which strengthened the "Europeanist" opposition. However, under pressure from the conservative "colonialists" the technocrats were forced out of the government by 1972 and many of them became associated with a group established two years earlier, called SEDES (Association for Social and Economic Development). In a booklet entitled *Portugal para onde vais?* SEDES outlined the economic options that would vie for acceptance: (a) Western European capitalism; (b) elite capitalism (e.g., the Caetano regime); (c) Western socialism (e.g., the USSR and Sweden); and (d) another kind of socialism (e.g., decentraliza-

17. F. Distler, "Angola: Preliminary Country Development Brief and Proposals for Technical Assistance" (mimeographed, December 4, 1974), p. 3.

tion along the lines of China or Tanzania). In the opinion of one observer, "SEDES favored the fourth option and they clearly had considerable influence on the opposition forces, including the MFA and General Spínola himself."[18]

The conflict between the "colonialists" and "Europeanists" was not simply one of economic theory or analysis. The Portuguese economy, without waiting for the resolution of the theoretical argument, shifted from its dependence on the colonies as trade with Europe expanded. From 1959 to 1972, Portugal's exports to the European Free Trade Association and European Economic Community (EFTA and EEC) increased from 40.3 percent to 61.3 percent, while its exports to the colonies were declining more precipitately, from 29.8 percent to 14.7 percent. Portugal's imports moved in the same direction, from the colonies to Europe, but not as sharply as exports.[19] Curiously, although these statistics appeared in the Lisbon newspaper *Expresso* on April 20, 1974, just five days before the coup, few observers recognized that the economic foundation of the "colonialist" position had been so drastically eroded. In fact, the capitalists who were assumed to be principal supporters of the colonial wars had recognized before the politicians and the foreign analysts that the cost of colonialism was too high. Guinea, which was almost a fief of CUF (Companhia União Fabril), Portugal's largest conglomerate, was the most striking example of the economic futility of the colonial war. PAIGC, the most effective of the anti-Portuguese nationalist movements, caused Portugal to escalate its defense budget for that tiny West African colony until it reached hundreds of millions of dollars per year by the 1970s.[20] At the same time, Guinea's balance of trade showed a steadily increasing deficit as exports remained stable and imports rose rapidly to meet defense demands. The Guinea-Bissau economy was tiny, even by Portuguese standards, but its economic crisis had a critically important impact on the struggle within Portuguese nationalism between "colonialists" and "Europeanists."

18. Gerald J. Bender, "Portugal and Her Colonies Join the Twentieth Century: Causes and Initial Implications of the Military Coup," *Ufahamu,* 4, no. 3 (Winter 1974), 121.
19. Ibid., p. 119.
20. Ibid., p. 120.

The Mello brothers, who were the principal owners of CUF and two of the most prominent capitalists in Portugal, realized that it no longer made economic sense to continue their support of the Caetano regime. According to the same observer, "Once these men and others in the large business sector adopted the position that their best interests were served by expanding trade abroad rather than with the colonies, the wars became liabilities rather than assets. And once these business oligarchs got off the Caetano bandwagon, the regime was in very serious trouble."[21]

Political Opposition

The disaffection of crucial economic interests within Portuguese nationalism was not commonly recognized until the Salazar-Caetano regime fell. The political opposition was more visible since it surfaced during each electoral period.

Salazar always identified his political program with Portuguese nationalism and defined the purpose of his dictatorship as being "the establishment of a political, economic and social nationalism . . . dominated by the uncontestable sovereignty of the Strong State."[22] Therefore he counted any opposition to his program or policies as antinational and antipatriotic. The political police (PIDE), the Portuguese youth movement (Mocidade Portuguesa), the volunteers of the Spanish Civil War who had formed the Legião Portuguesa, and the official censorship, all were organized to protect the New State and eliminate all opposition. Nevertheless, opposition persisted.

The republican and democratic forces in Portugal had been encouraged by the Allied victory in Europe in 1945 to form the Movement of Democratic Unity (MUD), which hoped to start in Portugal "a legal and orderly revolution in the internal political system with the affirmation of principle and ideas which rule gloriously in the countries of the most advanced civilization."[23] The government dissolved parliament and announced free elections for November 1945. However, the opposition soon recog-

21. Idem.
22. Oliveira Marques, II, 294.
23. *Eleições legislativas—subsídios para a história da vida portuguesa 1945/1973* (Lisbon: Edições Delfos, 1973), pp. 9–10.

nized that it needed more than the month allowed for the campaign to properly organize its ranks, and MUD petitioned the president to delay the elections for at least six months. When the petition was denied, the opposition decided to abstain and all the candidates of the official party, União Nacional, were elected as they had been in 1934, 1938, and 1942. Shortly after the election a wave of persecution against those who had supported MUD swept hundreds into prisons and others—including military officials—out of their government employment. It appeared that Salazar had not expected such strong opposition.

The united political opposition made its greatest show of strength in the presidential election of 1949, but it still lost. MUD nominated the elderly general Norton de Matos, who had been governor of Angola for two terms in the republican period. As had consistently happened, on the eve of the election the opposition withdrew because the government refused to change its regulations to allow for the free registration and voting by opposition supporters. However, in various regions of Angola where Norton de Matos' prestige was high and the opposition went to the polls, the opposition won majorities.[24]

The presidential election of 1958 not only produced a strong opposition candidate, General Humberto Delgado, but even revealed dissension within the regime. President Craveiro Lopes was not a candidate for reelection, either refusing because of disagreements with Salazar or being rejected by the dictator. Salazar chose his navy minister, Américo Tomás, as the official party candidate. He was opposed by Delgado, an air force officer and general director of civil aeronautics who attracted considerable support by his charismatic style. Contrary to the usual practice of opposition candidates, Humberto Delgado did not abstain at the last minute and he maintained that he had won. However, the official results gave Delgado only one-fourth of the votes and the regime followed its usual practice of punishing prominent opposition leaders. Delgado was dismissed from his government position and sought asylum in the Brazilian Embassy.

The repression of the opposition to Salazar's nationalism in-

24. Oliveira Marques, II, 351.

creased when Humberto Delgado was assassinated by the political police in 1965 and Mário Soares, the Socialist leader, was deported to São Tomé.[25] The increasingly senile Salazar seemed to have lost control of the country to his own creations, the censor and the political police. In the late sixties the legal opposition, which had courageously albeit futilely protested at each election period, became more frustrated and hoped for a change by means other than protest or elections.

In September 1968 change came in an unexpected way. António Salazar fell and suffered a cerebral hemorrhage from which he never recovered. President Américo Tomás called Marcelo Caetano to assume the post of prime minister.

One political anecdote at the time of transition from Salazar to Caetano described the latter as a driver who gave a signal to the left but turned right.[26] The signal was seen in the call to Mário Soares to return from exile and the readmission of many other political refugees; in the placing of PIDE under the restraint of the justice ministry; and in the slight modification in the powers of the censor. Also, the political opposition was allowed to hold a congress, and previously banned books began to appear. The signal that was watched most closely was the election of November 1969. For the first time in forty-four years the opposition went to the polls in Portugal and even participated in the inspection of the votes. A few independent candidates were allowed to run for the National Assembly on the official party ticket and, of course, they won.

These new "liberal" legislators were some of the first to recognize that Caetano had given a false signal. The conflict between the new prime minister and the opposition centered on the colonial question. He devoted more than half of his first policy speech to African questions, affirming that: "Portugal cannot abandon her people, of whatever color or race, to the whims of violence, to the fury of resentments, to tribal hatreds, or to the devious maneuvers of international politics.... We defend not one civilization, but civilization itself."[27] Caetano became more

25. Ibid., p. 357.
26. Ibid., p. 410.
27. *Africa Report*, 14 (Feb. 1969), 32.

rigorous than his predecessor in suppressing any discussion of Portuguese colonialism or of alternate solutions to the African wars.

The political opposition increased as the burden of the colonial wars became heavier, and the government allowed a Congresso Democrático to meet in Aveiro in April 1973, six months before the electoral campaign. Although discussion of the colonial war was still officially prohibited in Portugal, most of the speeches and the resolutions at Aveiro dealt directly or indirectly with the war and linked the establishment of democracy in the metropole with the decolonization of the African territories.

POLITICAL OPPOSITION IN EXILE

The Portuguese political opposition, frustrated within the system, also became active underground and in exile. General Humberto Delgado had helped to form the Frente Patriótica de Libertação Nacional (FPLN) in Algeria. This "front" was rent by internal strife, principally between Delgado's supporters, who proposed to infiltrate the Portuguese military and government through an internal underground, and the Portuguese Communist Party's strategy, calling for a long struggle leading toward a mass "popular uprising."[28] The Communists won control of the FPLN and the Algerian government ejected Delgado from his FPLN office. Within a few weeks, the slain body of the former air force general was discovered in Spain near the Portuguese border.[29] Under Communist leadership the FPLN continued its publications and broadcasts from Algeria, but Delgado's judgment was vindicated by the events of 1974, when the regime was overthrown by an underground movement within the military itself.

Religious Opposition

The opposition to the Lisbon regime came from elements in the Catholic Church as well as from economic interests and politicians. During the 1958 presidential elections, when Humberto Delgado was leading a strong political opposition, the

28. Marcum, II, 180.
29. Idem.

Bishop of Porto, Dom António Ferreira Gomes, not only[30] wrote
to Salazar insisting on governmental changes but even had the
temerity to circulate the letter. The bishop went into exile, but
this did not stifle the Church's criticism of the Salazar regime. In
fact, opposition was stimulated the next year when Pope John
XXIII announced his intention to call an ecumenical council for
the updating, *aggiornamento,* of the Catholic Church. The open
style encouraged by Pope John and many of the texts enacted by
the council threatened the conservative Portuguese ecclesiastical
and political hierarchies. Strong supporters of the Vatican
Council became suspect. The hierarchies feared, for example,
three Holy Ghost fathers in Lisbon who, with the encouragement of Vatican II, freely expressed their progressive ideas.
Inexplicably, the Portuguese officials sent the three missionaries
to Angola rather than disciplining them in the metropole. Indeed, they gave them strategic ecclesiastical positions in the colony where the war was escalating. Padre Jorge Sanches became
rector of the largest seminary, Cristo Rei in Nova Lisboa, and
Padres A. F. Santos Neves and Waldo Garcia, a Spaniard, were
assigned to his staff.

Inspired and supported by the Vatican Council documents,
the three progressive missionaries opened up theological, political, and sociological doors, not only to the seminarians with
whom they worked daily, but also to many clergy and lay members of the Church. The bishop of Nova Lisboa, Dom Daniel
Junqueira, with considerable misgivings, allowed the three
priests to establish the Instituto Superior Católico, which spon-
sored various lecture series and ecumenical encounters. The
impact of Sanches, Waldo, and Santos Neves, and indirectly of
the Vatican Council, was felt especially by the younger clergy.
Twenty-two Holy Ghost missionaries in Angola signed a statement sharply criticizing the Church's support of the Portuguese
colonial system:

What is the point of a society of baptized Christians . . . which lets a rich
communal life, such as the African peoples enjoyed, go to rack and
ruin? . . . How can such a society witness to brotherly love and poverty

30. Hugh Kay, *Salazar and Modern Portugal* (New York: Hawthorn, 1970), p.
360.

when it parades a style of life which shows an imposing, impressive, official and intimate connection with the powers of this world, and is conditioned by these powers? How can a church witness, as the Gospel demands, to understanding and peace, when, in an armed struggle that has been going on for nine years already, it does not publicly try to bring the opposing parties together round the negotiating table? How can people believe in the disinterestedness and full freedom of the bishops when public opinion can only see them as State officials with the same privileges as these high officials of the State in matters of salary, housing, transport, protocol and even retirement pension?

We feel that, as Portuguese, we have a special responsibility as preachers of the Gospel in this land where we want to stay. . . . We cannot, in conscience, accept a system of missionary activity such as it exists here at present, and to give it active support would constitute a grave mistake.[31]

The hierarchy, which had deported the three progressive missionary priests from the metropole to Angola, expelled them from the colony in 1968–69: Padre Sanches to the offices of the General Council of the Congregation in Rome, Santos Neves to Paris, where he later left the priesthood, and Waldo Garcia to Spain. The latter wrote an article describing the "Two Churches of Angola": one white, Portuguese, self-satisfied, the other black, African, suffering. Since the hierarchy belonged to the first of these churches, it did not allow the second to speak, which led to the defection of some of the more progressive seminarians and priests. The loyalty of the hierarchy to Portuguese colonialism hid the fact that more Catholic than Protestant missionaries were expelled from Angola during the war of liberation. Santos Neves became the chief publicist for the religious opposition by publishing five books between 1968 and 1975, composed principally of the papers, lectures, and reports of the short-lived but fecund Instituto Superior Católico de Nova Lisboa.[32]

31. *Governmental Policy and the Church in the Portuguese Territories of Africa,* IDOC International No. 43 (Rome, 1972), pp. 29–30. The complete correspondence, including the reply of the Episcopal Conference, is found in A. F. Santos Neves, *Quo vadis, Angola?* (Angola: Editorial Colóquios, 1974), pp. 235–54.

32. In addition to *Quo vadis, Angola?*, A. F. Santos Neves published the lectures and papers of the Instituto Superior Católico de Nova Lisboa in various forms:

The erosion of the support of Portuguese colonialism by the Roman Catholic Church became most visible on July 1, 1970, when three leaders of liberation movements from Portuguese colonies were received by Pope Paul VI in the Vatican. Agostinho Neto of MPLA, Amilcar Cabral of PAIGC, and Marcelino dos Santos of FRELIMO, who had been attending an International Conference in Support of the Peoples of the Portuguese Colonies in Rome, stayed over for the privately arranged interview. This outraged the Portuguese government, which had diplomatic relations with the Vatican through the Concordat. Prime Minister Caetano tried to assert that this audience implied no recognition of the movements:

Taking advantage of a routine event in the Pontiff's life, namely the weekly collective audience given to visitors, the terrorists insinuated themselves into the Pope's presence as Catholics and Christians, engaged him in a discussion which could scarcely be heard and later used this for spectacular effect with the aim of compromising our country.[33]

Radio Vatican, however, did not agree with this interpretation and answered:

That the audience of the leaders of the three movements struggling against Portuguese authorities in Africa was only able to take place by prior consent; that the delegates of the Decolonization Committee of UNO had attended the anti-colonialist conference in Rome, in company with the leaders of the liberation movements; that the attitude of the Church towards the independence of the new nations remains unchanged and is well known through the documents of the Council, the encyclicals and the allocutions of Paul VI."[34]

Although the Portuguese government withdrew its ambassador from the Vatican over this incident, it still had confidence

---

Ecumenismo em Angola: do ecumenismo cristão ao ecumenismo universal (Nova Lisboa-Angola: Editorial Colóquios, 1968); *Liturgia, cristianismo e sociedade em Angola* (Lisbon: Livraria Editora Pax, 1968); *Negritude e revolução em Angola* (Paris: Edições "Etc," 1974); and *Para um ecumenismo omnitotidimensional em Angola* (Angola: Editorial Colóquios, 1975).

33. Arslan Humbaraci and Nicole Muchnik, *Portugal's African Wars: Angola, Guinea-Bissão, Mozambique* (Dar es Salaam: Tanzania Publishing House, 1974), p. 204.

34. Idem.

in the Catholic hierarchy. A council on countersubversion in the Húila district of Angola expressed this confidence in a report:

We believe that the bishops of Angola have manifested very well their patriotism and their dynamic will for the expansion of the Catholic faith among the masses, with the accent on civilizing in the constructive sense of portugalization.[35]

The same council gave a negative evaluation of the influence of the Protestant missions:

In meetings of the District Council we have often spoken about the pernicious influence which the Protestant missions exercise through individuals who made harmful statements and propaganda. These are foreign agents who exert influence over the native masses. They generate admiration and enthusiasm for certain anti-Portuguese ideologies and movements. They surreptitiously undermine the idea of Portuguese citizenship. They create mentalities in the service of ideas inimical to Portugal. At best they limit themselves to propagating a religious ideology not in conformity with our tradition. They neutralize our efforts for portugalization and occupy key positions which make it easy for them to implant ideas contrary to our interests.[36]

For the Portuguese authorities, the crowning proof of the Protestants' subversive influence was the identification of the major mission-church agencies with the three liberation movements. Holden Roberto, named after a British missionary, was educated in Baptist Missionary Society schools. However, the tie between the FNLA, the Baptists, and the Bakongo was not simply in the person of Roberto. After the outbreak of the revolt in northern Angola in March 1961, hundreds of thousands of refugees fled to Zaïre, not only as individuals but in village groups. It was the church which provided the necessary cohesion to keep the bands together as they fled the military zone. It was also a Baptist mission in the lower Congo which provided food, clothing, tools, and seed as well as moral and spiritual support to the refugees.

Agostinho Neto was the son of a Methodist pastor and studied medicine with a scholarship from the Methodist Church. The

35. *Angola: Secret Government Documents on Counter-Subversion*, trans. and ed. Caroline Reuver-Cohen and William Jerman (Rome: IDOC, 1974), p. 119.
36. Ibid., p. 115.

Rev. Domingos da Silva, a Methodist minister, was vice-president of the MPLA, and Deolinda Rodrigues de Almeida, a cousin of Neto and also a Methodist Crusade scholar, held several important posts in the party before she died or was killed in the war. The arrest and expulsion of four American Methodist missionaries in 1961 for allegedly "running a school for terrorists, teaching courses with hidden meanings, and importing refrigerators filled with guns" certainly identified the Methodist missions with the liberation struggle in the minds of the Portuguese and of the Angolans.

Agostinho Neto, while on Methodist scholarship support in Lisbon, admitted to the mission board that he no longer considered himself a Christian believer. The MPLA also explicitly refuted religion and supernaturalism in its third-grade science book.[37] Nevertheless, the Portuguese knew that the sympathies of the Methodist Church in Angola were with the MPLA and in 1966–67 imprisoned many of the church's leaders, including a number of women, whom they suspected of giving financial aid to the movement.

Jonas Savimbi grew up in the Chilesso Mission and like the other liberation leaders studied abroad with a church scholarship. The Portuguese council of countersubversion considered the influence of the Dondi Mission nefarious.

Military Opposition

Civil and religious opposition within Portuguese nationalism persisted through the Salazar-Caetano regime, but it was not able to change the system. Military opposition to Salazarist nationalism also appeared regularly and finally it won the victory for anticolonial, democratic, socialistic nationalism. It was the Movement of the Armed Forces that played a crucial role in overthrowing the regime.

In 1946 a military revolt broke out in the north of Portugal, and although it was easily crushed by the government's forces, military opposition to Salazarist nationalism persisted. The next year another military plot was discovered in which even President António Carmona was suspected of participating.

37. Movimento Popular de Libertação de Angola, Departamento de Educação e Cultura, *Ciências naturias 3 classe* (Holland, 1972), pp. 103–6.

After the government declared Américo Tomás victor over Humberto Delgado in the 1958 election, the air force general pled with four other generals who were chiefs-of-staff to impede the inauguration of Tomás. They did not respond, but other lower officers and civilians formed the Movimento Militar Independente, which laid plans for a military coup. The Portuguese Communist Party was part of the movement but withdrew shortly before March 12, 1959, the date set to take control of the military establishments, radios, and newspapers. At the last minute the authorities suspected some subversive activity and just before the zero hour put the strategic barracks and headquarters on alert. When faced with the necessity of actually entering into combat, the leaders cancelled the coup and several of them were arrested.[38] Delgado's political charges during the campaign and the attempted coup made the armed forces sensitive to the criticism that the Portuguese military was a pretorian guard defending a dictatorship that it detested.[39]

In 1961 important elements in the military saw the specter of colonial war on three continents. The Minister of National Defense, General Botelho Moniz, told Prime Minister Salazar that the armed forces would confront "a suicide mission from which we could not come out alive."[40] As early as August of 1960 the conflicting views regarding the colonial situation became evident within the Portuguese military. One side included the Minister of Defense, Botelho Moniz, and Colonel Costa Gomes, Subsecretary of the Army, who believed that a political solution leading to self-determination was the only way to avoid this suicide. The most articulate spokesman for the "intransigent military defense of the colonies"[41] was Kaúlza de Arriaga, Subsecretary for the Air Force, who discovered the plot to oust Salazar in March of 1961. Salazar appointed himself as minister of defense, which removed the danger of the coup being led by Júlio

38. Avelino Rodrigues, Cesário Borga, and Mário Cardoso, *O movimento dos capitães e o 25 de Abril: 229 dias para derrubar o fascismo*, 3d ed. (Lisbon: Morães Editores, 1975), pp. 161–82.
39. Ibid., p. 164.
40. Ibid., p. 183.
41. Ibid., p. 186.

Botelha Moniz, and immediately implemented the hard line in Angola by sending troops *já em fôrça*, "in full force."

The support of the armed forces for Salazarist nationalism suffered another blow with the Indian conquest of the Portuguese enclave of Goa, Damão and Diu in December 1961. Salazar had exhorted the Portuguese to resist the invasion, but did not supply troops or supplies. The military opposition to the regime always presented itself as faithfully patriotic—but rebelled at being the scapegoat for the regime's ineptitude.

The Movement of the Armed Forces

The Movement of the Armed Forces, which finally ended fifty years of fascist nationalism in Portugal, started out as an elitist revolt of career officers and in nine months had become a revolutionary force which established a new anticolonial, democratic, and socialist nationalism.

In July 1973 the Portuguese government issued a decree to increase the supply of career officers to the infantry, artillery, and cavalry. The Military Academy was not attracting students and by 1973 only 72 of the 423 places in the school were filled. Therefore the government issued Decree 353/73, providing that drafted noncareer officers who were mostly students or professional men could become regular officers if they studied for two semesters at the academy. Career officers protested the decree which, they felt, discredited their professional training and prestige. After several weeks of pressure from the officers the government issued a revised decree which did not change the essence of the previous ruling but protected the majors and superior officers.

A group of career captains met August 21, 1973, and formed the first cell with the idea of organized, continuing action against the decree. Simultaneously, meetings were being held by officers in Guinea. The first mass meeting of the captains was held September in Evora, Portugal, with 136 officers present. They considered demonstrating against the government in Lisbon and formulated a statement to be presented to the prime minister. All the officers signed the document in Evora and another 190 added their names later. The petition was sent to the colonies, where officers supported it with their signatures.

The officers in Angola took the most radical action. Each one agreed to write his personal letter of resignation and also to sign a joint letter of resignation to take effect if and when the decrees were implemented. The Angolan meeting was also distinguished by the fact that the career officers invited noncareer officers to attend and lend their support.

On September 14, 1973 the military governor of Lisbon issued an official note warning officers against any unauthorized actions, but this did not deter the protests. In fact, the very next day the first information bulletin of the "Movement" was sent out to military units in the metropole and the colonies. The number of officers who committed themselves to resign if the decree were enforced increased rapidly and by October 30, 1973 there were 598, with the metropole accounting for 368, Angola 120, Mozambique 60, and Guinea 50.[42]

The rapid development of the movement was not only numerical but ideological. After three months of almost exclusive preoccupation with their own privileged status as career officers, the movement in November 1973 suddenly plunged into radical criticism of the regime's politics and especially of the colonial war. A lieutenant colonel affirmed: "We must awake from this nightmare. We must end, once and for all, this damned colonial war, which is consuming everything, including the dignity of military professionals of a civilized nation."[43]

A week after listening to this call to action the "captains" met in Obidos in Portugal and voted on three alternatives: immediate revolution; revolution after a more or less extended period of preparation; or revolution as the last resort after exhausting all means of negotiation with the government. The third alternative of revolution as a last resort received the most support, but the option of immediate revolution gained enough votes to surprise everyone.

What produced this rapid ideological shift from a conservative struggle to protect the prestige of the military profession to radical criticisms of the regime and its colonial war? First, the high

42. Dinis de Almeida, *Origens e evolução do movimento de capitães, subsídios para uma melhor compreensão* (Lisbon: Edições Sociais, 1977), p. 177.
43. Ibid., p. 206.

command, which became known as the "Rheumatic Brigade," had become so decrepit that it not only alienated the career officers by its first decree, and then the noncareer officers by its second, but offended the whole of the military by its ineptitude. Second, some political radicals were in the movement from the beginning and took advantage of the government's mistakes to lead the elitist protest to a revolutionary revolt. Third, most of the noncareer officers had come out of the radicalized academic or university communities of the metropole; when they joined the movement toward the end of 1973, they strengthened the few radicals who had been active from the beginning.

The dissension within the Portuguese armed forces did not reflect serious military problems for them in Angola. In fact, in eastern Angola the Portuguese had successfully carried out "Operation Attila" in 1972–73, using napalm and defoliants in scorched-earth assaults on nationalist villages. By May 1973 the Lisbon press carried articles confidently describing the decline in insurgent activity in Angola.[44] It was only in Guinea and Mozambique that PAIGC and FRELIMO were challenging the Portuguese militarily and politically.

Angolan Military Weakness

The Angolan armed forces, on the other hand, had suffered serious fluctuation in their fortunes during the thirteen years of the war of independence, and in 1973 they were at a low ebb. The MPLA's army, EPLA (Exército Popular de Libertação de Angola), had reached its peak strength in eastern Angola in 1970–71 when it carried out some 59 percent of the nationalist actions against the Portuguese. Guerrilla forces in Vietnam inspired the MPLA and it named two of its principal bases Hanoi II and Ho Chi Minh. At Hanoi II, Dr. Américo Boavida, the head of the medical services of MPLA, was killed during a Portuguese air attack in 1968. Ho Chi Minh surrendered to the Portuguese in 1972. EPLA suffered especially from Operation Attila. Whether as cause or effect, the military reverses were accompanied by political and diplomatic setbacks. In 1972–73, Agostinho Neto transferred 800 EPLA troops from the eastern

44. Marcum, II, 201.

front to Congo-Brazzaville and the Soviet Union withdrew support from MPLA. On the eve of the Angolan nationalist political victory the MPLA military was at its weakest.

ELNA (Exêrcito de Libertação Nacional de Angola), the FNLA's military arm, had the logistic advantage of exclusive access to Angola across the Zaïre border. Its major external base, Kinkuzu, in the Lower Congo district of Zaïre, also enjoyed a favorable location and the protection of the Zaïre government. However, these advantages contributed to the relative passivity of the ELNA forces, which were numerically larger than either of the other major movements. As Jonas Savimbi and the other rebels charged in 1964 (see Chapter 6), the FNLA fought a frontier war and did not use its logistical advantage to press aggressively into the interior of Angola. The FNLA did open an eastern front north of the UNITA-MPLA operational zones but, as in the north, sent patrols into Angola from a staging base in Zaïre, near Kolwezi.

Portugal in 1969 raided Mpinda, a Zaïrean border village that FNLA used as a rest camp and staging base. The Zaïre authorities then shut down three border camps and pulled the ELNA forces back to Kinkuzu from which it was more difficult to launch incursions into Angola.[45] ELNA actions declined and the Zaïre frontier was reopened to local trade.

The FNLA's military strength was struck another blow in 1972 when troops mutinied and Zaïrean forces had to intervene to rescue Holden Roberto from almost certain overthrow.[46] This placed the FNLA under closer Zaïrean tutelage and the Zaïre army more actively reorganized, retrained, and equipped the FNLA forces. At the same time the number of ELNA soldiers increased as large-scale recruiting—almost conscription—took place among the large Angolan refugee population in the Lower Congo. On the eve of the Angolan nationalist victory, the FNLA was able to mount an impressive parade of troops in smart uniforms before diplomatic representatives from twenty-two countries who had been flown to Kinkuzu by Zaïrean helicopters.[47] Yet the number and appearance of the FNLA troops were

45. Ibid., p. 219.
46. Ibid., p. 220.
47. Idem.

misleading. They proved disorganized and ineffective when the civil war broke out in 1975.

UNITA's military arm, FALA (Fôrças Armadas de Libertação de Angola), suffered for lack of an outside base and arms suppliers. Some of the Chokwe troops that had formed the core of UNITA's initial attack on Teixeira de Sousa on Christmas Day, 1966 defected to FNLA and MPLA when UNITA was not able to supply them with arms and munitions. In 1972 UNITA claimed 4,000 "well-trained men and women,"[48] though a Portuguese estimate of April 1974 went as low as 300 and a report published by the International Institute for Strategic Studies in London credited UNITA with something over 1,000.[49] Out of necessity, UNITA emphasized political education and self-reliance. "To liberate territory is of no interest to us, we want to liberate consciousness. . . . The army and the armed struggle are in a way secondary, for one does not conduct a nationalist war in the absence of national consciousness."[50] Foreign journalists who walked into Angola in August 1973 and attended the Third Congress of UNITA seemed to confirm that UNITA had established "a nation within a nation" although their military strength was minimal.[51]

Intermovement conflicts in Angola weakened Angolan nationalist forces so that they were not able to present the threat to the Portuguese authority that PAIGC and FRELIMO offered in Guinea and Mozambique. For example, the MPLA and FNLA could not exploit the advantages they had over the Portuguese of popular support and rugged terrain because of their internecine warfare. Since the FNLA's alliance with Zaïre gave them control of the border, it was able to apprehend the MPLA soldiers as they moved in and out of northern Angola. In March 1967, FNLA forces captured a group of twenty MPLA militants, including five women, returning to Zaïre from northern Angola. The most famous of those captured was Deolinda Rodrigues de Almeida, a member of the MPLA Executive Committee, whom Roberto imprisoned at Kinkuzu, where it is presumed that she

48. "The War in Angola," Harvard-Radcliffe student booklet, 1973.
49. Marcum, II, 217.
50. Idem.
51. "The War in Angola," p. 4.

was executed.[52] Later, Commander João Gonçalves Benedito, another member of the MPLA Executive Committee, was apprehended with nine other militants and also imprisoned in Kinkuzu, never to be seen again.[53] In 1968, Agostinho Neto claimed that the FNLA was keeping nearly 100 MPLA militants in Kinkuzu, which became as infamous as a prison as it was famous as a military base.

The FNLA also blocked attempts by the MPLA to reinforce its northern front, and as a result the northern headquarters base of BRNO fell to the Portuguese in 1968. "According to Portuguese officers, hatred between the two forces was such that MPLA informers 'often' disclosed FNLA positions and let the Portuguese wipe out an FNLA unit."[54] UNITA claimed to have captured arms from both the Portuguese and MPLA troops since it had no regular external supply. "In 1972 an MPLA deserter alleged that his unit had, in fact, done most of its fighting against UNITA."[55]

Not only this intermovement conflict, but also intramovement dissension weakened Angolan nationalism in its struggle with Portuguese colonialism. Holden Roberto kept control of the FNLA by ruthlessly eliminating anyone who challenged his command, and survived the two major challenges to his leadership: the Umbundu revolt and resignations led by Jonas Savimbi in 1964 and the Kinkuzu mutiny in 1972. MPLA's dissensions are associated with three names: Viriato da Cruz, Mário de Andrade, and Daniel Chipenda. Viriato rebelled against MPLA policy in 1963 and, after trying to align himself with FNLA, went to China, where he died in exile. Mário de Andrade abandoned his active role in MPLA in the mid-sixties and in February 1974 led the "active revolt" of a group of intellectuals who criticized Neto's leadership. Daniel Chipenda, the Umbundu who had been one of the principal leaders on MPLA's eastern front, revolted when Neto made an agreement with the FNLA and withdrew most of the MPLA forces from the east. Chipenda led what

52. Marcum, II, 198.
53. Idem.
54. Marcum, II, 211.
55. Idem.

was called the Eastern Revolt and almost gained control of the movement as the colonial war came to an end.

Perhaps because UNITA was smaller and more concentrated it was less subject to factionalism. However, some assassination attempts on Jonas Savimbi were reported.

Efforts Toward Unity

Even the search for unity by the Angolan nationalist movements became a cause for contention among them. Each movement professed to advocate a united front against Portuguese colonialism but claimed a position within the front that the other parties would not accept. As the name indicated, the FNLA considered itself already a front and that the other movements should merely join the UPA and PDA in the Frente Nacional. Holden Roberto and most of the FNLA leaders feared that a truly united front would be dominated by the MPLA because of its greater political sophistication. The MPLA also assumed its superiority and so initiated unity negotiations which usually broke down due to Roberto's intransigence. UNITA was a tireless advocate of unity since such negotiations would at least have given it the recognition that it lacked both on the part of the other movements and internationally.

The Organization of African Unity (OAU) succeeded in gathering representatives of MPLA and FNLA around a common table to sign two agreements, but both attempts aborted before they produced a united front. Under the auspices of the OAU Conciliation Committee, MPLA and FNLA signed an accord on October 13, 1966, calling for a political as well as military cease-fire and a release of prisoners, but the agreement was promptly repudiated by Roberto. In 1972 the OAU made another serious effort at reconciliation through four African presidents, Kenneth Kaunda, Joseph Mobutu, Julius Nyerere, and Marien Ngouabi. Only the FNLA and MPLA were involved since the OAU did not recognize UNITA.

Both the FNLA and the MPLA were weak in 1972 and considered that cooperation with the OAU's reconciliation efforts could give them advantages. MPLA had suffered from Portugal's offensive in eastern Angola and needed access across the Zaïre border to its constituency in the northwest. The Kinkuzu mutiny had weakened the FNLA and it sought arms and external support that the OAU might provide. After months of negotiations a formal agreement was signed on December 13, 1972 in Kinshasa.

This agreement seemed more promising than previous unity efforts because it provided a structure for political and military collaboration between the MPLA and the FNLA. A Supreme Council for the Liberation of Angola was created to coordinate a unified military command and a political council. Cadres of both movements met to negotiate the implementation of the agreement, but they made no progress. The MPLA had not gained its principal objective—access to northwest Angola across the Zaïre border—and its militants were still subject to arrest within Zaïre. Even more serious for MPLA was the internal dissent precipitated by the unsuccessful negotiations. Daniel Chipenda and the other MPLA leaders on the eastern front felt that they had not been adequately consulted regarding the agreement with FNLA so they attacked Neto's political leadership. Then, when Neto withdrew the best troops from the east to take advantage of the anticipated access to the northwest, they condemned his military leadership. The Neto and Chipenda factions in Zambia broke into open conflict and finally the dissidents formed the "Eastern Revolt." So this supreme effort by the OAU resulted in a further division within MPLA rather than the unity of Angolan nationalism.

Competition for International Alliances

The conflicts within Angolan nationalism were caused not only by such domestic factors as regionalism, personal ambitions, cultural differences, and ideology but also by competition for international alliances and support. Journalists frequently exaggerated the dependence of the movements on specific allies and simplistically identified MPLA with the Soviet Union, FNLA with the United States, and UNITA with China. The picture was much more complex. In their more candid moments, spokesmen for all the movements admitted that they would accept aid from any source as long as it was given without unacceptable conditions. Agostinho Neto, in trying to destroy the image of undue dependence on one foreign ally, declared: "No country or organization could claim a monopoly on aid to the Angolan struggle."[56] In 1962 he traveled to Washington with Bishop Ralph Dodge to put his case before the American government and press and to remove pro-communist coloring from his movement's image.[57] Evidently he had some success because a U.S. embassy official in Leopoldville was quoted as saying, "U.S. policy is not, repeat not, to discourage the MPLA [Neto-Andrade faction] move toward the West and not to choose between these two movements."[58] The Soviet Union gave the most consistent support to MPLA, but even that was not uninterrupted. In 1973 the Soviet Union, concerned with the internal strife within the movement, withdrew its support. The MPLA also actively sought Chinese aid as Neto visited North Vietnam, North Korea, and China in 1971.[59] During the same period, Agostinho Neto toured the Scandinavian countries and they contributed to "certain activities" of MPLA, FRELIMO, and PAIGC in 1972–73.[60]

The FNLA, which reputedly depended exclusively on the United States, also negotiated with many countries to receive assistance. Holden Roberto in 1963 met with Chinese Foreign Minister Chen Yi during Kenya's independence celebrations (December 12, 1963) and with Soviet and Cuban representatives at the United Nations and then announced that he had been assured of "whatever we need in arms and money."[61] The fact that such assistance was not actually delivered at that time was not due to the potential donor's reluctance to give or to any ideological scruples on FNLA's part about receiving aid from the socialist nations, but rather to Mobutu's requirement that all material assistance to the movement or to the government-in-exile had to be channeled through the Congolese Government."[62]

Ten years later (December 1973), Holden Roberto led an

56. Marcum, II, 14.
57. Idem.
58. Marcum, II, 16.
59. Ibid., p. 230.
60. Ibid., p. 232.
61. Ibid., p. 132.
62. Ibid., p. 133.

FNLA delegation to China and returned to Kinshasa with a promise of substantial Chinese aid. Almost immediately he flew to Bucharest and signed a joint declaration of cooperation and friendship between the Rumanian Communist Party and the FNLA. Back in Zaïre at the thirteenth anniversary of the outbreak of the war, and only a month before the coup in Lisbon that ended the anticolonial struggle, Roberto announced that this "very special aid" from China and Rumania would give the Angolan struggle a "new thrust."[63]

UNITA, which did not even exist when the other two movements were negotiating for foreign assistance from 1961 to 1966, received only limited aid from China. The frequent journalistic association of UNITA and China did not represent significant dependence, but simply the fact that the People's Republic of China was the only government to publicly contribute to UNITA's support. UNITA, however, prized the tenuous tie with China and at its Third Congress in August 1973 extended its "gratitude to the People's Republic of China for its continuous support of our struggle for national liberation" and saluted China's entry into the United Nations as a "resounding victory" for "oppressed people of the world."[64]

The movements sought arms and diplomatic support from governments, yet their operations were so small that even the minor assistance offered by voluntary organizations could provide significant "humanitarian" aid which the movements turned to political advantage by satisfying some of the needs of their followers. In Western Europe and North America, nongovernmental organizations and small voluntary associations gave support to all three Angolan liberation movements. The most prominent and effective association in Europe was the Angola Comité, founded in Amsterdam in 1961, which gave ardent support to the MPLA and to its CONCP partners, FRELIMO and PAIGC. In North America, the Liberation Support Movement (LSM), organized in 1966, sent medical supplies, tents, and food to MPLA,[65] but its most significant contribution was the

63. Ibid., pp. 230–31.
64. Ibid., p. 230.
65. Ibid., p. 238.

publication of eyewitness accounts of the fighting in Angola by LMS leaders and by MPLA military officers.[66]

The World Council of Churches also responded to the Angolan nationalist movements' requests for assistance by establishing the Special Fund of the Program to Combat Racism in 1969. From 1970 through 1974 the program made grants totaling $1,050,000 "to organizations of oppressed racial groups or organizations supporting victims of racial injustice whose purposes are not inconsonant with the general purposes of the World Council." Of the total of $656,000 that was granted to Southern Africa liberation movements, the Angolan movements received $176,000: MPLA $78,000, FNLA $60,500, and UNITA $37,500.[67]

Opposition to Aid to Portugal

The Angolan nationalist movements complemented their efforts to receive international aid by campaigns to reduce the assistance going to the enemy, Portugal. During World War II, Portugal had maintained a strained neutrality between sympathy for the anticommunism of the Nazi and Fascist forces and the ties with its traditional ally Britain and other western European neighbors. Recognizing that the war was going against the Axis Powers, and under pressure from Britain, Portugal tilted its neutrality toward the Allies by agreeing to embargo wolfram exports to Germany and by negotiating with Britain and the United States for use of the Lages Airfield on the Azores Islands in the North Atlantic. The strategic advantage of the Azores base loomed large in 1949 as Portugal was admitted to the North Atlantic Treaty Organization (NATO) although its Iberian

66. "Liberation Support Movement Interview—Daniel Chipenda," taped in Lusaka, Zambia, August 28, 1969, by Don Barnett; "Liberation Support Movement Interview on Angola—Spartacus Monimambu," taped in Dar es Salaam, Tanzania, March 21, 1968, by Don Barnett; Roy Harvey, *People's War in Angola: Report on the First Eastern Regional Conference of the MPLA* (Seattle: LSM Information Center, 1970); and "Interview in Depth MPLA—Angola #4," interview with Paulo Jorge, director of MPLA's Department of Information and Propaganda (DIP) (Richmond, B.C., Canada: LSM Information Center, 1973).

67. Elisabeth Adler, *A Small Beginning: An Assessment of the First Five Years of the Programme to Combat Racism* (Geneva: World Council of Churches, 1974), pp. 15–17, 92–95.

partner, Spain, was not welcomed. A bilateral agreement was signed by the United States and Portugal during World War II and renewed periodically.

When the agreement was renewed in 1951, the United States began to give Portugal military aid. By 1953, the total U.S. military assistance of $71.5 million actually exceeded the Portuguese defense expenditure from their own domestic receipts—$70.5 million.[68] From that high, the aid decreased and by 1960 it was less than $10 million.

When the war broke out in northern Angola in 1961, the United States made some moves indicating that it might take a stand for the independence of Angola in spite of its ties with Portugal. The United States voted in favor of the March 15 United Nations resolution calling on Portugal to introduce reforms in conformity with the resolution on the granting of independence to colonial countries and peoples. Ambassador Adlai E. Stevenson made a speech which Portugal and the African nations interpreted as supportive of Angolan liberation, saying: "The United States would be remiss in its duties as a friend of Portugal if it failed to express honestly its conviction that step-by-step planning within Portuguese territories and its acceleration is now imperative for the successful political and economic and social advancement of all inhabitants under Portuguese administration—advancement, in brief, toward full self-determination."[69]

Supporters of African liberation, such as the American Committee on Africa, worked to convince American public opinion and the U.S. government to cut off aid to Portugal even if they were not prepared to give full-fledged support to the Angolan liberation movements. The course of U.S. policy toward Angola, however, took the opposite direction. After voting for Resolution 1742 in January 1962, reaffirming the right of the Angolan peoples to self-determination, deploring "repressive measures," and calling for reform and for no support and assistance to Portugal, the United States turned around in the United Nations

68. William Minter, *Portuguese Africa and the West* (Middlesex: Penguin, 1972), pp. 45–46.
69. Ibid., p. 78.

and voted with Portugal on all major issues involving the Portuguese colonies. Consistent with this new turn was the ap-
pointment by President John F. Kennedy of Admiral George W.
Anderson, Jr., as ambassador to Portugal; he showed his sympathy with Portugal's "civilizing presence" in Africa as he visited
Angola and Mozambique in 1964.

In 1969 the Nixon Administration strengthened the U.S. support of Portugal on the basis of National Security Study
Memorandum 39. This memorandum presented five options
for U.S. policy in Southern Africa and, if not formally, at least in
in practice, the Nixon Administration adopted Option 2, which
took as its premise: "The whites are here to stay and the only way
that constructive change can come about is through them. There
is no hope for the blacks to gain the political rights they seek
through violence, which will only lead to chaos and increased
opportunities for the communists."[70]

In 1962, Portugal had refused to enter an agreement for
American use of Lages air base in the Azores because of its
resentment of the U.S. anticolonialist stand. For nine years, the
United States used the airfield without a formal accord. Then in
December 1971 the United States and Portugal renewed their
agreement on Lages Field. The new accord and the closer relations between the United States and Portugal were given greater
visibility by a meeting at the Azores base between President
Richard Nixon, Prime Minister Marcelo Caetano, and President
Georges Pompidou of France. In return for the continued use of
the air base the United States offered a grant of $1 million for
educational projects, $5 million in nonmilitary surplus equip-
ment, and Public Law 480 credits of $30 million for the export
of surplus agricultural commodities. Export-Import Bank credit
of $400 million was also made available to Portugal for projects
to be approved. An Angolan liberation leader condemned this
United States support for Portugal on the grounds that, "President Nixon has come to Portugal's rescue with the new economic
aid agreement in exchange for America's Azores bases. Ameri-

70. *The Kissinger Study of Southern Africa: National Security Study Memorandum 39
(Secret)*, ed. Mohamed A. El-Khawas and Barry Cohen (Westport, Conn.: Lawrence Hill, 1976), p. 105.

can aid will equal the entire amount of Portugal's military budget for a year. American credits will free Portuguese funds for pursuit of war aims. American aid is the main factor that keeps the Portuguese from pulling out of Africa.[71]

The Azores base proved strategically valuable for the United States in 1973 when other NATO allies refused to allow the United States to use their air space to fly supplies to Israel in the October War. The United States refueled C-5A and C-141 cargo planes at the Azores base, but the Portuguese permission was bought at a high price, according to reports: the Administration pledged to work against an anti-Portuguese amendment to the foreign aid bill being considered by the U.S. Congress.[72]

The Angolan nationalists and their friends in Western Europe were no more successful in decreasing British, French, and German aid to Portugal during the anticolonial war than they were in cutting off American aid. In Great Britain, missionaries of the Baptist Missionary Society inspired the Baptist Union of Great Britain and Ireland to start a public protest against British support of Portugal. The protest climaxed in a petition with 37,524 signatures, presented to the House of Commons on July 5, 1961 which viewed "with grave concern the continuing harsh and oppressive policy of the Government of the Republic of Portugal towards many of its subjects in its African territory of Angola" and humbly prayed "that no military supplies should be allowed to be sent from the United Kingdom of Great Britain and Northern Ireland to the Republic of Portugal and its overseas territories in Africa . . . while such repressive policy is continued."[73] Such protests, which were joined by liberation support groups and Portuguese opposition groups in London, did not weaken the centuries-old Anglo-Portuguese alliance. After supporting the 1961–62 United Nations Resolutions critical of

71. "America's Foreign Policy: Report of the First Africa-Based Conference of African and American Representatives, Lusaka, Zambia, Jan. 17–21, 1972" (New York, African-American Institute, 1972), p. 21.

72. *African News: An Information Service of the Southern Africa Committee,* 1, 36 (October 29, 1973), 1–2.

73. Len Addicott, *Cry Angola!* (London: SCM Press, 1962), pp. 101, 144, and *Angola: A Symposium—Views of a Revolt* (London: Oxford University Press, 1962), pp. 58–79.

Portuguese colonial rule of Angola, Great Britain either abstained or opposed subsequent resolutions designed to put pressure on Portugal to free its African colonies. Britain also supplied frigates for the Portuguese navy, light aircraft for the air force, and jeeps to the army. Both Great Britain and the United States required assurances from Portugal that military assistance would be used only "to meet Portugal's NATO obligations."

France's support of Portugal was given without any political inhibitions and with no official restriction as to where it could be used. The Alouette helicopter supplied by France became particularly important in the latter years of the anticolonial war when the fighting became a duel between the Portuguese helicopters and the guerrillas' land mines.

West Germany, not being a member of the United Nations until 1973, was under less pressure to restrict its support of Portugal. During the colonial war, West Germany became the most important supplier of imports to Portugal, including large amounts of arms and aircraft. The West German Air Force acquired use of an air base in Beja, Portugal, which was constructed with German aid. The German military mission in Lisbon, which coordinated military relations between the two countries, was the largest foreign advisory group in Portugal.

This continued support of Portugal by the United States and Western Europe was called by Angolan nationalists the "NATO-ization" of the war: "The napalm that burns our children is 'made in USA,' the planes that bomb us are 'made in Italy,' the defoliants that destroy our harvests are 'made in Germany,' and the helicopters that transport the Portuguese commandos are 'made in France.' This is what we call the 'NATO-ization' of the war in Angola. We are certain that halting this military assistance to Portugal would hasten the end of the war."[74]

The war did not come to an end because external military assistance to Portugal was halted. Rather, internal dissension within Portuguese nationalism overthrew the regime which was

74. Manuel Jorge, "Massive Aid Required to Hasten End of War and Assist National Reconstruction," *Objective: Justice*, 5, no. 1 (January–March 1973), 12.

prosecuting the war. In retrospect, we can trace the military opposition to the regime, as we have above, but very few persons inside Portugal or outside were aware of the tremors that finally issued in the coup d'état of April 25, 1974.

The Portuguese Coup d'Etat

Two months before the coup, all of Portugal and much of Europe was awakened to the strength of the opposition by the publication of a best selling book by the most charismatic of the Portuguese military officers, General António de Spínola. *Portugal and the Future,* published on February 22, 1974, articulated criticisms of the regime which the political, economic, religious and military opposition had been formulating, each in its own sphere, but had not expressed publicly.

Politically, Spínola, who had instituted people's congresses in Guinea,[75] advocated free debate of all issues and equal opportunity of access to positions of political power—i.e., the parliamentary democracy that opposition candidates had proposed at each election. Economically, the general, who was close to the major capitalists, used the Europeanists' arguments proposing a rapid increase in industrialization and integration into the Common Market as the necessary means to achieve the desired prosperity for Portugal. Religiously, Spínola recognized that the authority of the Church in the future must be based on the principal that "to govern is to serve the community."[76] Finally, the deputy chief of staff of the armed forces affirmed that to try to win a guerrilla war militarily meant certain defeat. He agreed with the Movement of the Armed Forces (MFA) that the role of the military is only to create and conserve the security conditions that would permit sociopolitical solutions.

Prime Minister Caetano himself might have accepted the platform presented in *Portugal and the Future,* but he succumbed to pressure from the reactionary military hierarchy and dismissed both Spínola and the Chief of Staff, General Costa Gomes. The

75. Manuel Belchior, *Os Congressos do povo da Guiné* (Povoa de Varzim: Editora Arcádia, 1973).
76. António de Spínola, *Portugal e o futuro: Análise da conjuntura nacional,* 2d ed. (Lisbon: Arcádia, 1974), p. 38.

dismissals strengthened the MFA by providing possible standard bearers for the junior officers and rallying support of some business interests as well of the general public. Before the publication of the book, Costa Gomes was considered the most likely choice of the MFA for president of Portugal. The enthusiastic response to *Portugal and the Future* made Spínola a more attractive possibility for the top post.

The public acceptance of the book and the more open criticism of the regime led the MFA to attempt an ill-prepared coup d'état on March 16, 1974. The coup collapsed when it was discovered by forces loyal to the government and the regime assumed that by arresting and rusticating some of its leaders, the MFA had been effectively destroyed. Such complacency allowed the movement to work clandestinely and make more careful plans for a second try during the week of April 20, 1974.

On April 25, five short weeks after the abortive coup, the MFA overthrew in an almost bloodless coup d'état the police state which had ruled Portugal for forty-eight years. At twenty minutes after midnight, the announcer on the Catholic radio station read the chorus of a prohibited song:

> Grândola, dusky village, Land of Liberty
> The People are the rulers within you, O city.

At this signal, the MFA detained the commanders of the barracks and occupied the government radio-television stations without resistance. Simultaneously, the young officers took control of the key highways leading to the capital, the national bank, and the international airport.

By 4:20 A.M. the MFA broadcast an appeal to all inhabitants of Lisbon to stay in their houses and keep calm. Commands were given to the police, national guard, and other militarized units that were not part of the MFA to avoid any confrontation with the armed forces. The only violent confrontation on April 25 was between the MFA and the political police, the *Direcção Geral de Segurança* (DGS), in which five persons were killed: two DGS agents, two civilians, and one off-duty soldier.

The population of the capital did not obey the appeal, but out of curiosity filled the streets and soon began to show enthusiastic support for the revolutionary forces. As the coup proceeded peaceably, except for the shots exchanged around the DGS headquarters, the public gave flowers to the soldiers who patrolled the streets in their military vehicles, and a red carnation stuck in the mouth of a rifle became the symbol of the coup.

The Portuguese did not know just who or what the MFA was, but within twenty-four hours they were convinced that the old Salazar-Caetano regime had been overthrown. At 8:00 P.M. the government announced the surrender of Caetano to Spínola. Just twenty-four hours after the coup began, the Junta of National Salvation appeared on national TV and pledged to govern Portugal according to the program of the MFA.

On April 26 all the newspapers carried the program of the MFA. The very first phrase of the document referred to the colonial situation: "Considering that after 13 years of war in the overseas territories, the regime in power had not succeeded in defining concretely and objectively an overseas policy which would lead to peace among the Portuguese of all races and creeds. . . ."

THE REACTION IN ANGOLA

The news of the April 25 coup reached Angola, but its significance was not immediately clear. Although the first reason for the coup was given as the unsuccessful colonial policy, the news was received with much more uncertainty in Angola than in the metropole. With the departure of Caetano, Tomás, and the rest of the Cabinet and the capture of the Secret Police headquarters, no one in Portugal doubted that a revolution had started, but in Angola the same officials continued in power.

The contrast between General Spínola's image in Portugal and that in Angola was one cause of the difference in Portugal's and Angola's reactions to the coup. In the metropole, Spínola had become the best-known spokesman for the political opposition with the publication of *Portugal and the Future*. Among Angolans, he was known as an arrogant colonialist riding in a military jeep with monocle and swagger stick. Spínola's record in Angola as a hard-line officer from 1961 to 1964 was different from the fame he established as a relatively liberal general in Guinea from 1968 to 1973.

In his first speech to the nation, Spínola pledged himself and the Junta of National Salvation to guarantee the survival of Portugal as a "pluricontinental" nation. This phrase and the argument for a Portuguese federation in Spínola's book did not sound to the Angolan nationalists like the rhetoric of independence.

The governor-general of Angola, Santos e Castro, who was a close friend of Caetano, was removed from office April 27 and replaced temporarily by Colonel Soares Carneiro. At a press conference on May 3, Carneiro conceded that although the Angolan people were happy with the change of government in Lisbon, there still prevailed a climate of unrest because no political decisions had been made regarding the future of Angola. Even those Angolans who were optimistic about the future noted certain inconsistencies. In Portugal the hated political police was immediately abolished, but it continued in Angola. Even São José Lopes, who had been its director since it was established in the colony in 1957 and had disappeared on April 25, returned to his post in Luanda a few days later.

General Francisco Costa Gomes, the first member of the Junta Nacional de Salvação to visit Angola, did not clarify the new Lisbon government's colonial policy. He appealed to the liberation movements for a cease-fire and recognized that the war still continued. However, Portuguese troops were staying in their barracks and soon tension and boredom was reported among the soldiers.[77]

On May 19 the Portuguese commander-in-chief of the 50,000 troops in Angola ordered suspension of all military operations to allow the guerrillas to come out into the open peacefully in the hopes that a cease-fire could be signed.

The uncertainty about what April 25 meant in Angola was heightened on June 11 at the investiture of the new governor-general of Angola, Silvino Silvério Marques, who had been a hard-line governor-general of Angola from 1962 to 1966. His reappointment cast further doubt on the intentions of the Lisbon government to grant independence to Angola. At the ceremony in which Spínola installed Silvério Marques, the president

77. *New York Times,* June 5, 1974.

said that immediate independence for the colonies would be the most blatant negation of the democratic ideal.[78]

The equivocal actions and statements of the Lisbon government caused more doubts and consternation in Angola than in Mozambique and Guinea-Bissau. In May, negotiations between PAIGC and Portugal began in London. In June, Mário Soares, the Portuguese foreign minister, went to Lusaka, Zambia, to initiate negotiations with FRELIMO. Portugal was pressed to negotiate with Guinea-Bissau and Mozambique by the effective military operations which had been mounted by PAIGC and FRELIMO, and neither of those movements had any serious competition as it claimed to speak exclusively for its country.

MPLA and FNLA repeatedly affirmed that they would enter negotiations only after Portugal agreed to immediate independence for Angola. Jonas Savimbi was reported to have declared that the population of Angola was not prepared for immediate independence.[79] Then, on June 17, UNITA agreed to a cease-fire with Portugal.

By the end of July, MFA pressure had forced Spínola to promise freedom to the African territories.[80] Although MPLA and FNLA had bitterly criticized UNITA for signing a cease-fire with the Portuguese, they followed suit in October.

The April 25 coup released much pent-up political energy in Angola. Within weeks, a score of political organizations had sprung up among both black and white communities. The prospects of an election or referendum in Angola prompted these new organizations to formulate platforms that would attract a constituency. Although the sudden proliferation of these parties was impressive, they did not gain significant followings in their short lives.

As soon as each of the three movements had negotiated a cease-fire with the Portuguese government, it set up offices in all the population centers of the country and began political activities. MPLA was the last to set up its offices, in late October 1974. It became obvious that none of the post-coup political parties

78. *Revista de Angola,* no. 313 (June 15, 1974).
79. Idem.
80. *New York Times,* July 28, 1974.

could compete with the movements which had been fighting the anticolonial war and had solid regional constituencies. Therefore, the parties that had burst on the scene in May and June disappeared just as rapidly in October and November when the three movements stepped up their political campaigns. The announcement in late November of a summit meeting of the three movements was the final blow to the new parties and from that time any Angolan, black or white, who wished to participate actively in the political process was forced to align himself with the MPLA, FNLA, or UNITA.

The rush of supporters to the three headquarters began soon after April 25. MPLA sympathizers and militants flew off to Brazzaville to affirm their loyalty, as did FNLA supporters to Zaïre. The UNITA adherents filled the trains going from Lobito, Nova Lisboa, and Silva Porto to the headquarters southwest of Luso. Such visits resulted in military recruitment, which enlarged the armed forces of each movement as well as creating political enthusiasm in adherents who could return to their homes and organize local party groups.

At a summit meeting in Mombasa, Kenya, January 2–5, 1975, the three movements recognized each other as independent parties with equal rights and responsibilities. All other parties were to be excluded from the negotiations that would prepare for Angolan independence. They also agreed, following the example of FRELIMO, that they were not ready to take over immediately, but that a period of transition was necessary. During the transition period the three movements would work together with the Portuguese in order to lay the basis for an independent Angolan state. At Mombasa they also proclaimed that the territorial integrity of Angola was to be maintained with its colonial borders, rejecting any separatist claim. According to the Mombasa agreement, every inhabitant of Angola regardless of race could become a citizen of the new country.

The Transitional Government

Ten days later, at Alvor in Southern Portugal, the three movements and Portugal signed an agreement which spelled out in greater detail the general principles accepted in Mombasa. November 11, 1975, was set as the date for the proclamation of independence and full sovereignty of Angola. Until that date, all power would be exercised by a Portuguese high commissioner and a transitional government to be inaugurated January 31, 1975.

The presidents of the movements did not take posts in the transitional government; rather, they named trusted lieutenants to the presidential college. FNLA named Johnny Eduardo, who had held posts as president of FNLA's youth section and representative of the Front in North Africa, as well as being the Front's secretary for external relations. The second presidential colleague, Lopo do Nascimento, had been an active militant of MPLA since its inception in 1956. He was arrested by the Portuguese in 1959 and 1963 and since 1974 had been secretary of MPLA's Politburo. The UNITA president, José N'Dele, a Cabindan, had been secretary general of the National Union of Angolan Students and later was UNITA's secretary for youth.[81]

Beside the thirteen civil ministries in the transitional government, the Alvor Agreement established the National Defense Commission, which was to command an integrated army to be formed by 8,000 combatants from each of the movements and 24,000 Portuguese troops. The agreement also instructed the transitional government to hold elections for a constituent assembly by the end of October 1975.

Angolans were euphoric when the transitional government

81. The transitional government inaugurated January 31, 1975 was made up as follows (M-MPLA, U-UNITA, F-FNLA, P-Portugal): Presidential Council—Lopo do Nascimento (M), José N'Dele (U), Johnny Eduardo (F); Ministry of Interior—Ngolo Kabanku (F), Secretaries of State, Geologo Henrique Santos (M) and Waiken (U); Ministry of Information—Manuel Rui Monteiro (M), Secretaries of State, Jaka Jamba (U) and Hendrick Vaal Neto (F); Ministry of Labor and Social Security—António Dembo (U), Secretaries of State, Cornélio Caley (M) and Baptista Nguvulu (F); Ministry of Economy—Vasco Vieira de Almeida (P), Secretary of State for Industry and Energy, Augusto Lopes Teixeira (M), for Fisheries, Manuel Alfredo Teixeira Coelho (U), for Commerce and Tourism, Graça Tavares (F); Ministry of Planning and Finance—Saydi Mingas (M); Ministry of Justice—Diógenes Boavida (M); Ministry of Transportation and Communications—Albino Antunes da Cunha (P); Ministry of Health and Social Matters—Samuel Abrigada (F); Ministry of Public Works, Housing and Urbanization—Manuel Alfredo Rezende de Oliveira (P); Ministry of Education and Culture—Jerónimo Wanga (U); Ministry of Agriculture—Mateus Neto (F); Ministry of Natural Resources—Jeremias Kalandula Chitunda (U).

was inaugurated on January 31, 1975. The anxieties and uncertainties that had reigned in Angola since the April 1974 coup d'état seemed to vanish. Portugal's colonial policy had been clarified as the talk of federation and referendum ended and a definite date for independence had been accepted by all parties. The myriad political associations that appeared immediately after the coup disappeared, leaving the political field to the three movements which had fought against Portugal in the war of liberation. The whole Angolan population, black and white, accepted the fact that to be politically active meant to align oneself to one of the movements. Angolans were heartened by the presence in the government of men who had accumulated academic qualifications and experience in Portugal and internationally. The plan for integrated armed forces also gave the Angolans hope that law and order could be preserved without the intervention of foreign troops.

Angolans wanted to believe that they were on a smooth path to independence and unity. In retrospect, it can be seen that the euphoria of January-March 1975 was precariously based on the principle of peaceful competition for power laid down at Alvor. The agreement would have been workable only under one of two conditions: either genuine consensus among the movements in keeping to the rules of procedure agreed upon, or the presence of an authority capable of enforcing these rules.[82] In a few weeks, events proved that neither condition prevailed.

The Angolan liberation movements had been formed as illegal, guerrilla organizations and during the war of liberation had acquired no experience of operating by consensus or of abiding by legal provisions. Even while facing a common enemy, the movements were unable to reach political or even strategic accommodations to present a united front against Portugal. When the self-interest of African states pushed the movements to agree to unity declarations during the war, they were always denounced or violated before they could be implemented. The movements were not able to break this pattern even when their activities were legitimated in the transitional government.

Yet Angolans were hopeful as the movements seemed to

82. Heimer, *Social Change in Angola,* p. 48.

undertake seriously their new responsibilities defined by the Alvor agreement. Each movement inaugurated intensive political campaigns to mobilize as large a part of the population as possible. The preindependence elections seemed to be an accepted goal and the parties utilized mass meetings, posters, wall inscriptions, local organizations, and the mass media to increase their constituencies. All three movements had women's and youth leagues to organize and lead rallies and carry on grassroots propaganda. It appeared that the movements had indeed adopted methods appropriate to a representative, multiparty democracy.

However, from the beginning of the post-Alvor period the movements had to divide their energies three ways: to staff and execute the transitional government, to organize partisan political campaigns, and to assume administrative, judicial, and police functions. It was the addition of this third responsibility that most seriously threatened the success of the Alvor plan.

The Beginning of Civil Strife

If the Portuguese had been willing and able to carry out the civil and paramilitary functions necessary to keep the country operating, the nationalist movements might have moved toward a working consensus as they cooperated in the transitional government and presented their programs to the public. However, the colonial administrative machinery was paralyzed, so the Portuguese invited the liberation movements to set up their own administrative offices in each provincial capital and allowed military units of each movement to police the areas where they had substantial popular support. A skeleton police force augmented by Portuguese army patrols was supposed to maintain overall order. The weakness of this divided authority was shown on February 1, 1975, in Luanda, just a day after the inauguration of the transitional government. In the MPLA-controlled Lixeira *musseque* a minor misunderstanding erupted into a shoot-out between FNLA and MPLA guerrillas. Seven persons, including two officers in a Portuguese patrol who had come to restore order, were killed.

Violence escalated in mid-February as the MPLA tried to "neutralize" the Chipenda faction or Eastern Revolt, resulting in twenty deaths.[83] As weeks passed, the conflicts between the movements increased in frequency and violence. At the end of March, Portugal's foreign minister, Major Ernesto Melo Antunes, and the minister for overseas territories, Dr. António do Almeida Santos, rushed from Lisbon to Luanda to bring the leaders of the movements together. The Angolan leaders and the ministers agreed to end the fighting. They also repeated the Alvor pledge to integrate the movements' military units with the Portuguese armed forces. The Portuguese ministers had hardly returned to Lisbon when conflicts broke out again in Luanda between FNLA and MPLA. A curfew was ordered in the capital, but this did not bring peace to the city and the surrounding African townships. Small clashes continued to disturb Luanda and at the end of April another major combat between MPLA and FNLA forces shook Luanda. Lisbon papers estimated the casualties at more than 500 dead and 700 wounded.

The Portuguese high commissioner, General Silva Cardoso, warned the leaders of the movements and the population of Luanda that if the "fratricidal struggle for power" continued, the integrated armed forces would use force against any unauthorized armed groups. Perhaps if he had been able to carry out his threat, law and order could have been maintained. Since that was not done, the two movements rushed to increase their own military strength and this became their primary concern, leaving their governmental and political responsibilities in a secondary position. FNLA received materiel from Zaïre. MPLA's aid came mostly from Eastern Europe, which presented both logistic and political problems. A communiqué of the National Commission of Defense, dated April 29, 1975, prohibited the unloading of military supplies destined for MPLA from the Yugoslav ship *Postoyna*, but the commission was not able to enforce its own decrees.[84]

The escalation of military activities reduced the importance attributed to the political process. Also, the prognostications of the electoral results made the MPLA and FNLA doubt that they should trust their futures to the political process. The MFA and

83. *Africa,* no. 43 (March 1975), p. 37.
84. *Diário de Notícias,* May 5, 1975.

the OAU visiting delegation estimated in mid-1975 that in any popular plebiscite UNITA would win a plurality, followed by MPLA and FNLA.

The FNLA still believed in mid-1975 that it had the greatest military force, and it was not willing to have its future decided by ballots, where the result would be certain defeat. At the beginning of 1975, FNLA disposed an estimated 15,000 troops, which were relatively well equipped and well trained on a low technological level. The Chipenda forces were officially integrated into the FNLA forces in March 1975 but in fact maintained a semiautonomous status. They had their headquarters in Menongue in the south of Angola.

The MPLA, combining ideological conviction with the solid support of the socialist bloc, was confident that it could gain power in Angola either by political maneuvers or by military strength. MPLA had about 3,000 guerrilla troops after the Chipenda breakaway. However, MPLA quickly recruited and trained several thousand men from its political constituency, mainly in the Luanda area. The USSR and Eastern European countries supplied the necessary arms for the expanding MPLA force. MPLA also armed its Poder Popular, the local units of political militants, which became an aggressive militia.

UNITA was the only movement ready to give itself wholeheartedly to the electoral process since that was its only hope to achieve power. Its trained military forces were small and its history of fighting from inside Angola had restricted its diplomatic contacts so it could not count on the sure support of any nation or bloc. Jonas Savimbi, in the midst of the first major FNLA-MPLA confrontation, declared the neutrality of UNITA.[85] It did stay out of the conflict from February to July of 1975. UNITA campaigned strenuously on the political front and projected the image of the movement most likely to bring peace and unity to Angola.

By the end of May 1975 the FNLA and MPLA were no longer responding to local isolated incidents as they clashed, but were setting the stage for a nationwide struggle in which each was preparing itself to gain exclusive power. This preparation re-

85. *Diário de Lisboa,* March 3, 1975.

quired the increase of outside aid, including materiel and ad-visors. UNITA proposed a summit conference (to avoid a direct confrontation between MPLA and FNLA) and the two movements agreed. However, the agreement seemed to be motivated more by a desire to gain time for the military show-down than by a commitment to the peaceful resolution of their differences.

The Nakuru Agreement

The summit meeting of Holden Roberto, Agostinho Neto, and Jonas Savimbi in Nakuru, Kenya from June 16 to 21, 1975, did not halt the rapid escalation of the civil strife into a civil war. It did, however, produce a succinct analysis of the "causes for the deterioration of the situation in Angola":

1. The introduction of great quantities of arms by the liberation movements after the 25th of April and especially after their move to Luanda. This race for arms is due to the fact that the liberation movements have maintained their mutual lack of confidence resulting from their political and ideological differences and their divergences in the past.
2. The lack of political tolerance which manifests itself in violence in the activity of the liberation movements and their militants.
3. The existence of so-called zones of influence and of regions of supposed military superiority.
4. The arming of the civilian population.
5. Military clashes among the liberation movements and their ten-dency to regionalize which in addition to causing numerous innocent victims, aggravates the situation by tending to increase tribalism, re-gionalism and racism.
6. The presence of reactionary agitation and of elements foreign to the process of decolonization.

The seventeen-page Nakuru agreement elaborated on these causes and proposed solutions to reverse the trend of events in Angola by preparing "a peaceful transference of powers at the moment of independence." Yet, even as the leaders were meet-ing in Kenya, the movements were stepping up the race for arms; the much-publicized handshakes and hugs among the leaders, presided over by President Jomo Kenyatta, had not changed the "mutual lack of confidence."

The transitional government did face the key issue of a united Angolan army after the Nakuru meeting, but again the result was only accurate analysis unaccompanied by practical solutions. Rui Monteiro, the minister of information in the transitional government, after saying that the government hoped to have an integrated army before Angola gained its independence in November, went on to comment: "It will be difficult because our country is not used to democratic processes and it is hard explaining to them the concept of non-partisan and integrated military units."[86]

In July, the MPLA evidently decided that instead of following the agreement at Nakuru to eliminate the "zones of influence and regions of supposed military superiority" it would aggressively establish complete control of its zone—Luanda-Malange. By the beginning of August, the capital, the whole Kimbundu corridor, and the Lunda district were cleared of all FNLA military and political personnel. The only area in which the FNLA successfully resisted the MPLA was north of Luanda, where the FNLA zone dipped within a few miles of the capital.

Until July, UNITA had not engaged in the military clashes. Then MPLA began pushing south and "invading" the UNITA zone of influence. Cuanza-Sul became the first district of active confrontation between the MPLA and UNITA. By mid-August, UNITA was forced out of its "peacemaking" position and became one of the combatants again. The MPLA drove south along the coast, taking Porto Amboim, Novo Redondo, Lobito, and Benguela. It also sent its forces by an eastern route through Lunda and into Moxico. Although UNITA formed an uneasy alliance with FNLA forces south of the Cuanza, they were not able to withstand the MPLA forces, which showed superiority in leadership and organization as well as equipment.

The escalated fighting forced all sides to look for increased support from outside. MPLA's military successes due to Soviet and Communist bloc support was matched by more aid for FNLA and UNITA. In June 1974, China had sent an advance party of Chinese military instructors to the FNLA base at Kinkuzu. The remainder of the Chinese team, totaling 120, arrived

86. *New York Times*, June 30, 1975.

in August together with materiel. For a year China assisted FNLA, but after recognizing that it could not successfully compete with the Soviets in an Angolan arms race, China withdrew its military instructors from Zaïre in October 1975.

Also in 1975, the United States increased its aid to FNLA in Zaïre and the Ford Administration sought to convince the American public that the national interest required a more substantial intervention to oppose communism in Angola. Overt and covert American aid to FNLA and UNITA increased in September.

There was no advantage, however, in sending more sophisticated equipment without skilled personnel to operate it. Events moved so swiftly toward independence on November 11 that there was no time for the advisors and technicians who had arrived from various countries to train the Angolans to use the new equipment. Therefore, each movement welcomed foreign forces. The Zaïrean troops could enter most easily across the northern border to reinforce FNLA as it fought to hold its zone of influence in northwest Angola. Cuban forces arrived in October through Pointe-Noire in the Congo and Pôrto Amboim to strengthen MPLA. In the same month, the Zulu column of white South African troops swept northward from Namibia. In three weeks they had recaptured Sá da Bandeira and the coastal cities of Benguela and Lobito, which the MPLA had taken in August and September. Two factors halted the drive of the Zulu column before it reached Luanda. First, the date of Angolan independence was fast approaching and all the movements wished to keep their foreign troops out of the headlines. Second, Cuban forces which had reached the Keve River by the first of November presented the first stiff opposition to the South African troops.

The strategic fact that Luanda was the center of the MPLA zone of influence had a dramatic, and perhaps decisive, effect in the first stage of the Angolan civil war. When the MPLA exerted exclusive military control over the Luanda-Malange districts in July 1975, the non-MPLA populations from the north and south fled the capital. The political leaders of the FNLA and UNITA felt particularly vulnerable without the military protection of their own troops so they also abandoned the capital. This meant the collapse of the transitional government, and on August 14 the acting Portuguese high commissioner in Angola, announcing the dissolution of the coalition regime, took over all executive powers. However, the order dissolving the coalition provided for the Portuguese take-over of only those ministries "abandoned" by the FNLA and UNITA. The posts were actually being filled by MPLA officials although the arrangement was an informal one. This allowed the MPLA to extend its control over the whole Angolan administration while the Portuguese were still formally in authority. Such administrative control also gave a direct financial advantage to the MPLA. All taxes paid in Angola came to the Luanda government, which was in the hands of the MPLA from August 1975 until independence.

Independence and Civil War

The proclamation of independence on November 11, 1975, was a subdued affair in most of Angola compared to the euphoric inauguaration of the transitional government nine months earlier. Only in Luanda did Angolans celebrate independence enthusiastically.

The four other Portuguese African colonies had come to independence without major civil strife. The Portuguese government handed the reins of power to governments that were recognized as being representative of the people of Guinea-Bissau, Mozambique, Cape Verde, and São Tomé and Príncipe.[87] The Lisbon regime could not decide what it would do in Angola, where the conflict between the three liberation movements was escalating with the approach of the independence date.

At the last minute, the Portuguese cabinet resolved that it would not recognize any of the competing movements. On November 10, the Portuguese high commissioner, Admiral Leonel Cardoso, announced in a brief ceremony in Luanda that he was transferring power to the "Angolan people," yet not a single Angolan was present. The Portuguese flag was lowered and some 2,000 Portuguese troops quietly boarded naval trans-

87. The independence dates for these countries are: Guinea-Bissau, September 10, 1974; Mozambique, June 25, 1975; Cape Verde, June 5, 1975; São Tomé and Príncipe, July 12, 1975; and Angola, November 11, 1975.

ports to return to Lisbon, retracing the route of Diogo Cão, who had arrived at the mouth of the Congo River almost five centuries earlier.

At midnight of November 10, thousands of Angolans gathered in the stadium near Luanda's city center to celebrate their independence and heard Agostinho Neto say: "In the name of the people of Angola, before Africa and the world, I proclaim the independence of Angola." Neto's forty-minute speech was punctuated by chants of "The struggle continues" and "Victory is certain." He acknowledged that the next phase of the struggle would be more arduous than the thirteen-year struggle against the Portuguese. Later in the day, Dr. Agostinho Neto was declared the president of the People's Republic of Angola (PRA).

The political struggle did continue. On November 11 the FNLA and UNITA proclaimed the independence of the Democratic People's Republic of Angola (DPRA). This loose anti-MPLA coalition formed a national council to act temporarily as the government with its capital in Huambo, the center of the UNITA zone of influence.

The military struggle also continued. At independence, the military power of MPLA and the anti-MPLA forces were in rough equilibrium. MPLA's forces were spearheaded by more than 1,000 Cubans,[88] who had at their disposal sophisticated Soviet weaponry such as T54 and T34 tanks. More effective for the MPLA than their other arms were the 122-millimeter rocket launchers (Stalin's Organs), which terrified the FNLA and UNITA soldiers and the general population.

The FNLA forces in the north with Zaïrean troops and 150 former Portuguese commandos[89] reached the Morro da Cal, twelve miles from Luanda, but on the eve of independence they failed to make the all-important breakthrough into the capital. The FNLA-UNITA troops in the south did little fighting, but gave support to the column of white soldiers organized and manned principally by South Africans who, for political and military reasons, were stalled on their push to the capital.

88. Marcum, II, 273.

89. Pedro Silva, Valdemar Moreira and Francisco Esteves, *Angola: Comandos especiais contra os cubanos* (Braga-Lisbon: Braga Editora, 1978).

Independence was followed by a decisive shift in the military balance between the MPLA and the FNLA-UNITA coalition. The MPLA control of the capital not only provided the political and administrative advantages noted above, but also gave the MPLA the most strategic military position. It had internal lines of military communication and could move out from its base, which contained Angola's only international transportation and communications center.

The international allies of the MPLA were able with impunity to increase their aid in both materiel and personnel. Both the port and international airport of Luanda were available to the Russians and other socialist bloc nations, which rapidly increased the resources at MPLA's disposal. The Cuban combat troops tripled in the three weeks following independence, reaching at least 3,000 by the first of December.

On the other side, pressure mounted against those supplying materiel and personnel to the anti-MPLA forces. The Ford Administration argued for increasing aid to the "anti-Marxist" forces, but the Vietnam backlash was very strong and congressional opposition against involvement in the Angolan civil war increased rapidly. In December, the U.S. Senate voted to prevent the Administration from continuing intervention in Angola. Although this prohibition was only enacted into law when it was supported by the House of Representatives in February 1976, it was clear in November and December that the United States would not be able to balance the massive aid coming from the USSR and the socialist bloc to the MPLA.

The United States' inability or unwillingness to continue its military support of the anti-MPLA coalition had a cooling effect on France, Belgium, and other Western European countries which had also been supplying aid to UNITA and FNLA. The most direct military effect of the U.S. withdrawal was the pulling back of the South African personnel, who had led the FNLA/UNITA columns and dislodged MPLA from the coastal cities in October and November. South Africa had assumed, on the basis of promises that are difficult to document, that the United States and other Western nations would give substantial support to the anti-MPLA coalition. South Africa was left out on a limb when the other aid to FNLA/UNITA decreased instead of equaling the greatly increased aid to MPLA.

South Africa also faced domestic opposition to its Angolan
adventure. The governing Nationalist Party was unsuccessfully
challenged by weak opposition parties accusing the government
of failing to take the public into its confidence and to explain the
actions and objectives of the South African troops in Angola.
Some of the chief black leaders in South Africa also spoke out
against the South African intervention.[90]

South Africa's withdrawal from Angola shifted the military
balance decisively in favor of the MPLA. The South African
presence had hurt the FNLA/UNITA more politically than it
had strengthened them militarily. On November 27, Nigeria
announced its recognition of the People's Republic of Angola,
citing South African intervention as the reason. Nigeria then
made a financial contribution of $20 million to the Luanda gov-
ernment.

The MPLA took advantage of its military and political advantage and launched a New Year's offensive in the north of Angola, led by Cubans and Katangese. By January 6, 1976, MPLA
captured Uíge, the FNLA's headquarters in Angola, and effectively eliminated any serious military threat in the north. This
victory had political as well as military significance, since it took
place on the eve of the meeting of the Organization of African
Unity (OAU) in Addis Ababa.

The OAU made the last international effort to reconcile the
combatants in the Angolan civil war. The 1976 meeting was
evenly divided between those nations supporting the Nigerian
resolution to recognize the People's Republic of Angola and
those voting for Senegal's resolution calling for a cease-fire,
withdrawal of foreign troops, and reconciliation of the three
movements in order to form a government of national unity.
The deadlock of twenty-two votes for each resolution was in fact
a victory for the MPLA. More than thirty nations had already
recognized the MPLA regime in Luanda and not a single nation
had recognized the FNLA/UNITA coalition government in
Huambo. If the OAU had passed the Senegalese resolution,
probably some nations would have recognized the Huambo government.

90. *Washington Post,* January 24, 1976.

Returning politically victorious from Addis Ababa, the MPLA turned its military force southward, and if there had been any possibility of an MPLA-UNITA coalition it was then completely ruled out. João Filipe Martins, the Angolan minister of information, made it clear: "We have always stated that the FNLA and UNITA are our enemies. There is only one movement in Angola and that is the MPLA."[91] The MPLA, with Cuban forces and Russian equipment, swept through the south almost as easily as they had the north. On January 25, defense Minister Pieter W. Botha told the South African parliament that South African troops were withdrawing from the front lines in Angola.

When MPLA troops arrived within fifty miles of Huambo, the coalition forces withdrew eastward along the railway to Silva Porto, which had been the military headquarters of the UNITA forces during the civil war. This strategic retreat did not strengthen the coalition's military position and within two weeks the MPLA had achieved its major military objectives.

Just three months after independence the MPLA with the support of 10,000 Cuban troops and massive Russian aid took control of the major cities of Angola. February 11 can be taken as the date of the end of this phase of the Angolan struggle, which the MPLA called the Second War of Liberation. On that date Huambo, the UNITA capital, and São Salvador, the last FNLA stronghold, were captured. The OAU recognized the People's Republic of Angola, and President Gerald Ford signed the bill prohibiting further U.S. aid to Angola.

The confrontation between Portuguese and Angolan nationalisms produced the political rhetoric of the anticolonial era, but the most decisive actions were the result of dynamics within each nationalism. The clash between the Salazar-Caetano regime and the Portuguese opposition issued in the coup on April 25, 1974. This in turn led to the end of Portuguese colonialism and the independence of Angola. Conflict within Angolan nationalism then generated a civil war which invited broad foreign intervention and led to the victory of the MPLA, which established the People's Republic of Angola. The anticolonial

91. *The Times* (London), January 20, 1976.

war fought externally between Portuguese troops and the three liberation movements from 1961 to 1974 was so low-key that it did not interfere seriously with Angola's economic growth, nor were the casualties high. When the Angolan conflict became an internal struggle, the violence escalated. From 1974 to 1976 the civil war destroyed the Angolan economy and infrastructure, as well as killing more Angolans than did the whole thirteen-year anticolonial war.

Portuguese and Angolan nationalisms shaped each other as they developed through five centuries of conflict. The events of the last decade have severed that tie and Angola is establishing new relationships that will help form the next phase of its history.

Conclusion: The
Struggle Continues

The title of this chapter is paradoxical. How can we come to a conclusion if the struggle continues? We can only do so by recognizing that the conclusions drawn in this final chapter form a brief résumé of the current situation in Angola and do not imply that the five centuries of conflict have come to an end. Unfortunately, we see no signs at the beginning of 1979—the fourth year after independence and after MPLA's victory in what it called the Second War of Liberation—which would lead us to conclude that Angola is emerging from this long, painful period.

Angola in 1979 is marked by four characteristics: (1) The Portuguese suddenly dropped out of Angola's history and are no longer a significant factor. (2) Angola has shifted its dependency from Portugal and the Western nations to Cuba and Eastern European nations. (3) The Luanda government is attempting to reorganize the shattered administrative system and reconstruct the destroyed infrastructure at the same time that it is fighting resistance forces in many rural areas. (4) Angolans are still struggling to assert their African culture and resist the imposition of foreign ideology, politics, and economics.

The Movement of the Armed Forces effectively eliminated Portuguese dominance of Angola when it executed the successful coup d'état in Lisbon on April 25, 1974. The flight of 300,000 Portuguese settlers from Angola in the summer of 1975 and the quiet withdrawal of the last Portuguese troops on November 10, 1975, physically ended the Portuguese presence in Angola. Politically, however the Portuguese had abdicated their role earlier. After presiding over the Alvor agreement and setting up the transitional government in January 1975, Portugal was unwilling or unable to enforce the conditions of the agreement. This abdication contributed significantly to the strife which developed into the full-scale civil war with international involvement.

Other European colonial nations—Great Britain, France, and Belgium—that gave independence to their colonies in the late 1950s or early '60s have continued economic and even some military involvement in the territories formerly under their control, involvement classified by some as neocolonialism. But Portugal's own political instability and economic decline since the coup foreclosed the possibility of renewing its prominent position in Angola's life.

The end of Portuguese colonial control has not created an independent Angola. Angola has merely shifted its dependency from Portugal and the Western European nations to Cuba and Eastern Europe. Neither Angola nor Cuba has published the number of Cubans serving in Angola, but estimates placed it at about 23,000 in early 1978. Of this total, 19,000 were military and 4,000 civilian. In 1976, rumors in diplomatic channels suggested that Cuba would withdraw its personnel from Angola, but in late 1977 it was officially announced that Cuba would send an additional 10,000 technicians.[1] Whatever their exact number today, Cuban military personnel were responsible for the MPLA victory in the civil war and are essential to maintain the government of the People's Republic of Angola.

Cuban civilian personnel played key roles in reorganizing the coffee and sugar industries after production fell sharply from the 1973 levels. They also provide a large share of the technicians in the field of health and education. Special instructors were sent from Cuba to direct courses in political education for the Department of Political Orientation and courses for trade union personnel. Cuba has also received hundreds of Angolan students for technical and professional courses.[2] Angola's dependence upon Cuba is extremely visible. Less visible but just as vital is Angola's dependence upon the USSR. The Cuban military personnel were effective in the civil war because they knew

1. *Tempo*, November 24, 1977.
2. BBC-ME (British Broadcasting Corporation Moderating Europe)/5560/b/6, ME/5562/B/8.

how to operate the superior arms and equipment supplied by the USSR. Although Cubans occupy many command posts, Russian advisors are in direct control of the Angolan Ministry of Defense.[3] Angola's dependence on the USSR was formalized by the signing of a twenty-year friendship pact in October 1976.

After Cuba and Russia, East Germany is the third main support for the present regime of the People's Republic of Angola. It has provided advisors for the economic reorganization of Angola and has furnished a large contingent of civil servants who work in a broad spectrum of services from administration to the police.[4] Other foreign personnel from Bulgaria, Yugoslavia, Algeria, Italy, and the Scandinavian countries are also bolstering Angola's political, administrative, and economic structures.

Angola's dependence has even spread to the provision of the basic necessities of the population. It is estimated that Angola produced 90 percent of its food supply in 1973. Two years after independence, perhaps 50 percent of the food for the Angolan population under the government's control was imported. The exports to pay for these burgeoning imports were, ironically, produced by firms that are the remnant of Angola's dependence on the Western economy: Gulf Oil provides Angola with $1 million a day from its oil production and Diamang continues to market Angola's diamonds.

The Luanda government has been taxed beyond its own resources to organize this large new nation which had been reduced to near anarchy by the civil war. Lopo do Nascimento, the prime minister, classified the public administration situation as one of "institutionalized anarchy."[5] One hundred and twenty highway bridges were destroyed in the most intense phase of the civil war, from October 1975 to February 1976, and thousands of kilometers of roads and railroads were put out of service. Some port facilities were damaged. Sugar and coffee plantations were devastated. Of the 28,000 trucks circulating in Angola before independence, 22,000 were taken by the departing Portuguese or wrecked by inexperienced drivers.

3. *The Times* (London), November 22, 1976.
4. *O Jornal,* April 1, 1977.
5. *Diário de Notícias,* September 24, 1976.

The replacement of the vehicles and repair of the roads and rails would have been a major effort in a peaceful setting. However, MPLA's military victory in early 1976 did not end the military resistance to its rule. From Cabinda in the north to the Cunene in the south, the Angolan government has faced persistent military and political resistance.

On May 1, 1977, the Frente para a Libertação do Enclave de Cabinda (FLEC), which had taken up arms sporadically in 1974 and 1975, announced the establishment of a provisional government of the Republic of Cabinda in what FLEC claimed to be a liberated zone of the enclave. Henriques Tiago Nzita was declared president of the provisional government. FLEC was so weak militarily that this declaration might seem to pose no serious threat to the Luanda government. However, the heavily wooded hills of Cabinda make it the most favorable area for guerrilla warfare and the Cabindans' ethnic and regional sympathy for "its own movement" require the Angola government to maintain a major troop contingent in the enclave. The danger that FLEC presents to the People's Republic of Angola depends on the willingness of the Congo and Zaïre to provide a safe refuge for guerrillas making forays into Cabinda.

The FNLA was so shattered by the MPLA/Cuban forces in December 1975 and January 1976 that it was presumed incapable of offering further resistance to the MPLA government. However, the FNLA continued to mount ambushes against MPLA/Cuban forces in the Kikongo area. For a time, Angolan officials denied that FNLA existed in Angola, but on November 23, 1977, President Neto announced that the FNLA would be crushed before January 1978, which confirmed the existence of FNLA as a threat. There is no evidence that MPLA forces have indeed accomplished the task set for them by the president.

The strongest resistance to the Luanda government has been organized by UNITA. This movement has certain advantages in its efforts to resist the Luanda regime. First, UNITA has its support in the central highlands, which is the most populous area in Angola. No regime can securely rule Angola without the backing of the population of the Huambo-Bié districts. Second, UNITA has experience in fighting this kind of guerrilla operation since it opposed the Portuguese from inside Angola for six years. Third, educational opportunities expanded rapidly in the late sixties and early seventies so that UNITA has a large number of men and women with secondary education. Many had military experience in FALA or the Portuguese army and others have training that enabled them to set up rural education and health networks.

The strength of UNITA resistance is demonstrated by several facts. Into the fourth year of independence, UNITA troops are able to traverse most of central and southern Angola with impunity. The operation of the Benguela Railway, which traverses this territory, is regularly disrupted by UNITA: some limited sections are operative but there has been no international traffic. The Fourth Congress of UNITA, with several hundred in attendance, was held within sight of Huambo in March 1977. Outside of the cities, no area of central and southern Angola is safe from UNITA ambushes.

Resistance to the MPLA government has also appeared within its own ranks. On May 27, 1977, two members of the MPLA politburo, Nito Alves and José Van Dunem, led a coup against the government in Luanda Although unsuccessful, it resulted in the death of six top MPLA leaders and revealed the disaffection of thousands of Angolans from the geographic and ethnic constituencies that have generally supported MPLA.

As long as serious resistance continues, the regime can be expected to depend heavily on foreign economic and military aid to maintain power.

Chapter 2 described cultural patterns of Angolan ethnolinguistic groups as they were in about 1920, at the beginning of Angola's colonial period. The economic and political developments of colonialism, the nationalist revolt, political independence, civil war, and foreign intervention could be expected to have moved Angolans away from those older patterns. Contrary to this expectation, the breakdown in administration, the destruction of the infrastructure, and the declining economy caused by the continuing civil war have thrown Angolans back on their precolonial practices and wisdom. That chapter may again be an accurate description of daily life in many parts of Angola.

It seems safe to predict, at least, that two relatively constant features of Angolan life which have persisted through the five centuries of conflict will continue to shape this new nation.

First, most Angolans have identified themselves by their ethnolinguistic relationships. Their most persistent rivalries have followed the same social lines. The FNLA-MPLA battles at the Dande River thirty miles north of Luanda in November and December 1975 were replays of the conflict between the Kongo and Kimbundu at the same spot in 1556. In the sixteenth century, both sides were supported by Portuguese advisors and troops. Four centuries later, the combatants were the same, with supporting troops and advisors not only from Portugal but from Zaïre and South Africa, Cuba and Russia.

The several Angolan nationalist movements grew out of the same ethnolinguistic soils. Personality, ideology, international pressures, and economic interests bent and shaped the three principal movements, but fundamentally they continued to draw sustenance from the three main ethnic areas.

A second relatively constant feature in Angolan history is the confrontation between European and African cultures, which cuts across these ethnolinguistic lines. In fact, this conflict of cultures has rent the lives of many Angolans ever since the sixteenth century when the famous King of the Kongo tried to be true to his two names: Nzinga Mbemba and Afonso. This conflict has sharpened in Angola as the MPLA moves to become an officially Marxist-Leninist party in the European tradition and UNITA tries to appeal to African loyalties.

Jonas Savimbi attributes the continuing struggle in part to the culture conflict between European and African world views:

What is being imposed on Angola today is a carbon copy of European political thought and action. . . . If Neto were informed in his actions by African culture, he would not have avoided the dialogue between UNITA, FNLA and even FLEC. . . . Because, in the end, our conception in Africa is to dialogue. . . . But Neto, as he has a European conception of politics does not understand this. . . . He also acts in a foreign way. We therefore have a war which cannot end while the Angolan rulers do not begin to think as Angolans.[6]

The present form of the war may soon end since the opposi-

6. *O Diabo,* November 8, 1977, p. 16.

tion movements are being pressured externally and internally. The accord signed in 1978 by Zaïre and Angola to respect each other's boundaries and impede foreign incursions will hamper the military activities of the FNLA and FLEC in the north. The independence of Namibia will threaten UNITA's ties with South Africa and other allies that use the southern border to aid the resistance in Angola. Internally, the MPLA government is increasing its military, administrative, and cultural control.

FNLA, FLEC, and UNITA may disappear, but the struggle will continue. Ethnolinguistic loyalties and African-European culture conflict are so basic to the Angolan reality that whatever the fortunes of particular leaders or parties, these features will exert a profound influence on the continuing struggle in Angola.

Index

Library of Congress Cataloging in Publication Data

Henderson, Lawrence W   1921–
    Angola: five centuries of conflict.

    (Africa in the modern world)
    Includes index.
    1. Angola—History. I. Title.
DT611.5.H46   967'.3   79-5089
ISBN 0-8014-1247-1